GODS OF POWER

A Study of the Beliefs and Practices of Animists

$9.27

PHILIP M. STEYNE

GODS OF POWER

A Study of the Beliefs and Practices of Animists

ISBN # 1-880828-64-2

Library of Congress Catalog Card Number: 90-70844

Published by Touch Publications, Inc.
Box 19888, Houston, TX 77224
(713) 497-7901
Fax (713) 497-0904

TABLE OF CONTENTS

DEDICATION

To all Christian workers who recognize that
we wrestle not against flesh and blood
but against principalities and powers.

PREFACE

"You really don't believe that evil spirits can effect miracles, do you?" The incredulity implied in the question does not reflect on those who believe that this is possible, but on what Scripture says. The secular mind set has long since come to believe that the spirit world is powerless if not nonexistent. But for most two-thirds world people the question deserves no answer.

Since I've learned how extensive and persistent animism is around the world, not only as one religion alongside others, but as the basic underpinning of all non-biblical religions, my secular mind set in approach to the Bible has been substantially challenged. I have come to appreciate more than ever before the fact that the Bible is a revelation of God who is distinct from all other gods. This God requires from those in relationship with Him a distinct lifestyle of trust and obedience. His interaction with man demonstrates that His revelation of Himself is the bulwark against animism (all other gods vying for man's allegiance) in whatever form it presents itself.

The Bible highlights the presence of two religious options open to man. Both these options are presented as living faiths. Both have to do with spirit sources. Both claim man's total allegiance. Both have a singular motivation and objective. Both claim to offer man the meaning of, and the means to deal effectively with, life. But the Bible also states categorically that these options are not of equal value, power or authority. Only one of these options can rightfully claim for itself the presence, power and authority of the Omnipotent God. Only one can rightfully claim the allegiance of man. Although the other religious option claims for itself a superior power, the claim is false and the actual encounter with the biblical God—the God of Abraham, Isaac and Jacob—significantly and adequately exposes the powerlessness of that fallacious claim.

The Bible reveals man's propensity to substitute God's mandated approach to life with his own finite knowledge in dealing with life's issues. The Bible describes man's constant drive to establish himself as his own god with his own agenda for life. This counterfeit religious system is most attractive to man and frequently seems to triumph in claiming his allegiance. The tragic consequences are seen in personal, family and community life worldwide. Perhaps more subtle is the way man tries to be a part of both the real and the counterfeit at one and the same time. The exclusive biblical option does not allow for that interrelationship. Nevertheless he persists because the alternative religious option is all-inclusive. It allows both to function together, always favoring man's interpretations. The result is syncretism, issuing in a weak Christian presence and failure to deal with the deceiving and destroying powers determined to rob God of the glory due His Name. It is my hope that learning about this counterfeit system will cause readers to seek out the truth of the Bible vis-a-vis other religions. There is a fine line between the true and the counterfeit, and all too frequently the counterfeit has effectively robbed Christians of the whole Gospel. In much of Christendom too much of man's relationship with God is poured into sterile molds, built on lifeless dogma and expressed in meaningless forms. Surely the Christian life is dynamic, life-changing and radical in its effect on society! Is not the Gospel God's power unto salvation in every area of life? This book attempts to deal with the realities of animism, the counter-religion, in the belief that biblical Christian faith is dynamic and successfully confronts all other religious challenges.

I owe a great deal to several special people who helped to bring this project to a successful completion: I am indebted to the Administration of Columbia Bible College and Seminary, which released me to give attention to the writing of the manuscript; to those who made it possible for me to travel to different countries to do field research; to members of my family in South Africa—William and Lydia Crew, who opened their home to us, cared for our daily needs, and provided the use of a computer and the needed software; to missionaries and others who gave of their time to read and helpfully critique the manuscript; to those who in particular spent a great deal of time on the project, namely my beloved wife Jeanne, who amidst great difficulties produced the original manuscript on computer discs; Lamar Brown, a faithful friend with the gift of helps, who cared for many trying details and successfully transposed the original discs into a useable form for word processing in the U.S.A.; my daughter Linda, who designed the first manuscript cover; and our family, colleagues and dear friends who encouraged and prayed very specifically for this project. To all who made this project possible, we are deeply grateful. To each one I say "thank you." This I know— God has privileged us to be workers together for His glory. I pray that this book in some small measure will contribute toward the declaration of His glory among all people groups.

FOREWORD

This book is long overdue. Contrary to what Western theologians have been saying in recent years about "man coming of age," becoming more secular and less religious, the hunger for spiritual power is abundantly evident in today's world. My own missionary experience in Latin America made me deeply aware that this widespread quest for spiritual power is found on all social and educational levels.

Many people are animists. They worship spirits. Fear is their constant companion. To tell them that this is superstition is to ignore their deepest convictions. They seek a power greater than the power to which they are in bondage. They need to know and experience that "greater is He that is in you than he who is in the world" (I John 4:4). The New Testament teaching about a malevolent spiritual realm whose works the Son of God came to destroy is not only an accommodation to first-century cosmology, but a guide to present day spiritual warfare as well. No church that stresses theological doctrine and moral teaching without also emphasizing that the preaching of the Gospel is "the power of God unto salvation" will flourish and grow in much of today's world.

In this comprehensive volume, Dr. Philip Steyne, professor of missions at Columbia Biblical Seminary and Graduate School of Missions, presents animism as a religion supremely concerned with spiritual power. This book is not a quaint anthropological study of primitive tribal religionists isolated from the mainstream of human progress, but a knowledgeable treatment of a religious perspective that pervades and underlies both the classic world religions and such contemporary religious developments as the New Age movement.

Steyne's view that animism is the basic underpinning of all non-biblical religions causes anthropologists and missionaries to rethink previous presuppositions. He argues that although biblical religion took shape in the midst of animistic society, it stands in stark contrast to the animistic belief systems which surrounded both the Old Testament people of Israel and the New Testament church. He views Elijah's encounter with the animistic priests of Baal as paradigmatic of the confrontation

11

between biblical faith and all religions which do not share that faith. His analysis of animism as the prevailing worldview into which God revealed Himself will shed new light on our understanding of the Bible. Christians in general and missionaries in particular will find much help in this volume.

Replete with numerous examples and personal experiences, this book explores the beliefs and practices of animism. He challenges the presupposition that animism can be dismissed as primitive superstition. He maintains that the gods of animism are indeed "gods of power," and that their power source is linked to a malevolent spiritual realm in rebellion against the Creator.

Steyne is well qualified to author this work. Born in South Africa, and trained at Roosevelt University, Northern Baptist Seminary and the Fuller School of World Mission, he has served as a missionary among animist tribal peoples and animistic Hindus. He has preached and taught the Word of God with power on six continents and from many of North America's most significant pulpits.

This book will give you a new appreciation for the distinctiveness of biblical revelation as well as a broadened understanding of animistic religion. Your horizons will be expanded, your preconceptions challenged, your faith enlarged.

Kenneth B. Mulholland
Dean and Professor of Missions and Ministry Studies,
Columbia Biblical Seminary and
Graduate School of Missions

INTRODUCTION

It all started in the late 1940's. As a South African born of European parentage, I became aware of another Africa. Beyond the Africa generally experienced by visitors to this diverse and startling continent lies an African world of mystery and intrigue. It is a world motivated by strange forces and yielding to even stranger powers which do not hesitate to exact human sacrifice if need be. It is a world that lies beyond the natural and the visible but exerts enormous influence upon all that emanates from an African cosmology. It is a dynamic world, a very real world, a world that has deeply embedded itself in the African world view.

The Africa of the Africans was to remain to me an unknown world for many years. Whatever could not conform to my Western world view did not belong to the real world and was therefore classified as merely imagination, or at best superstition. For example, one thing that I had concluded rather early in my life was that African people are very irreligious. The usual structures I had come to associate with religion were obviously absent. There were no regular meeting places, no obvious praying that I could discern, no recognition of God as Westerners would practice that belief and no particular rituals which could be inferred to be religious.

And yet there were rituals, such as deliberately spilling a drink on the ground. There were the sacrificing of goats and the sprinkling of blood here and there. There were the times when the spirit of the deceased would be welcomed back to the homestead with a celebration of significance. There were those who could "read" the entrails of animals and then foretell events about to take place or explain events that had taken place. There was drum-beating and loud singing for hours on end and then the occasional newspaper article reporting the grisly findings of another alleged "ritual murder." Surely, I thought, none of this qualified as religion. These were merely the superstitions of uneducated, primitive people. They had no basis in fact. The day would come when, after having received a Western education, they would look at life as good Westerners do, emphasizing the visible and material world, and underrating, if not ignoring the spirit realm.

13

When my wife and I were assigned to missionary service in an African country, my previous perceptions were quickly confirmed. Now more than a decade later I saw somewhat more clearly how desperately the people needed to be rescued from their imprisoning superstitions. Like my fellow Western missionaries, I, too, believed that the people lived in fear of the spirit world. Little did I know that that fear was not without recourse to sources of power, available to these superstitious people through a variety of ritual practices.

I had all the preparation I thought I needed to effectively and adequately deal with the challenge of superstitions. Along with the regular classroom teaching of secular school subjects, systematic Bible teaching was part of the daily instruction program. When told that my teaching and preaching were greatly enjoyed and appreciated, I believed I was making progress. But my hope was dampened by the added postscript "But we don't understand what you mean." I redoubled my efforts, but a good measure of disillusionment began to set in. There was great appreciation for the Bible, but not much understanding of its message.

To add to my communications concerns, I was called to deal with actual spirit manifestations. Of course, I didn't believe what was told me. I assumed that overactive imaginations conjured up these apparitions. That the people had actually encountered and experienced a nonmaterial being was all too evident in the obvious presence of great fear. And yet I responded in total disbelief. My Western, secular world view could find no parallel category to accommodate this new information. I did, however, have a sense of uneasiness which caused me to query those converts to Christianity who evidenced a commitment to the Christian faith concerning these sightings. The response was consistent. "We know you don't believe it, but we, too, have had these encounters and we know these apparitions are real."

Once in a great while, missionary discussions would raise these matters and related issues. The general attitude was that the people are merely superstitious and should be taught that these things do not exist. Even if they did exist, they should, like good Western Christians, simply ignore them. Any reference to ancestors was censured, and national workers were instructed to teach and preach against belief in ancestors and the practices involved in such belief. Few, if any, really understood the African world view and the resulting beliefs.

Our next term of service landed us squarely in the Indian culture of South Africa. These people were by and large Hindu in religious orientation. Here our awareness of a spirit realm grew, but we still found it hard to accommodate what we heard and actually saw within our Western, secular world view. I still tried to explain it away, and when I could not, I simply ignored it and continued teaching as if the people were totally conversant with my Western secular worldview. Perceptive national pastors sought to help me understand what they knew to be a part of their regular ministry in bringing deliverance to spirit-troubled people, but with little success. My enculturation kept me captive to an understanding of life which made little, if any, allowance for an active spirit realm. Again I rationalized that proper counseling techniques and appropriate medicines would be just as effective, if not more so, than the deliverances effected by national Christian workers and on occasion by a Western missionary. Deliverance ministries, or power encounters, were quite suspect in the thinking of the greater part of the missionary family.

A change, however, had come. I conceded that there was something real in all of this practice of superstition. This was no mere imagination. There were powers with which these people were involved. These powers were greater than anything I knew. Indeed, these people were involved with "gods of power" unknown to me and most of those who share my world view. If I was to bring to them a message of salvation, as I surely wanted to, I had better acquaint myself with their metaphysical culture which appeared to be significantly informed by the spirit world. But where and who could help me understand this spirit world? Most source books on the subject are strongly influenced by Western evolutionary and rationalistic thought. Like typical Westerners, these authors also disbelieved the reality of the spirit world even as they sought to describe the practices of the people. I learned to identify some practices, but the power structure which integrated and undergirded these practices continued to escape me.

Providentially I was led back to the classroom and under the perceptive and biblically focused instruction of Alan R. Tippett, former missionary to Fiji, my understanding of animism began to take form. I began to understand, in some measure, what we had encountered in our missionary activity. Many of our problems related to the persistence of animism, even though people had become acculturated to Western material culture and, to a lesser degree, Western social culture.[1] By and large this metaphysical culture had remained intact, and the Christian message as we proclaimed and taught it had not penetrated every level of their metaphysical world. Many of our converts held the Bible in one hand and their traditional religion in the other. Rather than helping them we only knew how to berate them. Frankly we did not know how to help them.

The two courses which gave me direction were entitled Animism I and Animism II.[2] Not only were these titles not very creative, but their use was rather frequently challenged and questioned. Some felt, and still do, that animism is a derogatory term while others consider its use not a proper description of the religious system it supposedly defines. Alternative terms have been used and are thought to be better suited. Why not use a term like primal religion, or folk religion, or traditional religion or natural religion? In their own right these terms do indeed have value. But by the same token, each of these terms assume that mankind started his religious life in the context of a world left to its own devices in which man had to find and make a religious system for himself, void of divine revelation. This premise, which is a hypothesis, cannot be proved. It is a concept rejected by those who believe Romans 1:18-32 to be the description of the human condition which actually prevailed in the early history of mankind. It is also accepted that divine revelation was subsequently given in the context of a world that had rejected God and therefore specifically answers to the issues under consideration in animism. No other term I know of evokes the concept of spirit involvement like the term animism. And so animism was selected for the course title and content. For such reasons I too have elected to use the term animism throughout this study.

Since my first formal study of animism, I have done extensive research in libraries and as a participant-observer in a number of countries. In time I began to perceive commonalities which are typical of animistic peoples in all religions and cultures. But this was not just my evaluation. In teaching a course on traditional religions, students from different parts of the world and converts from different religions confirmed that they, too, had known and encountered these practices among their people. The degree to which a particular practice would be in evidence and the relative importance associated with it might vary from culture to culture, but the basic function was present in some way. This being the case, I thought there must be reasons why man in such diverse parts of the world would be committed to and involved in the same religious practices. What are these reasons?

Now that I knew somewhat more about animistic practices, I began searching the Scriptures for an explanation of why animism is so widespread and is subsurface in all religions, including Christianity. In the first place I discovered specific animistic practices mentioned in Scripture. In each case we're warned not to be involved in such practices, to turn away from them and to submit to and recognize the Lord God

16

of the Bible. It also became quite clear from the biblical context that in using animistic practices, man wants to determine his own destiny; he wants to secure his own salvation; and he wants to exercise power over all his environment. In other words, his knowledge of his world is superior to that of the God of the Bible, he thinks. Essentially man wants to be his own God, omnipotent over all. Of course, that challenge came to man in the very beginning of time—when the serpent challenged Eve by saying, "in the day that you eat thereof, (the tree of knowledge of good and evil) you shall be as god." And it appears under all religious guises for the most basic reason that man wants to be his own God. This is exactly what the Apostle Paul stated in Romans 1:18-32. The biblical revelation of God and His providence is quite unlike that of animism or, for that matter, any other world religion.

For such reasons, which will be encountered in this study, my definition of animism is not as narrow as that of some researchers.[3] The way I understand animism and the way I prefer to use the term has reference to the search for and the discovery of power sources by which man may manipulate the spirit world to execute his will. The term animism not only recognizes spirits but describes spirit involvement with a view to achieving human objectives. Therefore, I prefer the term animism to any others suggested by students of comparative religions or the science of religion. Furthermore, this study does not evaluate one particular animistic system. Rather, it seeks to isolate the occurrence of animism in all religious systems. It is a general study of animism, and here and there a particular religious group may disclaim a practice. However, over all, I believe it is fair to say through what I've discovered that animism to varying degrees persists in all religions because of man's strong sinful motivation to be his own god. What superstitions have grown up around these practices simply serve to further perpetuate and entrench this religious system.

I have taught in the topic of animism for the last eight years. Repeatedly former students will write from the mission fields to express appreciation for the help received through the course content. However, students and instructor alike sensed that more understanding was needed.

I compiled a reader on animism in hopes that the selected readings might help students understand to a greater degree what they were up against. The resulting anthology, though helpful, did not deal with the subject from a biblical perspective. So few Western authors who had made valid research in the field actually accepted the reality of the spirit world and its influence on mankind, let alone recognized the Bible as the standard of evaluation for all beliefs and practices. Furthermore, my own attempts to deal with this subject biblically left much to be desired. As those concerned for the growth of the church and the influence of syncretism within Christian structures, we owe Christian workers better preparation and sources to deal with animism and its continuing persistence in many Christian churches. If we are to see biblical Christianity practiced in animistic cultures, we must understand what we are up against. This study attempts to do that, but much more needs to be done and can be done to help Christian workers in specific animistic cultures. This study is too broad and general for such purposes.

This study is missiological in nature. It is an attempt to make Christian workers aware of the context in which they are seeking to apply the Christian message, and to propose a methodology. I believe that this information can be helpful in understanding a religious context in which Christian workers are seeking to teach biblical Christianity and to help contextualize its message. For true contextualization to take place, God's Word must inform and if need be change the metaphysical culture of a given people group. This study, in part, helps to achieve that goal. While it is not written primarily for the student of comparative religions or science of religion, the student may find its assumptions interesting if not challenging. It may be necessary for him to re-evaluate what the Bible claims for itself vis-a-vis other world religions. However, I fully expect him to challenge my basic assumptions on my understanding of animism and the biblical response to it. Furthermore, this study does not pretend to be a theological treatment of the subject, although my theological assumptions will surface rather frequently. It attempts to deal with animism as a power religion and discusses how to effectively counter it.

This study is divided into three parts. The first part seeks to establish the function of religion, the religious basis for animism, its definition and its occurrence in all religions. To understand how animism can be compatible with most religious systems, it is necessary to define religion and then know its role and function in human society. Once this is understood, it becomes relatively easy to grasp how animism can be quite satisfactory, if not preferred, in serving man's religious needs. The same will hold true for all other religions. Furthermore, it also becomes somewhat clearer why a power religion is sought after and why animism is so appealing to man.

The second part deals with the actual beliefs and practices of animism. The most common practices are defined and discussed with a view to understanding their role and function in the overall world view and practice of the animist. Some practices are illustrated but only where it was felt necessary to create a clearer understanding of the subject. Terms are introduced and not always defined. The wider context usually explains what is meant by a given term. Where the practice needed definition, I provided it, but I assumed overall a measure of preunderstanding of the subject. Each practice is seen as a potential power source in man's pursuit for omnipotence, finite as he may be.

The third part exposes the student to biblical perspectives on animism. In this section I attempt to highlight some biblical references to animism, the wholly otherness of God and the task the Christian worker faces in dealing with this religious world. The need for a power encounter is seen as the actual orientation of animism is discussed. Once one discovers the basic motivation in animism, the actual power sources man seeks to tap, he will more clearly understand that this system of religion is indeed one of power of no mean consequence. Therefore, the title *Gods Of Power* is quite appropriate.

It will also become quite obvious that short of a counteracting religious power, a greater power than that evidenced in animism, little headway will be made in establishing vital and truly biblical Christianity among animistic peoples. Either the resources available to Elijah and the Apostles are available to the church today, or else Christianity must take its place alongside other living faiths as only one alternative among others. Christianity will then be seen as equally valid with the others except that, along with one or two other religions, it demands a higher degree of ethics.

I am persuaded that Christianity is a power religion par excellence and that it must be so proclaimed and demonstrated. It is indeed unique and its gospel is God's power unto salvation. The animist works with spirit powers, and to doubt that is to be ignorant of the system. Christian workers need to seek those opportunities where they can give a clear demonstration that Jesus Christ is indeed Lord of all and over all other powers. It is well for Christian workers to think upon and then to practice the fact that,

> Though we walk in the flesh, we do not war according to the flesh, for the weapons of our warfare are not of the flesh, but divinely powerful for the destruction of fortresses. We are destroying speculations and every lofty thing raised up against the knowledge of God, and we are taking every thought captive to the obedience of Christ.
> (2 Corinthians 10:3-5)

ENDNOTES:

1. Culture may be best understood when divided into three constituent parts. Material culture covers matters such as technology, artifacts, clothing, housing, etc. Social culture refers to patterns of kinship, family and interpersonal relationships, etc. Metaphysical culture covers matters such as world view, beliefs, values, the world of the supernatural, the religious factors which bind the sociocultural structures into a functioning whole.

2. Alan R. Tippett, "The Evangelization of Animists," in J. D. Douglas (editor), *Let The Earth Hear His Voice* (Minneapolis: World Wide Publications, 1975), p. 844. I am indebted to Dr. Tippett for many insights regarding animism as this study will reveal.

3. *Ibid.*, pp. 844-845.

PART ONE

ANIMISM:

THE POWER RELIGION

Chapter 1

WHAT IS RELIGION?

How many ways are there to God? Is there only one god or are there many? Do all people have the same god in mind? Are there other powers to which man may turn for help in handling the problems of life? Does man indeed need a superior power to deal with the challenges of life? These and other questions come into focus in the discussion of religion. Of course, the basic question we must answer is, "What is religion?"

A UNIVERSAL PHENOMENON

All people have some form of religion—some body of beliefs and some way of dealing with those aspects of life that are beyond normal control. Religion is a universal phenomenon. It is the cement that holds the sociocultural structures of society together. Every human being has some kind of religious system. It establishes for him a set of beliefs and a scale of values with which he approaches and handles life's experiences. It is only in the West that secular man dares to claim he has no religion,[1] arguably because of his very narrow definition of religion.

DEFINITIONS OF RELIGION

When does a system of beliefs and values qualify as merely a system of philosophy or ethics rather than religion? Some have proposed that the difference lies in the fact that religion postulates a relationship with a power beyond man, whereas a philosophy or system of ethics does not. Religion gives one confidence in the outcomes of life's struggles because it offers personal connections with superior powers. For that reason every religion does many things for its followers as well as for society. First of all, it provides the individual with access to a power. It also helps him to face the troubles of life with fewer complaints, in part by providing an explanation for the problem of evil. It adds quality to life, projects the hope of a better future, proposes an ideal society, and offers salvation.[2]

Some students of religion point out that religion is an acknowledgment that man needs help from beyond himself. Whatever the source of that help, be it nature, spirits, or even the potential of science, man seems to understand that he is not an independent agent. He is not alone in this world. Forces and powers act upon him and he may exercise some influence in return. These forces penetrate all spheres of life and call for a response. Man is certainly not all that matters.[3]

Searching for a definition of religion is, therefore, much more difficult than it seems at first. No definition is agreed on by everyone. Furthermore, religion is never simple, but always a complex system of belief and practice. It is intimately bound up with and integrated into the sociocultural structures of any given group of people. While the idea of religion brings many images to mind, any definition must be sufficiently comprehensive to include the dimensions of belief, behavior, and the divine itself, however that divine may be defined.

Definitions of religion generally fall into one of two categories, the supernatural and/or phenomenological and the humanistic. These categories are not necessarily mutually exclusive. The supernatural definition emphasizes man's need for a point of reference outside the normal, such as a father figure. It highlights his need for a source of help from beyond the ordinary, a Wholly Other. Freud postulates that man's vulnerability and insecurity in a hostile world—a world of tenuous existence, natural disasters and inhumanity—drives him to invent a means to preserve courage and maintain equilibrium. He does this by creating a heavenly father—consistent with his childish ideas of an earthly father— who then becomes the object of his hero worship.

In keeping with Freud's concepts, some have concluded that religion is nothing more than exploitation, with God bribing man and man repaying the compliment. As such, religion, or more specifically, the focus on a deity however defined, is nothing less than a system of placation and subjugation which keeps people enslaved and dehumanized. [4]

Some more serious students of religion have a higher opinion of man's interaction with and need for the supernatural. In his volume,

African Traditional Religion, Idowu contends that:

> Religion results from man's spontaneous awareness of a Living Power. "Wholly Other" and infinitely greater than himself, a power of mystery because unseen, yet a present and urgent reality, seeking to bring man into communion with Himself . . . Religion, in its essence, is the means by which God as a Spirit, and man's essential self communicate.[5]

Idowu's definition recognizes man's finitude and the transcendence of the supernatural. Furthermore, he suggests that God is a searching God, a concept consistent with biblical teaching. Idowu's definition also suggests that man's religious impulse comes from his essential nature, a nature that, by Christian definition, claims that man has a conscience informed by God.[6] Religion may then be defined as essentially a search for a relationship to and with the supernatural. Although Tillich's definition does not require a personal god, it may very well summarize the above when he says:

> Religion is the state of being grasped by an ultimate concern, a concern which qualifies all other concerns as preliminary and which itself contains the answer to the question of the meaning of our life.[7]

Others maintain that religion starts and ends with man. It relates primarily to man and as such it is and can only be centered on him. Therefore it must be so defined. Kenneth L. Schmitz, in *Philosophy of Religion and the Redefinition of Philosophy,* claims there are three interacting dimensions in religion: sociology, anthropology and phenomenology.[8] Concerning sociology he notes, "community, rite, and symbol form the institution of religion."[9] In regards to anthropology, he states:

> . . . religion provides a group with a consecrated bond which helps to secure basic needs and to reserve both individual personalities and group identity from disintegration in the face of recurrent crises. Through myth men come to know how they stand with regard to the profound forces of life; through a system of values they are given norms with which to measure actions in relation to the basic needs of the group and its members; through rite they know how they might come into touch with ultimate reality and receive help or protection from its power.[10]

Schmitz describes phenomenology as "the pre-philosophical phase of religion." In this state man is aware of the numinous—what Rudolph Otto calls "a vague something."[11]

In summary, religion encompasses "a theory of being and a theory of meaning."[12] This definition by Schmitz refers to the ultimate (we assume he means the supernatural) in the context of the anthropological dimension and introduces the phenomenological as a "vague something." Nonetheless, he does include two vital aspects normally omitted by the supernaturalists, namely, the sociological and the anthropological.

THE NATURE OF RELIGION

In Primitive Religion, Its Nature and Origin, Paul Radin perceives religion to consist of two parts:

> ... the first an easily definable, if not precisely specific feeling and the second, certain specific acts, customs, beliefs, and conceptions associated with this feeling.[13]

J. O. Buswell, Jr.'s definition is not unlike Radin's. "Religion," says he, is:

> ... the set of beliefs, attitudes and practices which indicate and express the feeling of conviction of a group of persons that they are bound fast to something which is supreme to them.[14]

These two descriptions of the nature of religion may be divided into three categories: feeling, behavior, and beliefs. Feelings may be manifested in thrills, exaltation, awe, exhilaration, and occupation with internal sensations. Examples of religious behavior include rites, rituals, customs, and socially mandated behavior patterns. And these behavior patterns are motivated by beliefs. These include beliefs "in spirits outside of men, conceived of as more powerful than man and as controlling all those elements in life upon which he lays most stress."[15] These beliefs are interconnected with and related to physiological facts such as birth, reproduction, disease, death; to man's encounter with the forces of nature; and his relationship to his fellow man. The ensuing behavior patterns may show that man has a sense of control, confidence and well being. Or, on the other hand, they may show that he feels fear, uncertainty, confidence, or even frustration.

Religion thus serves several purposes. First, it provides a system of belief and practice to deal with the struggles and problems of human life. Second, it deals with man's sense of powerlessness and the feelings he derives from what he believes. Together these give man a sense of order and understanding which provides him with a measure of security and a sense of control, however limited, over the tenuousness of human existence.

In *Understanding Religious Life*, Frederick J. Streng states that religion deals with three dimensions: the personal, the cultural, and the ultimate. The personal dimension covers "internal reactions, decisions, and meaning." The cultural dimension refers to "a cultural context in which alternative values, ultimate claims, and pressures are significant influences in their lives." The ultimate dimension deals with "questions of truth, reality, meaning, and problems involved in living a full life." To sum it up, says Streng, "Religious life . . . involves a personal subjective element, takes specific cultural forms and expresses an ultimate, supreme, or comprehensive reality."[16] Reduced to its essentials, we have feelings, behavior and beliefs, with man being the central focus. However, Streng emphasizes an oft-excluded, but very necessary, function of religion, when he observes that "religion is a means of ultimate transformation."[17] Therefore, it is never passive or neutral. Instead it demonstrates itself in and through the total fabric of life.

Evolutionary theory defines totemism (kinship between a human group and certain creatures) as the original religion. Here religion is thought to be a way of honoring oneself by ascribing to oneself or to a family, clan, or tribe the attributes of selected creatures. The totem comes to symbolize man's devotion to family, tribe, clan, or nation, with its specific values, ambitions, and customs.

Nida and Smalley define religion as "a set of beliefs about the unexpected, unpredictable and mysterious—the uncharted region of human experience."[18] In addition, they claim that the purpose of religion is to "help people to have a more organized picture of the universe around them and visualize their relationship to the nature that is so close to them...to make the world a more intelligible place in which to live."[19]

Besides providing a way to cope with the reality of the unknown, religion is also the most important means for maintaining sociocultural life values. As such, it is not primarily a philosophical enquiry into the nature of being and becoming. Rather, it preserves and maintains values which undergird and uphold the infrastructure of a given sociocultural system. Life values are more basic than religious beliefs, although they may arise out of them. Only when other means (philosophies) of maintaining or establishing life values become popular, does an accepted religion fade from the corporate life of the community.

For the religious pragmatist, religion maintains three life values most prominently and tenaciously. They are self-glorification (having dominion over one's environment and success in all of life); self-realization (searching for happiness, overcoming feelings of inadequacy, lack of acceptance, and guilt); and self-preservation (the desire for a long life). Man's concepts and perceptions of his world, formulated without the aid of divine revelation, lead him to conclude that success is the purpose of life. Man is the center of his world—a world of his own making.

A psychosociological definition of religion maintains that religion is a system of symbols. The symbols reflect a source of beliefs, written or unwritten. Such sources include the Bible, the Vedas, the Koran, Lenin's writings, Mao's red book, tribal folklore, and myth. Each of these sources of belief has given rise to a distinct set of doctrines, which posit systems of reward or retribution, such as nirvana, karma, class war, a classless state, heaven or hell. They offer means to achieve success or predict defeat when improper means are used. And they postulate an ideal state brought about by a messiah, such as Marx, Buddha, a Hindu god, or an ancestor. Devotees are thus drawn into the solidarity of a common identity.

Commitment to the belief system may be demonstrated through rituals, May Day parades, worship, or other ceremonies. The system of symbols establishes powerful, pervasive and long lasting motivations and moods in man. It elicits his allegiance and provides materials with which he formulates conceptions of a general order of existence. These conceptions are clothed with an aura of reality which he accepts as uniquely true.[20]

In summary, the definitions of religion highlighted above suggest one or a combination of the following: an awareness of and reaction to a living power; an ultimate concern which qualifies all other concerns and which contains the answer to the question of the meaning of life; a way of honoring oneself (by elevating symbols which signify man's devotion to a people group); a means to maintain courage (by conceiving of benevolent powers worthy of worship); a way of exploitation whereby deities bribe man and man in turn bribes deities (and thus a system to placate gods, which subjugates people); an impulse to discover what is right and what is wrong; and a search for security, success and happiness. Animism, as we will see, combines all of the above. The animist's approach to religion is essentially pragmatic. He wants a religion that he can use to meet his needs and provide for his wishes.

A WORKING DEFINITION OF RELIGION

To delve into the world of the animist and understand his perspective on, and approach to, life, we need to arrive at some definition of religion that fits his world view. Such a definition would have to include the personal, the sociocultural, and the supernatural or phenomenological. As a religious pragmatist, the animist recognizes his own key role in making his religion useful. And in order to make it useful, he realizes that a personal relationship (one that produces feelings of presence, power, and pleasure arising out of a sense of success) with spirit beings is essential.

For the animist, life revolves around, and is totally integrated with, the realm of spirits. Meaning in life comes from the effective manipulation of spirits to do man's bidding. This relationship does not depend upon moral or ethical preconditions. But neither is it one-sided; the spirit beings are thought to be both legalistic and capricious. The animist must practice the proper rites, rituals, and liturgies to ensure a favorable response, but the spirits may change the needed rite at will. If the correct rite, ritual, or liturgy is used, however, miracles do happen, and results are achieved.

TWO CONTRASTING DEFINITIONS

The animist defines religion as a system of beliefs, feelings, and behavior which issue in rites, rituals, and liturgies. By these he manipulates familiar spirits to provide success, happiness, and security in all of life.

How does this definition compare to biblical Christianity? Would a Christian define his religion as that "aspect of one's experience in which he attempts to live harmoniously with the power or powers he believes are controlling the world?"[21] No, Bible-believing Christians define religion as an ultimate concern with a seeking and self-revealing God, which morally and ethically qualifies all other concerns, which motivates God-centered patterns of life, worship, and mission, and answers the question of the meaning of life.

Having sought to understand some of the differences among religions, let us consider why we should study them.

WHY STUDY OTHER RELIGIONS?

Pascal once said that we cannot understand man unless we consider him both in his greatness and in his misery. Without noting man's presuppositions about life as reflected in the practice of his religion, we cannot hope to understand him in depth. Religion, as we shall see, is "an institutionalized way of valuing most comprehensively and intensively"[22] what is important to man.

As Christian communicators, we widen our comprehension of other religious systems with a view to introducing people to the Jesus Christ of the Gospels. He came to show what the life of a free man is really like. Using the raw materials of a hostile world, He worked out the perfect pattern of human liberty, in total dependence upon God the Father.

To enter another's religious frame of reference requires both understanding and compassion. Compassion is not sentimentality, nor even acceptance. It demands that we respect and recognize another's belief system. We must have some understanding of the other person to perceive as he does.

To understand, we must first know the content of a given religion—or, in the words of Kraemer, "unveil the stupendous richness of (another's) religious life".[23] Secondly, understanding comes when we evaluate and measure the religious life from within the frame of reference of that religion: when we seek to know why people believe what they believe, why they behave as they do, and what hope their behavior shows them to have. Thirdly, understanding comes when we contrast Christianity's inherent humaneness with the baser elements in other religions.[24]

There are other reasons why the study of religion is so vital to the Christian communicator. Knowledge of these reasons is indispensable in establishing a truly indigenous Christian church, and one which will be true to biblical standards. If it is true that religion is the cement that holds together all facets of human society, then obviously we must understand the religion of a society to understand the society itself.

THE FOCI OF RELIGION

Religion basically revolves around two factors—the sacred and the manipulative or supplicative. The practice of religion may involve common material objects, paraphernalia, persons (practitioners and devotees), sacred places, and special times and events. Every religion has its own system of beliefs about the sacred and prescribes its own rituals for interacting with it. The clergy have definitive rituals outlining and prescribing the use and handling of objects such as idols, shrines, temples, and sacred utensils. Improperly approaching or using these objects not only brings censure but life-threatening judgment. The sacred is a source of absolute meaning. It provides believers with a validated place in the scheme of things. They know where they belong and how they should act on matters of ultimate concern. If we treat the sacred as inconsequential and easily displaced in the old religious system, it should come as no surprise when a new convert shows little fear or respect for the sacred in Christianity. But in the process of spiritual growth after conversion to Christianity, the convert may become aware of the lack of the truly sacred in his previous world view.

Not all religious practices are transferable to Christianity, but those that are should be safeguarded for their value. When indigenous forms of the sacred are treated with respect, they play an important role in regulating both individual and group behavior. Religion's hold on a people should not be treated lightly. God's truth has consequences and so does its counterfeit. The ramifications of religious practice are far-reaching.

If syncretism is to be lessened, every level of a people's culture—especially the metaphysical—must be invaded and informed by the Christian message. Failure to do so undergirds a spiritual dualism, in which some areas of life are influenced by Christianity and others serve and are informed by the previous religious belief and practice. The religious methodology (praxis) will show whether the approach to, and the use of, the sacred is manipulative or supplicative. Is the world of the supernatural viewed as something to be manipulated to secure desired objectives, or is there an attitude of dependency, and therefore a supplicative approach? In this respect the use of rituals may very easily be misinterpreted. Is a particular posture in worship or prayer, or the use of special religious terminology, merely supplicative, or is it manipulative? Are objects associated with religious practice endued with power, or do they merely facilitate worship? Are some rituals, liturgies, or sacred things seen as efficacious, and therefore inherently moral, totally apart from ethical considerations? Because religion is primarily experiential, many such questions can only be considered when a religious system is studied and observed in practice. Its impulses are largely translated into observable sociocultural forms. In this respect, religion serves some general as well as specific functions which are largely psychosocial rather than metaphysical.

FUNCTIONS OF RELIGION

The Christian communicator wants to know how a religion functions, what it does for its adherents, and what part it plays in the life of the society. Without a knowledge of and response to the general and specific functions of religion, he will miss much valuable information. The general functions of religion are to:

- provide order and cohesion to society through belief in and practice of common values and beliefs;
- relate adherents to a source of power beyond themselves and thereby create a sense of well-being;
- provide symbolic solutions to fundamental human problems;
- offer access to counter-forces for both the mysterious and other dimensions beyond normal control;
- postulate an explanation for vexing human problems; and
- validate society's value system.

The specific functions serve to:

- reduce fear and anxiety and so alleviate the helplessness of the human condition;
- provide a source of help for man's substantive needs;
- give life meaning and quality by steering life to the sacred;
- call man beyond himself to an ideal;
- provide distinctives which establish an identity; and
- hold out hope for maturation and thus mastery in the face of human frailty.

Christianity, like other religions, also does all the above. Christianity is not without its sociological and psychological functions, and it is practiced much like other religions. However, if Christianity is to be true to biblical faith, it will also call its adherents to a radical value system and lifestyle, modelled after the life of its founder and Lord, Jesus Christ.[25] His parting words and mandate for His people are:

All power is given unto me in heaven and in earth. Go ye therefore, and teach all nations, baptizing them in the name of the Father, and of the Son, and of the Holy Ghost: Teaching them to observe all things whatsoever I have commanded you: and lo, I am with you always, even unto the end of the world. Amen.[26]

Why study a religion? Because to attempt to bring the Gospel to a people without knowing how their specific religion orders human life and how it functions to provide sociopsychological mainstays for life in a given society is to invite catastrophe. The imported message, unrelated to the sociopsychological needs of a people will at best be "anaemic, precious, uninteresting, and the plaything of a small elite."[27] For this reason we will begin our study of animism by proposing a definition of the term "animism."

ENDNOTES:

1. George W. Peters, *A Biblical Theology of Missions* (Chicago: Moody Press, 1972), pp. 87-88.

2. Robert E. Hume, *The World's Living Religions* (New York: Charles Scribners Sons, rev. ed., 1959), pp. 3,4.

3. John B. Noss, *Man's Religions* (New York: McMillan Company, 1969), p. 2.

4. Marx, Lenin, Mao, *et al.*

5. E. B. Idowu: *African Traditional Religion* (London: S.C.M., 1973), p. 75.

6. Romans 1:18ff.

7. Paul Tillich, *Christianity and the Encounter of the World Religions* (New York: Columbia University Press, 1973), p. 4.

8. Frederick Ferre, *et al.*, eds., in *The Challenge of Religions* (New York: Seabury Press, 1982), p.6.

9. *Ibid.*

10. *Ibid.*, p. 7.

11. Rudolph Otto, *Das Heilige,* trans. as: *The Idea of the Holy,* by John Harvey (New York: Oxford University Press, 1958), p. 7.

12. Ferre, 1982, p. 9.

13. Paul Radin, *Primitive Religion: Its Nature and Origin* (New York: Dover Publications, Inc., 1957), p. 3.

14. J. O. Buswell, Jr., *Systematic Theology of the Christian Religion* (Grand Rapids: Zondervan Publishing Co., 1971), p. 3.

15. Radin, 1957, p. 3.

16. Frederick J. Streng, *Understanding Religious Life* (Belmont: Wadsworth Publishing Co.), 1976, p.7.

17. *Ibid.*

18. E. A. Nida and W. A. Smalley, *Introducing Animism* (New York: Friendship Press, 1959), p. 4.

19. *Ibid.*, p. 6.

20. See Philip M. Steyne, *Missionary Anthropology* (Columbia Biblical Seminary, Unpublished Manuscript, 1987), p. 138.

21. Josh McDowell & Don Stewart, *Understanding Non-Christian Religions* (San Bernardino: Here's Life Publishers, 1982), p. 10.

22. Frederick Ferre, *Basic Philosophy of Religion* (New York: Scribners, 1967), p. 73.

23. Hendrik Kraemer, *The Christian Message in a Non-Christian World* (New York: Harper and Brothers, 1938), p. 108.

24. *Ibid.*

25. Among others, see "The Sermon on the Mount," Matthew 5-7.

26. Matthew 28:18-20.

27. Stephen Neill, *Christian Faith and Other Faiths* (London: Oxford University Press, 1970), p. 214.

Chapter 2

WHAT IS ANIMISM?

Religious systems may be classified under one or several of the following categories: a belief in an impersonal power; a belief in spirit beings which indwell everything and everyone; a belief in gods, co-equal or in a hierarchy; or a belief in one supreme deity.

BELIEF IN IMPERSONAL POWER

Animists believe that an impersonal power is present in all objects. This power may be called *mana*, or life force, or force-vital, or life essence or dynamism. It may be likened to electricity—an essence with which everything is charged, which flows from one thing to another. The person in possession of this force may use it as he sees fit but always stands the chance of losing it. This is a type of pantheism.

BELIEF IN SPIRIT BEINGS

Animists also believe that spirits inhabit certain rocks, trees, mountains, idols, shrines, geographical areas and persons, both alive and deceased, and that these spirits may be manipulated to serve man.

BELIEF IN GODS

Polytheists believe in a plurality of gods, both co-equal or in hierarchy. These gods are believed to have specific spheres of control: spatial, personal or chronological.

BELIEF IN ONE SUPREME GOD

Belief in one supreme deity is called monotheism, but few people actually practice it in pure form. Some believe in a supreme god above lesser deities. Generally, in such cases, the concept of a supreme god is deistic, since this god is not considered to be intimately involved with or concerned for man and his world. Instead men seek out the lesser powers to meet their desires.

The above belief systems are found in societies where religion is valued for its power, sometimes in combinations. Animism is such a combination.

NATURE OF ANIMISM

Animism is simultaneously pantheistic, polytheistic and deistic. The animist lives in a spiritual world, instead of the techno-scientific world of the Westerner. His culture is humanitarian and socialistic rather than individualistic and/or democratic. He strives for a world of balance and harmony rather than one of competition, although he is not without competitive motives. In the face of life's demands, he is ultimately concerned with the who and why rather than the what and how.

PURSUIT OF POWER SOURCES

To survive in such a world and control it, man needs access to power to ensure equilibrium and remove conflict. The key to a successful life is the ability to manipulate the powers or forces. If man does this effectively, he will be rewarded. If he fails, he can seek an alternative means. The following incident illustrates the animist's understanding of power:

> "Pastor, this Bible you sold me is no good. I tried it and it doesn't work," said the young man with finality. "I have twice tied it with cords and cast the spell, but nothing has happened. Will you please show me how to make it work?"[1]

Or take the case of the man who wanted to be shown some especially powerful verses in the Bible, so that he could place his fingers on them to cast a spell on a woman he was seeking to seduce. He was so sure of the Bible's power he even burned a love candle on the Gospel of John. Animists believe that a sacred object like a Bible has inherent power beyond the power of its printed message. This power can be released and used for man's purposes.

The presupposition underlying both of these incidents is that there are forces or powers available for man's use. These men only had trouble finding the correct approach to coerce, awaken or release the inherent powers. That is what the shamanist (sometimes called fetishist) does. But shamanism is only one aspect of animism.

Shamanism, as practiced today, is essentially the same as animism. The Esalen Institute offers a course entitled "The Shamanic Journey and Healing: An Experimental Workshop." This is the catalog description:

Shamanic journey is one of the most ancient visionary methods used by mankind to enter non-ordinary reality and explore the hidden universe otherwise known mainly through myth and dream. Participants will undergo an experiential initiation into the journey, aided by traditional drumming and dancing. Using the spirit canoe and other methods, they will learn how the shaman's journey can be used to restore power and health, to acquire knowledge, and to solve personal problems. Participants will be introduced to shamanic seeing, to shamanic interaction with the powers of nature, and to the practical application of shamanism in their daily lives.[2]

A group called Ubu, Inc. describes its course on Shamanism like this:

This workshop will introduce the technology of shamanism, which operates by manipulating the energies of the spirit realm—the potential energy of reality. The class will provide conscious realization of, and access to, the subliminal energy forces that influence and even determine experience.[3]

Animism—what religious historian Mircea Eliade describes as shamanic experience—is a fundamental part of the human condition and the history of religions.[4]

ORIGIN OF THE TERM ANIMISM

The word "animism" is derived from the Latin *anima* which means "breath" or "breath of life." It carries with it the idea of soul or spirit. The word was first coined by Edward B. Tylor in 1871, in his study of pre-literate societies.[5] Tylor contended that the belief that man is constituted of two elements, namely body and soul, solved two enigmas for man. The first is: "What makes the difference between a living body and a dead one; and what causes waking, sleep, trance, disease and death?" The other is, "What are those human shapes which appear in dreams and visions?"[6] These phenomena were explained by the doctrine of the soul. The soul is able to leave the body temporarily, to undergo various experiences which may be recorded as dreams, or to depart for good, leaving the body without life.[7]

Tylor also observed that in pre-literate societies the concept of the soul is not limited to mankind. All objects, both animate and inanimate have their own power or force, thus giving rise to the belief that there are countless spirits in the universe.[8] This concept of a spiritual world produces a mindset very different from that of the typical Westerner, one that should be understood if a Christianity is to be clearly presented to animistic societies.

CHARACTERISTICS OF ANIMISM

Although the animist world may appear to be a neat dichotomy of the physical and spiritual, animist practice shows that it is in reality one fabric. This world is in essence spiritual rather than material, and any distinction between the religious and the secular is meaningless. What happens in the physical world has its spiritual coordinates and vice-versa. The whole universe is interconnected through the will and power contained in both animate and inanimate objects. Everything man is, does, handles, projects and interacts with is interpenetrated with the spiritual. His sociocultural structures, down to their finest details, are under the control of spiritual powers or forces. Nothing in man's environment escapes the influence or manipulation of the spirit world. The world is more spiritual than it is physical, and it is spiritually upheld.

If life is affected by spirits, then it is of utmost importance to maintain good relations with the spirits and secure their favor. To do this effectively animist man must discover who is in power and why this power acts as it does. This is an unending pursuit.

QUESTION OF MEANING

Meaning is always understood in a spiritual way. When personal resources fail, religious specialists will divine and supply satisfactory meanings. Life's questions and answers revolve around the spiritual rather than the physical. For example, after an impassioned presentation of the Christian Gospel, the preacher was asked: "What would you do if a stranger murdered a villager and confessed that a spirit had made him do it?" It would be simplistic to respond with talk of legal retribution. The answer must be spiritual in nature. The animist would want to know who the actual murderer is, who forced him to murder and why. Another Christian missionary was asked what he would do if a herd of elephants trampled the villagers' crops? Recommending the erection of a good solid fence would not have been enough. The questioner wanted to know who directed the elephants toward that particular area and why. The animist looks for reasons beyond the obvious and found only in the spiritual realm. Catastrophes, natural disasters, disease, untimely death and other exigencies of life are all evaluated spiritually, with a view to establish or restore harmony and balance to life's context.

A POWER-CONSCIOUS SYSTEM

To get the spirit world to serve man's objectives, man needs life force—power. The search for it occupies a great deal of his time, for without it he is helpless. Power is needed to make rain, give good crops, secure employment, heal diseases, guarantee fertility, or pass school exams. Protection is needed from disease, evil spells cast by malevolent persons, catastrophes of all sorts, failure, sorcery and witchcraft. These can only be dealt with effectively if one has power. Ways to secure power include contacting religious specialists, performing rituals, using medicines, contacting spirit beings or ancestors, worshiping ancestors, using charms and fetishes, participating in ceremonies, observing taboos, and going on vision quests. Some individuals are thought to be more powerful than others because of their success in making contact with power sources, whether through lineage, spirit-beings, magical paraphernalia or the practice of rituals. The search for a superior power is endless although not always vigorous.

This power could be totally objective. The officiant in the ritual may be no more than a catalyst. When the prescription for securing power is performed correctly, power follows. The relationship with the source of power is not dependent upon ethics or morality, but on expertise that gets results. Nida and Smalley affirm:

> ... if only one knows the right formulae, the spirit world can be made to do one's bidding, whether for good or for evil. The animist is not concerned about seeking the will of his god, but in compelling, entreating, or coercing his god to do his will.[9]

38

The power may belong to an individual, in which case it is thought of as life force. The person possessing the power can use it for personal aggrandizement and/or other purposes. It may be passed on to others or secured by them through touching or transferring objects associated with the possessor. Life force can be increased, threatened or diminished. When a person's life force is maintained or increased, he is well. When it diminishes, he is tired or sick, and it needs to be checked. The happiness and prosperity of the individual, the family and tribe depend on the conservation and strengthening of life forces. Wright correctly observes that in animism, man seeks to experience wholeness in this life. He writes:

> Animism is a method for the integration of man with himself and nature. To achieve this situation the devotee seeks a source of power. The animist acknowledges an ideal state, and that he is estranged from that state, and that beliefs and practices will lead to a return to wholeness. The concept of "wholeness" varies from good hunting or success in love, to union with the supernatural.[10]

By nature then, a passive approach to religious life will never satisfy the animist. His religion must be one of works, and he must have faith in his own ability to make things work in his favor.

In summary, in animism the world is essentially spiritual, and the material and the spiritual are totally integrated. Man needs power from outside himself to control his environment. Life's purpose is to seek and maintain the balance and harmony that result in success, happiness and security. To do this man must deal with the spirit powers correctly. Thus by rites, rituals and liturgies, he must impress and manipulate spirit beings to produce success, happiness and security. Life's pursuit and religious motivation is, in modern parlance, to find and sit in front of a console of a formulae computer and coerce and compel the whole universe, both spirit and material, to do man's bidding and serve his selfish ends regardless of what they may be. Man is the focus of life and all forces (powers) are solely for his benefit.

CONCLUSION

In a most helpful study on the difference between the God of Israel and the spiritual world of natural religionists (another term for animists), G. Ernest Wright helps us to understand that there is absolutely no compatibility between a faith centered in the God of the Bible and a faith focused on animistic beliefs. He writes:

Israelite faith . . . was an utterly unique and radical departure from all contemporary pagan religions. The latter were all natural and cultural religions . . . . Natural religion in Biblical times analyzed the problem of man over against nature. In the struggle for existence the function of religious worship was that of the integration of personal and social life with the natural world . . . . The life of the individual was embedded in the rhythm and balance of nature which was thus to fit into the rhythm and integration of the cosmic society of nature . . . In the faith of Israel . . . there is a radical and complete difference . . . The Israelite did not analyze the problem of life over against nature. The latter plays a subordinate role in the faith, except as it is used by God to further his work in society and history. Instead, the problem of life is understood over against the will and purpose of the God who had chosen one people as the instrument of his universal, redemptive purpose. This election of a people was not based upon merit, but upon a mysterious grace . . . . Here then, is an utterly different God from all the gods of all natural, cultural and philosophic religions. He is no immanent power in nature nor in the natural process of being or becoming . . . He transcends nature, as he transcends history . . . He is unique, *sui generis*, utterly different.[11]

The revelation of God's Word was given to a people whose beliefs had regressed to the point that they had come to accept that what was natural religious practice for most people—animism—was normative for them as well. A look at world religions in practice will reveal that animism lies very close to the surface of all of them.

ENDNOTES

1. Jimmy Aldridge, "Faith of Fear and Fetish" in *Heartbeat* 22 (Nashville: Free Will Baptist Foreign Missions, March 1982), p. 3.

2. *The Esalen Catalog* (May-October 1981), p. 17.

3. *SCP Newsletter* 9, no. 1 (Berkeley, California, March-April 1983), p. 2.

4. *Ibid.*, p. 4. Cf. Eliade Mircea, *The Sacred and The Profane: The Nature of Religion* (New York: Harper Torchbooks, 1961).

5. Edward B. Tylor, *Primitive Culture* (London: John Murray, 1871): II, p. 2.

6. *Ibid.*

7. *Ibid.*

8. *Ibid.*

9. E. A. Nida and W. A. Smalley, *Introducing Animism* (New York: Friendship Press, 1959), p. 54.

10. Michael A. Wright, "Some Observations on Thai Animism," ed. W. A. Smalley, in *Missionary Readings in Anthropology* (South Pasadena: William Carey Library, 1984), p. 116.

11. G. Ernest Wright, *God Who Acts* (London: SCM Press, 1973), pp. 19-21.

Chapter 3

HOW ANIMISTIC ARE WORLD RELIGIONS?

Man has an innate desire to want to control what happens to himself, to others and to the environment. The illusion of omnipotence is intrinsic to humanity and can be traced back to our first parents in response to the serpent's challenge in the garden in Genesis 3. Man desires to be the center of the universe and to control everything and everyone. Arthur S. Gregor claims that man attempts "to gain control over nature by supernatural means." The means consist of "spells, charms and other techniques to give man what he cannot achieve with his normal human powers."[1] Are these features confined to primitive and tribal peoples?

THE UNIVERSALITY OF FOLK RELIGION

The desire to exercise control over life's circumstances is universal. It is interesting that contemporary advocates of witchcraft (also called the craft of the wise) claim that they can guarantee man such omnipotence. For example:

If you are tired of frustration, bewilderment, and helpless bafflement, tired of having guilt and fear yelled at you, give our way—the Old Way—a try. Witchcraft will open new vistas for you . . . The School of Wicca conducts a serious . . . study course . . . it results in a thorough theoretical and practical knowledge of Witchcraft as a religion. The course consists of . . . (among others), . . . use of your powers, use of spirit powers . . . freeing the mind (meditation); standard Wicca services (includes Eshbats, Sabbats, and casting the circle); initiation and fertility services; . . . prayers, songs, and incantations (spells); perils and precautions (includes exorcism); forming and running a coven;

healing; telepathy, clairvoyance, and clairaudience; prediction; and harmony . . . The Church and School of Wicca . . . is a loosely knit organization . . . in the group are churches of many persuasions using their own rituals and calling on their own deities.[2]

How does one become adept at passing on such desired knowledge to help man realize his supposed omnipotence? The advertising material tells the potential initiate how the instructor came by such valuable expertise:

After extensive theoretical studies in England and Wales, he continued into various practical religious exercises, passing tests demanded by various mountain sects of witches from Cumberland through Wales and into the high Alps of Bavaria. From these experiences where all fear of bodily death was eradicated, he continued into the required study of other religions, spending time in work with Hindus, Haitians, Sikhs, Thais, Japanese, and Australian Aborigines, all in their native lands.[3]

Writing on Baal worship, Caquot and Sznycer in *Ugaritic Religion* and Boyd in *Baal Worship* point out the same practices mentioned above. These practices also characterize animism. For example, they list the use of enchantments, dealings with spirits, wizards, and mediums, witchcraft, soothsaying, divination, fortune telling, necromancy, fertility practices, incense and candle burning and many other rituals, as remedies for "frustration, bewilderment and helpless bafflement."

Generally, classical world religions stress the importance of orthodoxy (correct doctrine and correct understanding of practice), whereas folk religion (practiced religion) is of the heart and seeks to meet the felt needs of a people.

Folk religion largely dispenses with cognitive knowledge, but unlike most Westerners, Easterners integrate the two types of religious approaches. Manipulating and accruing merit are common as well. Man must by all means seek to secure the favor of the deities, however these may be perceived. As a pragmatist and practitioner, the folk religionist "is convinced that it is the world—not himself—that is out of synchronization with life."[4] It is, therefore, man's responsibility to either cajole or manipulate it to perform correctly.

The New Age Movement is also in the stream of the so called Old Way. Here, too, the search is for harmony, and for power to synchronize the world with human desires. One of its more famous and outspoken advocates, Shirley MacLaine, speaks freely of the fact that she consults with ancient souls via a medium, meditates in a mountain mineral bath (mountains are the traditional abode of superior spirit beings), and meets a man who has befriended an extraterrestrial. The actress defends her newfound spirituality by noisily proclaiming, "I am God, I am God."[5]

The New Age Movement, the Way of Wicca, Baalism and animism (or shamanism) are all cut from the same cloth. All place man at the center of his world, all ascribe to man a sense of omnipotence—a god within. All consult spirits and claim they know how to channel or manipulate spirit power. All believe life can be transformed by techniques applied to mind, body and spirit. All claim that there is no such thing as sin—i.e., offending a righteous God. All seek to dispense with guilt as merely an outside imposition. All would basically ignore the fact that history is moving toward final culmination.[6] And all would claim that spirit involvement produces self-knowledge and awareness of one's identity, issuing in success, happiness and security.[7]

THEORETICAL DIFFERENCE BETWEEN ANIMISM AND WORLD RELIGIONS

Religious scholars place belief systems into either of two broad categories: tribal and world religions. Tribal religions, also sometimes called folk, primal or traditional religions, hold that spirits of various kinds inhabit the universe; that they may be manipulated to serve man's purposes; that life continues after death, and that the deceased is accessible to living man and vice-versa. Tribal religion encompasses all aspects of life, and includes the unborn, the living and the dead. The spiritual is the real fabric of life and therefore also of culture.

In contrast, world religions are institutionalized. A world religion may have all the trappings of animism but is further distinguished by a legendary founder, sacred writings, and appointed places of worship. Although membership may appear optional, it is often socially required, and frequently synonymous with national citizenship. In world religions the practices of the sophisticated may vary greatly from those of the masses, but only qualitatively so. The teachings are generally symbolic and ritualized, with a significant difference between the real and the ideal. These religions have taken on different forms at different times and known periods of renewal and decline.

Religions which are normally placed in the category of world religions are Buddhism (and its many variations), Christianity, Confucianism (though its classification as a religion is debatable), Hinduism (and its many variations), Islam, Shintoism, and Taoism. Some form of animism has impinged on each of these religions, as will be pointed out. Seldom, if ever, are any of these belief systems practiced in their wholly pure form. However, even in their pure forms, all religions with the exception of biblical Christianity (which is not very widely practiced in its pure form) have levels of animistic influence.

ANIMISTIC PRESENCE IN WORLD RELIGIONS

Writing on Islam in West Africa, Trimingham[8] has a very helpful model of the interrelationships of three impinging cultures which qualify, modify and condition each other. He breaks it down into a six-fold scheme, three of which are helpful in understanding the presence of animism in a religion. He writes of three cultures: animist, Muslim and Western. He proposes that when the animist culture is in ascendance in Islam, there is a reversion from Islam to animism. He says that local custom holds out against Islamic law. Dynamism, spiritism, ritual practices and ceremonies then become associated with Islamic institutions such as circumcision, marriage and death, and are practiced in the traditional way. When Islam is in ascendance and animism is subservient, pagan myth and ritual are informed by Islamic myth and ritual, while retaining their animistic root. When animism conditions Western thinking, it gives rise to African separatist sects, which practice African Christianity informed by animistic concepts, thus giving animist meanings to Western forms. The result in each case is syncretism, although the degree of syncretism differs. Trimingham's model goes on to cover three other possibilities of syncretism: "Western conditioning Animist"—in which case there is breakdown and decay in African religions through the secularization of political, economic social and religious theory; "Muslim conditioning Western"—where Islamic law is officially recognized and Christian propaganda is prohibited; and "Western conditioning Muslim"—where there is resistance and reaction to secular civilization because Western law and procedure are applied to Muslims.

These three schemes of cultural and/or religious encounter are characteristic of all religions. In each case either animism, secular culture or a specific religion are at any one time in history ascendant, but the religion will never be free from the influence of animism. As previously stated, man has an innate desire to want to control what happens to himself, to others and to the environment. Animism claims for itself such power. Animism also discounts personal responsibility, sin and guilt. It guarantees success, happiness and security as products of the use of proper means and/or the manipulation of spirit beings. Such animistic concerns all too frequently motivate religious activity, providing man with the illusion of omnipotence to the point that he may even believe that he is above the orthodox practice of the religion.

In the practice of all religions there is this animistic tendency in which man wants to be his own god and control the world as it affects him. This innate desire, and the belief and practice which result from it, influence the orthodox practice of various religions at different levels.

LEVELS OF INFLUENCE

There are four broad levels. On Level One, animism dominates the religion. At Level Two, animism has significant effect on the religion. Folk Christianity (also called Folk Catholicism), like that practiced in the Philippines, operates on Level Two. All folk religions (such as Folk Islam) are also classified here. Many of the African Independent churches qualify for this level, although a number have moved into Level Three. At Level Three, no blatant, overt animist practices are evident. Devotees of the religion have not only adopted the religious forms of their chosen faith, but they have kept its traditional meanings. Religious practice is claimed to be orthodox, and any aberration is supposedly only some innocent superstition of little consequence. However, practice fluctuates between orthodox and animistic. The religious cult is central but by no means pure. The syncretistic animistic aberrations provide answers where the religious cult does not. The desire is still for power, with a view to success, happiness and security.

Level Four is characterized by orthodox practice. However, such practice is not altruistic. Correct belief and correct behavior here is only legalistic—a way to manipulate the deity or spirit by impressing it with the devotee's commitment. Man's innate desire is unchanged. He wants success, happiness, and security, and it is not beyond human nature to use right belief and right practice to manipulate the gods and so secure it. On this level motivations for religious activity are open to question. In the words of James 4:3, "You ask and do not receive, because you ask with the wrong motives, so that you may spend it on your pleasures."

Mysticism may appear on any of the four levels, and piety may be seen on Levels Three and Four. However, both may be forms of manipulation on the fourth level. Only when a religion is practiced for its own sake will there be an absence of animism. The words of Satan to God concerning Job presupposed an impossibility: "Will man serve God for naught"—for absolutely no benefit?[9] The unfolding drama reveals that anything short of worshiping God for His own sake is an insult to the character and nature of Sovereign God. The framers of the Westminster Catechism correctly intoned that the chief purpose of man is to glorify God—not for what He does for man, but because He is God. That kind of altruism can rightfully claim that animism's influence is minimal or nonexistent.

(See diagram on next page)

EXAMPLES OF INFLUENCE ON WORLD RELIGIONS

In Christianity

Some very informative articles have been written on Folk Christianity, especially in Latin America.[10] What is true in Latin America also applies elsewhere. For example, in Filipino Christianity animism still provides meaning and motivation for religious practice. Though Roman Catholicism is the espoused faith, for most Filipinos the shaman or babaylan is the recognized expert in reading the signs of the gods, the spirits and the ancestors. He has power to heal or kill, powers given by the spirit world. Amulets and charms (in the forms of brightly colored beads for infants) and medals and scapularies (with images of saints and holy inscriptions for others) are worn to ward off evil spirits and obtain blessing. Herbs of many varieties, either fresh or distilled in holy water, promise quick relief from illnesses.

Professional praying women (also religious specialists) offer their services to pray for desired blessings for those too busy to do it themselves. Speaking in tongues is deemed more effective at producing results than intelligible prayer. Words have power.

Images of patron saints are claimed to have magical power, and any personal contact with them assures the devotee of healing, spiritual strength, blessing on children, or any of a variety of positive responses to human longings. Christian saints have replaced the epic ancestor heroes of the past, and are endowed with magical charms and miraculous wonders. They are appeased, worshiped and entreated, in very much the same way as was done traditionally. Saints now serve as intermediaries between the gods and man.

Instead of the fertility rituals of the past, a patron saint referred to

LEVELS OF ANIMISTIC INFLUENCE

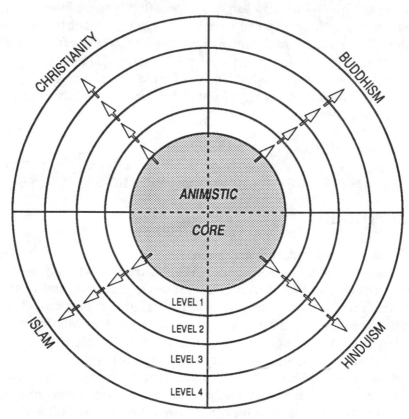

ANIMISTIC CORE:

1. Fear.
2. Absence of consolation.
3. Little differentiation between good and evil.
4. Fatalistic approach to life.
5. A search for a means to manipulate.

LEVELS:

1. Strong influence—little or no distinction.
2. Significant effect.
3. More or less influence.
4. Little, if any, influence.

as the "miraculous *Senora de Penafrancia*," is invoked for a good harvest. Bedecked in semi-precious stones and a gilded costume, the image is prayed to and worshiped that it may look kindly on the land.

Merit may be secured by participation in a *penetencia*—a re-enactment of the sufferings of Christ. Devotees scourge themselves with steel-tipped lashes until they bleed and fall down in pain and exhaustion. Some carry heavy wooden crosses, travelling by foot, from one town to another. Others even have themselves nailed to crosses, while others crawl on hands and knees over rough pavement. This is not the biblical fulfilling of the sufferings of Christ, but rather an attempt to secure the favor of God in some particular respect. An anthropologist observed that Filipinos are not consciously seeking for salvation as much as increased potency of their religious life. Filipinos are forever seeking for a demonstration and experience of power.[11]

In Islam

Several recent works have sought to highlight the practice of animism in Islam.[12] Up until very recently few scholars were even prepared to acknowledge its presence in the practice of religion. Dr. J. Dudley Woodberry, former missionary to Pakistan and other middle-eastern countries, and now Professor of Islamics at Fuller Theological Seminary, said:

I had been through what many considered to be the best program in Islamic Studies in the West, yet I never took a course in folk Islam. When I arrived in Pakistan in 1968, I soon realized how little I understood of what was going on there . . . I had been taught that Muslims viewed God as holy, other and distant, and that they believed that no mediator existed between God and man. Yet, in Pakistan, what appeared to be a majority of the people were visiting holy men, thus creating a mediator between God and human kind.[13]

When questioned concerning the origins of folk Islam, Woodberry replied:

Its origins go back to religious beliefs existing prior to Islam . . . For example, Mohammed preached against polytheism and against the idols in the Kaaba . . . But at the same time, when he adopted into Islam the essentially pagan pilgrimage to Mecca, though he changed its content (making it refer to the one true God instead of the various gods of the desert), he included the sacred black stone found in the

Kaaba in the pilgrimage. So even today, people touch the stone and expect to receive blessing from doing so ... Although magic is condemned in the Koran, certain magical practices or spells are admitted. You may use a spell, (according to orthodox tradition), to counteract the evil eye, snake bites, scorpion bites, and yellowness in the eye, so long as you do not associate anyone else with God. Mohammed allowed these and other practices ... formerly associated with the spirit world.[14]

In response to the question, "How does Folk Islam affect the way of a Muslim?" he said:

Many Muslims go to holy men ... for guidance, healing, and other immediate concerns (like when a family hopes to give birth to a baby boy). Sometimes, as in the Zar cult (found all across North Africa, throughout Egypt and the Arab world, on into Iran, and down into black Africa), you find people practicing divination as a means of determining or deciding questions about the future. An individual in the Zar cult might invite the Zar spirit into him or herself with the use of music, sacrifices, and things of that nature. While the spirit is within them they decide what is going to happen or what they should do in the future. Then they try to exorcise the spirit ... Many Muslims have little amulets fastened to them at a very early age. These amulets may include entire miniature copies of the Koran, select verses from the Koran, magical numbers, or the names of various angels or prophets. These are meant to ward off evil.[15]

Woodberry also mentioned other animistic practices in Islam. He tells of rubbing the brass knob at the edge of the saints' tombs for blessing, of reciting the names of God magically and of using names to bring reconciliation in the family, gain forgiveness and experience healing and deal with other felt needs.[16]

In some parts of the Muslim world, the head of the mosque will provide people with written amulets and prescribed rituals with which to achieve their goals. He is at one and the same time traditional shaman and teacher of Islamic law.

Other sources, such as *The Gospel and Islam,* edited by Don McCurry, discuss the presence and practice of animism in Islam. Several desires are highlighted. The less acceptable and more acceptable animistic responses are then posited along with biblical Christian answers. Animism may respond to the fear of the unknown with idolatry, stone worship, fetishes, talismans, charms or some less obvious superstition. Fear of evil is met with sorcery, witchcraft, amulets, knots or exorcism.

Fear of the future calls for angel worship, divination, the casting of spells, fatalism or fanaticism. Shame of not being in the elite requires magic means, curses or blessings, and use of hair and nail trimmings with which to practice sorcery.

If someone is powerless in the face of evil, the answer lies in worshiping a saint, or securing special blessing (baraka) from saints and angels. The feeling that life is meaningless can be eradicated by the acquisition of a familiar spirit, and sickness can be dealt with by magic means. Certain trees have healing power and saints may be implored. So too the creed and pillars of the religion are reinterpreted and given animistic functions.[17]

In Buddhism

Classical Buddhism is a theoretically atheistic and intellectual pursuit. In its many variations it has influenced a large part of the Asian world. More recently it has appeared in the West in different forms. However, as Michael C. Wright contends, few if any devotees practice pure Buddhism. He asks how Buddhism has then survived, if it needs an "intellectual turn of mind" so uncommon among man? In reply, he states that Buddhism has survived because it finds "its basis, not in intellectual principles, but in the aspirations of mankind . . . it survives grafted onto another system."[18]

That system, in every case, is folk religion. Buddha is both divinity, and when convenient, no more than a significant teacher. Devotees may both petition Buddha for his divine power, and subscribe to his apparent atheism when they are threatened by the demands which the existence of God would make on them.[19] Eugene Nida observes:

> The average Buddhist in a small town in Thailand is only vaguely aware of the importance of self-mastery by the denial of the ultimate reality of human existence. It is much more important for him to show respect for the spirit house which stands in the yard, to buy a little patch of gold leaf to decorate his favorite buddha, or to discover his fortune by whirling a numbered wheel after appropriate ritual.[20]

Folk Buddhism looks on the Buddha as a magical, swirling source of power. He is worshiped like the spirits and resides in the images of him, not as a person but as a power. Shrines or spirit houses (where spirits are appealed to, implored and worshiped) are very much a part of the religious system. Spirits serve as guardians of lands, buildings, material objects and all that relates to man. Sometimes this guardian function encompasses ownership also. Says Wright concerning Folk Buddhism in Thailand:

> Thai skilled artisans and traditional performers have ceremonies when they pay their respects to their teachers, and behind the immediate teachers, to the spirit masters of their profession . . . The approbation of the spirit master makes the drummer a drummer. Should he offend his master, he would lose his art . . . The human, historical teachers share in the spirit power of the original master . . . .[21]

Buddhists believe that ultimately everything works because of its relationship to a power source. Without this power source (phra) impotence reigns. The phra is nonmaterial, and it can increase or decrease, depending on what rituals are performed or omitted. But it is personal, and it demands respect.

The folk Buddhist lives in a spirit world. He thinks and acts in terms of spirits, constantly seeking to secure their favor to facilitate success in life. Whatever will arouse the interest, sympathy and compassion of the spirit world becomes a means of appeasement and cajoling. Prayer wheels, prayer flags, temple offerings, alms, the use of symbolism, burning of incense, festivals, bonfires, dragon floats, shooting off firecrackers or whatever is suitable—all serve to positively influence the spirit world and put it in the devotee's debt. Building decorations illustrate this relationship to the spiritual world:

> Earthenware cocks came to stand as symbols of beneficent powers, as did the ugly dragons, whose images used to scare away evil spirits, and came to be posted as guardians of entrances and rooftops. Bonfires and torches, and later, lanterns and candles and noisy firecrackers, served a similar purpose. Chinese festivals, even today, properly require firecrackers, lanterns, and huge dragon floats to celebrate good fortune in surviving evils that beset us in the course of our lives.[22]

As part of the spirit world, ancestors figure largely in daily life. They are worshiped along with other divinities. Says Newell:

> In its external appearance the butsudan is an altar to the buddhas and bodhisattvas, but in its essence it is a Buddhist-style altar consecrated to the family ancestors.[23]

The living are obligated to maintain the deceased ancestors by symbolically transposing to them the comforts and necessities of life. To fail to do so would be to chance the dire consequences of their wrath. But ancestors have obligations too. They act as intermediaries, securing for their families the blessings of the spirit world, which are translated into material blessing. The greatest difference between the Folk Buddhist and his counterpart in tribal religion is that in the former, practice is institutionalized. The motivations and results obtained are essentially the same.

In Hinduism

Although Hinduism supposedly consists of meditation, clean living and acts of piety, in actual practice it is nothing less than a system of rituals with which to manipulate spirit beings. Lamin Sanneh says:

> I have yet to know of the case of a man who sincerely believes in God and doesn't adopt ways of influencing his God, whether it be with a phrase or with some material object made of wood, iron or earth.[24]

All of the Hindus' rites and rituals are designed either to bring them information or to manipulate the forces around them in such a way as to better their existence. Life is wrapped up in ritual practice. There are five daily obligations:

> ... the offering to the gods, the offering to the seers, the offering to the forefathers, the offering to lower animals, and the offering to humanity. Then, obligations are embodied in the daily religious practices in the home. Starting before sunrise, the religious Hindu purifies himself and performs morning worship; at "midday" . . . he performs his worship before the image, and offers food to animals and to guests; at dusk he once more worships according to prescribed ritual, and after that he takes his evening meal.[25]

If "religious practices are a means to an end," as claimed by Sivaprasad Bhattacharyya, and "use the quickest and surest devices which have been discovered . . ."[26] then the religious craft of the Hindu is exactly like that of the animist. Rituals serve to program the deity or spirit world for action, namely positive action. For example, in the temple rituals, the god must be awakened, he must be bathed, fed, anointed and decorated. And the purpose? How else may a family, or community, or an individual get the god(s) to act favorably in its behalf? One veteran missionary to India describes it this way:

> The day's work is punctuated with little acts of worship. For instance, the bus driver starts his day's driving with an act of reverence for the steering wheel—or more accurately, for the god in the steering wheel—thus hoping for safety on the road.[27]

For the Hindu, all of life is religious. Religious practice is not confined to the home, the temple and other ceremonial occasions. Auspicious times to take on life's challenges must be divined, and protection must be secured against evil spirits which cause illness and other life-threatening calamities. Charms, sacred threads, amulets, magic, sorcery or other means must be used to guarantee success in life's pursuits. There are many magical religious practices. Holy men write out their prayers, chew them up and throw them at an idol, believing that if the paper sticks the prayers will be answered. Women practice imitative magic, bathing in a pool or river containing phallic symbols, believing that this will guarantee them ability to produce children. There are many such examples of Hindu pragmatism.

Hindu gods are estimated to number roughly three hundred thousand. Hindus try to pay respect to all gods of all peoples, fearing that missing one might have a negative effect on life. The variety and plurality of gods in the Hindu pantheon reflect man's diverse desires, even as do the plethora of spirits in the experience of the animist. Like the animist, the Hindu is too utilitarian to leave the events of life to chance. Through ritual means, gods are manipulated to meet a particular need. The challenge is to match the god to the need. Should the task be too much for the devotee, there are specialists who can help—the priest, guru, pundit, astrologer, sannyasin, sadhu, swami, shaman and yogi.

Hinduism is a religion of works, and though its object may be to so blend man with his world that man and universe are truly integrated, in actuality it is a means to place man at the center of the universe and have all of creation serve him. All religions appear to foster man's desire to control what happens to himself, to others and to the environment. What means has man found to effect that control? To understand the rationale for the use of these various means, we must review, first of all, basic animist beliefs.

ENDNOTES

1. Arthur S. Gregor, *Witchcraft and Magic* (New York: Charles Scribner's Sons, 1972), p. 1.

2. Garvin Frost, "Church and School of Wicca" (New Bern: North Carolina, n. d. A letter of introduction.)

3. *Ibid.*

4. Phil Parshall, *Bridges to Islam: A Christian Perspective on Folk Islam* (Grand Rapids: Baker Book House, 1983), p. 71.

5. *USA Weekend,* Washington, D. C. (January 9-11, 1987), p. 4.

6. G. Ernest Wright, *God Who Acts* (London: S. C. M. Press, 1972), pp. 16-19.

7. *USA Weekend,*(Washington, D. C., January 9-11, 1987), pp. 4, 5.

8. See J. Spencer Trimingham, *The Christian Church and Islam in West Africa,* (London, 1955).

9. Job 1:9.

10. William A. Smalley, editor, *Readings in Mission Anthropology* (Tarrytown, New York: Practical Anthropology, 1967), pp. 17-25.

11. Source of information: *Filipino Religious Beliefs,* (Manila, Philippines: Institute for Studies in Asian Church and Culture).

12. Bill A. Musk "Popular Islam: The Hunger of the Heart," in *The Gospel and Islam: A 1978 Compendium,* ed. Don McCurry (Monrovia: MARC., 1978), pp. 208-219. Cf. Phil Parshall, *Bridges To Islam: A Christian Perspective on Folk Islam* (Grand Rapids: Baker Book House, 1983). Samuel Zwemer's volume on *Islam and Animism* is most helpful.

13. *Pulse* 121, no. 6 (Wheaton Ill.: Evangelical Missions Information Services, March 21, 1986), p. 2.

14. *Ibid.*

15. *Ibid.,* pp. 2,3.

16. *Ibid.*

17. Don McCurry, editor, 1978, pp. 208-219.

18. Michael A. Wright, "Some Observations on Thai Animism," in *Missionary Readings in Anthropology,* ed. W. A. Smalley (South Pasadena: William Carey Library, 1984), p. 115.

19. *Ibid.*

20. Eugene A. Nida, *Customs and Cultures* (New York: Harper & Brothers, 1954), pp. 168, 169.

21. Michael A. Wright, in W.A. Smalley (1984), p. 117.

22. Archie J. Baum, *The World's Living Religions* (Carbondale: Southern Illinois University Press, 1964), p. 154.

23. William H. Newell, editor, *Ancestors* (Paris: Moulton Publishers, n. d.), p. 150.

24. Lamin Sanneh, "Amulets and Muslim Orthodoxy," in *International Review of Missions,* 63 (October 1974), p. 522.

25. Kenneth W. Morgan, editor, *The Religion of the Hindus* (New York: Ronald Press, 1953), p. 154.

26. *Ibid.*

27. Howard F. Vos, editor, *Religions in a Changing World* (Chicago: Moody Press, 1959), p. 195.

PART TWO

BELIEFS AND

PRACTICES

Chapter 4

BASIC ANIMIST
BELIEFS

The preceding pages have briefly dealt with some of animism's widespread influence. There are, however, particular beliefs and practices which characterize animism. None of these particulars can be fully understood apart from the whole. Each practice and belief is part of a complex and cohesive whole. The composite makes animism a viable, functioning, powerful religion.

APPEAL OF ANIMISM

Animism, as a total religious system, holds out the promise of success in the face of the difficulties, challenges and routine experiences of life. Animism works, and it encompasses all spheres of life from cradle to grave. Animism is not merely an attempt to respond to man's fears. It delivers on its promises, providing a degree of success, security and happiness.

Animism appeals to both the human mind and spirit. One of its foundational postulates is that man can master his own destiny. It is not necessary for man to be helplessly imposed on and buffeted by life's events. Using rituals, he can effectively deal with life's exigencies in the spirit world, the physical world and the world of human relations. By using power sources he can meet any challenge and attain success in life.

Animist man has come to believe that spirit powers can be manipulated by correct rituals. James Leyburn captures the animist's confidence in his beliefs as he spells out the Haitian voodooist's creed:

> I believe in scores of gods and spirits, guardians of earth and sky, and of all things visible and invisible. I believe that all these spirits are potent, although less majestic than *le bon dieu* (the good god), of the Christians; that some of them came with our ancestors from our former home in Africa, while others we have learned about in our Haitian Fatherland; that these spirits have power to possess us, their worshipers, informing us of their needs and desires, which we must faithfully satisfy; that these *loa* (spirits), like us, are capable of good and evil; gentleness and anger; I believe in the efficacy of sacrifice, in the pleasures of the living, in the careful cult of the dead, who may return to our abodes; in the spiritual causation of diseases and misfortune; in the possibility of interfering with the normal flow of events by means of magic.[1]

Although animism does not have an enscripturated belief system, it does have a comprehensive theology, as we shall see. Nothing in life is left to chance. The specialist (one who has demonstrable access to spirit power) has a ritual for everything. The animist puts into practice his firm belief that it is supernatural power (spirit power), and not mere head knowledge, that is of overriding importance. The actual use of power counts more than does cognitive reflection. A man's actions influence his feelings; therefore, acting out what he feels and believes provides emotional relief and brings him a sense of peace. Thinking without acting is a wearisome exercise in futility.

FOUNDATIONAL BELIEFS

Animist beliefs cover four broad areas: Holism, Spiritualism, Power, and Community.

Holism

Holism is a philosophical term for the view that life is more than the sum of its parts. The world interacts with itself. The sky, the spirits, the earth, the physical world, the living and the deceased all act, interact and react in consort. One works on the other and one part can't exist nor be explained without the other. The universe, the spirit world and man are all part of the same fabric. Each needs the other to activate it.

In this schema man enters the surrounding world in all of its dimensions—physical, material and spiritual—and it in turn penetrates him. He feels at one with his world, and his world mystically reciprocates. Therefore, distinctions between the physical, material or the spiritual are not only unthinkable but absurd. There is no category of thought for them in traditional animism. That would be beyond the bounds of animist reality.

The animist does not draw a line between the sacred and the profane, or the secular and the religious, or his profession and his community responsibilities. They are all knit together in a whole. The animist, therefore, is not likely to analyze the parts of his world. If he should he would likely give paramount importance to the world of the spirits. Holism is foundational to animism and leads logically to pantheism.

Spiritualism

Another foundational animist belief is spiritualism, a belief which is implicit in holism. Spiritualism holds that spirituality is the very essence of life and that life is saturated with supernatural possibilities. Everything in life can be influenced by, and responds to, the world of spirits. Whatever happens in the physical realm has a spiritual coordinate, and, likewise, whatever transpires in the spiritual realm has direct bearing on the physical world. Man is related to and dependent upon the unseen. For that reason all of life is to be understood spiritually. The correct response to any situation is a spiritual one, whether the matter is a family affair, sickness, or ceremonial practice.

Animist man does not think of spirituality as a state to be achieved, nor does he think of it as a tool to get what he wants out of life. To him, the spiritual nature of reality is a given, requiring that man carefully listen to the constant communication between the visible world of nature and the invisible world of the supernatural. The unseen is present in all phenomena. Therefore the universe is not always orderly. Tragedies, catastrophes and other events that are difficult to understand are the sport of the spirits. Their caprice reigns. To harmonize with life and even control it, one must correctly understand it. To miss this dynamic is to miss life's meaning.

Meaning in life springs from the fact that the world is spiritually alive and can be channelled to serve man's purposes. Spiritualism and the spirit world are closely related, if not synonymous. Where life force is thought of as an impersonal power, not a kind of spirit power, then life force will be seen as another kind of spirituality. Where life force is seen as synonymous with spirit power, then spiritualism will refer to the presence and power of spirit beings operating in the physical realm.

All animists share the belief that the constant dialogue between the seen and the unseen invades and pervades man's psyche. Spiritualism is that feeling which man has when he realizes he is in harmony with his total world. He may or may not have the help of the spirits but he senses his ability to better his lot in life by conscious or unconscious exertion. Spiritualism is intrinsic to man's desire for omnipotence. The animist's holism is integrally related to his spirituality. But if his religious system is to serve him effectively, he needs power, and he is keenly aware of his lack of it.

Power

Life's essential quest is to secure power and use it. Not to have power or access to it produces great anxiety in the face of spirit caprice and the rigors of life. A life without power is not worth living.

The drive to acquire power is a very strong and basic one. Power offers man control of his uncertain world. The search for and acquisition of power supersedes any commitment to ethics or morality. Whatever is empowering is right.

As pointed out previously, various terms describe this power—e.g. life force, force vital, life essence and dynamism. This power may be secured by ritual manipulation which may be in the form of sacrifices, offerings, taboos, charms, fetishes, ceremonies, even witchcraft and sorcery. The power may also be secured by the laying on of hands or by encountering a spirit being, either directly or through ritual means. The power may be transmitted through contact with persons of superior religious status or by using clothing or something previously associated with such a person. How it is secured is a secondary concern. It must be acquired whatever the cost.

In this regard the actual behavior and beliefs of an animist have no bearing on the validity and effect of a ritual. Ritual acts may be perfunctorily performed. They may be done in total indifference to moral or ethical concerns. Animist man may think what he likes, provided his ritual and customary conduct is proper. Any innovations in the practice of rituals will arouse the anger of the spirit world, but not so with the devotee's behavior and thoughts. In fact a person's thoughts are not known or heard in the spirit world. In the search for power, all else is dispensable and of little consequence.

This power is transferable to anything and anyone. It permeates everything, though unequally, but it may be focused to serve man's purposes. Since man's needs cannot be met without it, a powerless religion is valueless.

Community

Another characteristic of animism is the practice of community. Animistic man understands community holistically. He relates not only to people, but to almost everything else. In turn, this world affects him. He does not see himself as an individual but believes that his real life is in community with his fellows. He believes he is incomplete and inadequate without them. He needs the support of the community and only feels normal when he is in relationship with it. In fact, a broken relationship is a serious breach in animist theology. If anything in animist religious life may be termed sin, it is a broken relationship between persons of the same group.

Animist man is integrally related to his community. He is properly defined in terms of what he is becoming—a full member of society. His community has rites of passage for him to undergo at various times in his life. The final rite occurs at death, when he becomes an ancestor. As he enters into the cycle of generations, step by step (or rite by rite), he becomes fully human. He does not think of himself as an individual. A man is inadequate and incomplete without the others.

But community entails more than the above-mentioned experiences. Ancestors, especially the more recent dead, are an essential part of community. Man encounters his ancestors in the ways that society approves. Without ancestors and their influence in life, man loses both his focus and reason for being. Life without ancestral focus is empty and meaningless. The belief in reincarnation provides communities with a link to the past through its ancestors and a link with the future through the unborn.

The concept of community also sets the parameters of the normative in life. Community is designed for harmony. Whatever encourages the maintenance of harmony, such as ceremony and communal ritual, supports and strengthens community. Therefore, idiosyncrasies, withdrawal or undue publicity are feared. Though animist man is self-centered, conceited and self-conscious, he tends to do nothing without the group. As a member of society he conforms emotionally and intellectually to societal customs or pressures. He accepts these with little or no objection. Diversity or non-conformity is costly to the community and may signal the activity of evil spirits. Independent thinking about life's issues is an unaffordable eccentricity. There is overt and covert pressure to conform to community norms. Each member of society has a prescribed role, and he is subtly reminded of his responsibility to carry it out lest he incur the censure of the spirit world.

Although animist man fears to act outside of community sanctioned norms, he thinks of himself as essentially amoral until affected by circumstances. Should he misstep in ignorance or deliberately, he believes himself to have para-human possibilities which will enable him to supersede his just due. He firmly believes that he can negotiate with the spirit world. One may get the impression that the practice of community is a convenience, whereby man can profit from his fellows, and it would not be a very wrong conclusion.

The animist's participation in community is essentially self-serving. His goal is to attain power within the community and over his own destiny. Whatever stands in his way must be dealt with, surreptitiously if need be. There are sources of power available to help him do this.

Supplemental Beliefs

In addition to the aforementioned animist beliefs are the following subsidiary but significant tenets. First, man exists for himself and carries within himself the justification of his existence and of his religious and moral perfection. Outside codes or beings are only significant as they facilitate or support man's pursuit of self-significance.

Second, his religion is humanistic. His existence is the most significant fact of reality. Everything is from man, to man and for man. Divinities enter his affairs in the same way as do other beings which are close to him—he uses them for his own ends.

Third, everything he does is self-centered. He prays, implores, and sacrifices, not out of devotion, but in order to manipulate the spirit world. He venerates divinities for his own purposes, and to realize harmony and order in his environment so that he can accomplish them.

Fourth, he seeks to be at the master controls of life. Man is the central element of the cosmos and everything must serve him. Animists assume that the spirit powers are controllable. Man claims omnipotence if he can discern the correct ritual for any given situation. He believes he can discover these ritual secrets to command matter, to master nature and to coerce the spirit world. He therefore has para-human possibilities. Man even has the potential to metamorphose and also to communicate with the spirit world. Clairvoyance is a normal experience, as man is the vital link in the chain of existence for both the visible and the invisible, the go-between to whom they respond.

The spirit world is motivated to action through correct formulae which induce the spirits to do man's bidding. The formula may be the use of words, incantations, liturgies or rituals. Man seeks to align himself with good spirits unless he discovers that an evil spirit can help him achieve his own ends more to his liking. The evidence of his ability to master or manipulate the spirit powers is his success, status, security and contentment.

Rituals are also practiced to accrue merit in order to avert catastrophe. Animist man believes that he can compel the spirit powers by modeling—showing the spirits what he desires to have done. Should he fail in manipulating the spirits, the spirits deserve the blame. Failure lies with the ritual or the spirit, but not with man. Man's will cannot be subjected to question; it is always pre-eminent. Man does not confess his wrongdoing. Sacrifice and offerings are not made to expiate sin but rather to maintain filial relations with the spirit world.

In summary, the animist belief system deals with the spirit world practically. Spiritual life is experiential and rituals are productive; it is relational and communal, including ancestors and the spirit world. Spirituality is supersensory, encompassing dreams, visions, trances and states outside the body. Nothing escapes it, nothing is meaningful without it and nothing can be achieved aside from it. Animism is a spiritual religion, focused on and motivated by the spirit world. To evaluate animism within its own context we must understand the animist's concept of human nature and man's kinship with nature.

ENDNOTES

1. James E. Leyburn, *The Haitian People* (New Haven: Yale University Press, 1966), p. 143.

Chapter 5

THE ANIMIST CONCEPT OF HUMAN NATURE

We are all born into this world by no choice of our own. We do not choose our family, the country we will be born in, the culture we will be a part of or the circumstances of our lives. Yet all these factors will influence our choice of a belief system and the kind of a person we will become. The way we view ourselves, others, and the world, is a direct result of the sociocultural values we imbibe.

BECOMING A MEMBER OF SOCIETY

The animist's view of how a member of a family becomes a member of society differs from that of the average Westerner. The animist perceives that all of man's comings and goings are tied in with the spirit world. Birth, life and death are not happenstance events. Man is psychologically akin to spirits, and life must be understood spiritually. The traditional animist believes there is both a temporal and an eternal association between ancestors and their descendants. Social relationships must therefore include the deceased as well as all of the unborn. There is free concourse between the living and the dead. Ancestors are thought to be the guardians of the living, determining which ancestor shall return to inhabit the body about to be born, or if the spirit of the living should be reclaimed. Outside of this ancestrally chartered system there lies no possibility of life. Man's life is condi-

64

tioned by the whole spectrum of these relationships. Personhood is meaningless apart from them.

Man is made a member of society and becomes a person through rite and ritual. As E.A. Hoebel writes in *Man in the Primitive World:*

> The Omaha Indian child was touchingly introduced to the entire cosmos on the eighth day after birth in a traditional ritual always performed by the priest of a given subclan. On the eighth day the priest was sent for. When he arrived, he took his place at the door of the tipi in which the child was born. He raised his right hand, palm up to the sky, and intoned a beautiful invocation. Yet even this ritual did not make the child a real member of the tribe, for a baby did not complete its transition until it could walk. Then it went through a 'turning of the child ritual' wherein it discarded its baby name and got new moccasins. Baby moccasins always had a hole cut in the sole, so if a messenger from the spirit world came to claim the little infant, the child could answer, 'I cannot go on a journey—my moccasins are worn out!' New moccasins without holes were an assurance that the child was prepared for the journey of life, and that its journey would be a long one.[1]

Most animistic societies have some type of ritual with which to formally integrate the child into the membership of the society and associate him with both the physical and the spiritual worlds. Among some peoples a child is not even considered a human being until it has been made a member of the community in this way. The ritual may be postponed until the uncertain early years of childhood are past.

MAN IN RELATIONSHIP TO OTHERS

Generally animistic peoples do not seem to place much worth on individual life, but rather on life in relationship to others. Man is only man in relationship, as he participates in family and village life. A Zairean proverb states: "A man outside his clan is like a grasshopper which has lost its wings." One's humanity arises out of relationships, and relationships span both the physical and the spiritual dimensions. A Tiwi proverb reads: "It is man who counts. I call upon gold, it answers not; I call upon drapery, it answers not. It is man who counts." Relationships are the fabric of life, and life itself. They are the cradle, nursery, grammar, middle and high school through which a person is brought to maturity. This concept is also reflected in a monologue given by a Pomo Indian of California:

What is man? A man is nothing. Without his family he is of less importance than that bug crossing the trail, or of less importance than the sputum or exuvial. At least they can be used to poison a man. A man must be with his family to amount to anything with us. If he had nobody else to help him, the first trouble he got into he would be killed by his enemies because there would be no relatives to help him fight the poison of the other group. No woman would marry him . . . he would be poorer than a newborn child, he would be poorer than a worm. If a man has a large family. . . and upbringing by a family that is known to produce good children, then he is somebody and every family is willing to have him marry a woman of their group.[2]

Marriage is more than a physical relationship. It has eternal consequences. Not to marry is to cease living now and in the hereafter. Marriage establishes essentials in life and in death. Begetting children guarantees eternal life. Not only do children provide for the reincarnation of the ancestors, they also sustain the ancestors through prescribed rituals such as sacrifices and offerings. In other words, a man without lineage or relatives, or a group to whom he belongs, is like a man without citizenship, identity or allies in this world or the next. He is a nobody with nowhere to go, either in life or death. He might as well not exist.

The most terrible punishment that can be inflicted on anyone is to be cut off from the tribe, and so indeed be a lonely man, cut off from the vital support of his fellows at all the points at which he most needs it.[3]

MAN IN RELATIONSHIP TO THE SPIRIT WORLD

Animist man's concept of human nature is further reflected in his everyday experience. It is reflected in his every system of thought and action. His behavior is ordered by the spirit world. If the spirits will it, the circumstances will be good. But malevolent forces may also exercise control. Generally, man seeks to harmonize with his world. In order to do this, every behavior pattern is conceived of in terms of kinship relations. He must maintain specific patterns of conduct, fulfill expected social roles and conform to societal values. Any disregard of these has spiritual ramifications. Every effort must be made to avoid giving offense to the spirit world. Kinship provides ideological identity and also security. Within the kinship community there is a moral obligation, and each individual is expected to conform to custom. To break relationships or disregard custom is to sin. Says Anderson:

> Good and evil are generally judged by a very simple rule—whether or not the behavior in question does harm to the well-being of the community or threatens its members' health.[4]

Ideally, in the animist world, individuals may have rights, but they have them only by virtue of the obligations they fulfill to the community. Legality is not conceived of in terms of individual rights, but in terms of individual obligations to the natural world, the extended family, the tribe, the clan, the ancestors and the spirit world. Inversely, the community has rights only by virtue of the obligations it fulfills to the individual. Dominique Zahan writes, "The individual does not constitute a closed system in opposition to the outside world."[5]

Feeling, experiencing and participating are what make life meaningful, not ideas or cognitive knowledge. Animist man is emotionally engaged—he feels. He is mentally engaged—he believes the world to be an extension of himself. And he is physically engaged as he participates in whatever way the flesh and the spirit may be satisfied. The world indwells him and he in turn is an extension of it. Every aspect of his world is available to him to bring meaning to life. Animist man has

> . . . a sense of affinity, a mysterious knowledge of the relationship between man and the living world. He lives his life in a relationship of expanding ripples of community both within the seen and the unseen world. This can be seen both in the extended family system of interdependence and community and in the inclusion of the `living dead' in the family, clan, and tribal circle.[6]

THE ISSUE OF ACCOUNTABILITY

Animist man claims that he is not individually responsible for his actions. Because he believes himself to be the extension of the spirit world, the corporate family and the tribe, these must all share responsibility and blame for what he is and does. He is acted upon by powers he believes are beyond his control. He believes himself to be basically good, custom-abiding and pious. If he is not, then there are means to discover who or what is actually responsible. He believes he is totally within his rights to be offended if accused of a wrongdoing. By the same token, should something happen to him, such as sickness, the cause is to be discovered in the world.

In the animist world life is a complex composite, and individual man is an integral part of it, but only a part. Human nature cannot be understood apart from the total fabric of his culture. Man is the product of what the family, the clan, the tribe and the spirits have made him and therefore cannot rightfully be held responsible for his actions. He thinks of himself as part of the whole, a cog in a machine that must turn. And yet, if he can secure the needed power, he will attempt to short-circuit the system for his own gratification.

THE STATUS OF AGE

Old age bespeaks wisdom and respectability, and elicits reverence. Here too, the principle of indwelling and interaction applies. The aged are closer to the deceased ancestors than are the young, and this allows for the life essence (man's soul) to shine through and out. Old age is the honor and crown of life. The aged person must be respected and treated with dignity and honor lest recrimination follow after his decease, or even before. If man is an integral part of his culture, what is his relationship to the world of nature?

KINSHIP OF MAN WITH NATURE

There is a cosmic oneness in the animist's concept of his world. All things share in essentially the same nature and have the same interaction upon one another. In the words of John V. Taylor:

No distinction can be made between sacred and secular, between natural and supernatural, for Nature, Man and the Unseen are inseparably involved in one another in a total community.[7]

A DYNAMIC PANTHEISM

The animist's world is dynamic and not mechanistic. Nature, and with it the universe, is alive and pulsating with life, though much of this life is other than human. The visible world of nature is not alone. It is enveloped in the invisible spirit world, but not as something apart from and merely acted upon by the spirit world.[8]

The universe, which includes man's world, is an extension of God, but it does not merely reflect God; in a sense it is God. The animist's concept of his world is pantheistic, and this colors his understanding of God. For this reason nature is more than physical or material. Intertwined with nature and within it lie powers which can be used for either good or bad. That invisible power can be experienced in, through and by very visible, concrete phenomena in life. Man looks on the visible but he has potential to experience the invisible—a source of power. In the words of G. Ernest Wright in *The Old Testament Against Its Environment*:

> Nature is alive and its powers are distinguished as personal because man has directly experienced them. There is no such thing as the inanimate. Man lives in the realm of a throbbing, personal nature, the Kingdom of the holy gods. He is caught in the interplay of gigantic forces to which he must integrate his life. They are known to him because he has experienced them, not as objects, but as personalities so much greater in power than his own, that of necessity he worships and serves them.[9]

The most institutionalized form of man's kinship with nature is found in Shintoism. A major feature in Shintoism is the concept of *Kami*. *Kami* refers to sacred power (life force) in both animate and inanimate objects. Ninian Smart explains it as:

> . . . a powerful sense of the presence of gods and spirits in nature. These spirits are called *kami*, literally "superior beings," and it is appropriate to venerate them. The *kami* are too numerous to lend themselves to a systematic ordering of stable hierarchy . . . Izanagi and . . . Izanami, male and female deities of the second generation of gods . . . through the process of sexual generation . . . produced the land, and the kami of the mountains, trees, and streams . . . and so on.[10]

However, man does not worship and serve the powers of nature as ends in themselves. He has an ulterior motive, i.e., the desire to discover ways to control his environment and make it serve his purposes. In the words of Zahan, "he obliges God . . . to descend to him in order to divinize him."[11]

MAN'S ATTITUDE TOWARD NATURE

Man's desires to harmonize with nature, be subjugated to it or to manipulate it are for personal goals. By harmonizing with, or being subjugated to, nature, animist man is merely recognizing the spiritual nature of his physical world. In both of these responses he seeks to avoid giving offense to the spirits and other powers of nature, but instead enlist their favor. Even when it appears that man is totally overwhelmed by his environment, he sees this not as a limitation, but rather an invitation to enter into it, just as it enters into him. As Zahan explains:

> Between these two realities there exists a constant communication, a sort of osmotic exchange, owing to which man finds himself permanently listening, so to speak, to the pulse of the world.[12]

Thus, man lives in a dynamic world, where nature and the universe are constantly in the process of communicating. Since animist man views himself as being in the center of the universe, he understands that this communication is intended for him and for his welfare. It is up to him to decipher these messages. Animals, plants, rivers, rocks, mountains, and heavenly bodies may all carry messages. All of these phenomena are indispensable to human life. In one way or another they are there for man's sake.

TOTEMISM

Totemism relates man to nature. It affirms his interrelationship with all of his environment. But his finiteness limits his ability to relate. Through totemism he selects the parts of nature he will be in closest contact with. These closer associations provide each group of people with their own domain of relationships. However, some groups of people choose to relate to all of nature, finding it all of equal significance.

In totemism certain taboos apply to the totem animal(s) and/or plant(s). Totem objects are not to be killed, spoken of by name, eaten or even looked at in some cases. They elicit feelings of brotherliness. They are believed to have souls of similar nature to man's. They may be emblematic of abstract and emotional attitudes claimed by a group of people. The totem also serves quite a number of other sociocultural functions.

Some creatures are thought to be more akin to deity than others and are, therefore, more useful to achieve man's goals, whatever they may be. Fierce animals are associated with manifestations of God's immanence, and certain parts of their bodies such as the claws, teeth and eyes, may serve to ward off evil. Other parts may be included in medicinal potions. This is also true for several other creatures and plants. Serpents figure significantly in most religions. They are thought to be symbols of immortality. They are likely to be incarnations of ancestors and bearers of news. Some animals are thought to be more suited to sacrifice, while others, like the owl, are assumed to be evil.

THE WORLD OF NATURE

Some plants are considered sacred and believed to have special power to ward off evil and bring blessing. Apparently the marigold serves this purpose for many Hindu devotees. Some trees are considered sacred, being the habitats of spirits. Any part of them makes potent medicines. Offerings, sacrifices and prayers made in close proximity are considered most efficacious. Groves of trees are believed to harbor spiritual beings and are therefore considered excellent sites for religious rites. In Baal worship such groves served as venues for fertility rites. Rocks and boulders may serve as dwelling places of spirits or ancestors and must therefore be revered. Mountains and high places are closely associated with especially powerful spirits. Contact is more readily made with superior divinities from such places. Recognizing these practices, the Psalmist (Psalm 121) asks, "Shall I look to the hills? Does my help come from there?" But he categorically denies that his help came from high places. His help came from the Lord, the God above all gods.

THE ELEMENTS OF NATURE

The elements of nature have religious meanings. Some say that rain is the saliva of God, bringing man blessing. Thunder is His voice and a demonstration of His wrath. Lightning is the movement of God from one place to another, thereby making anything struck by lightning especially sacred and powerful.

Heavenly bodies have always held special fascination for men. They speak of the reality of the spirit world and are a visible expression of deity. They proffer power, omniscience and everlasting endurance. Astrology is an age-old, worldwide practice, in which it is assumed that these luminaries provide man messages to interpret.

But plants, trees, animals, mountains, and other natural phenomena do not only provide contact points or abodes for the spirit world. They stand in their own right as spirit vessels; not in the same way as spirits perhaps, but they do nonetheless have spiritual essence. As carriers of valuable information they play an indispensable part in man's spiritual life.

A WAY OF LIFE

Man's kinship with nature does not merely affect his view of reality. It is immensely complex and inextricably woven through the fabric of life. Animist man has come to know that there are powers in nature which he can make to serve him.

From this brief sketch of the animist's concept of human nature and man's kinship with nature, it may be more easily perceived why man believes and feels that it is totally right for him to manipulate his world to serve him well. Why should he seek to know and do the will of his god? As a part of the world, he is already doing the will of his god. The task is rather one of "compelling, entreating and coercing his god to do his will." And how does he do that? One of the quickest and surest devices discovered is through his relationship with the spirit world.

ENDNOTES

1. E. A. Hoebel, *Man in the Primitive World* (New York: McGraw-Hill, 1949), pp. 279-280.
2. *Ibid.*, p. 237.
3. Stephen Neill, *Christian Faith and Other Faiths* (New York: Oxford University Press, 1970), p. 138.
4. Sir Norman Anderson, editor, *The World's Religions* (Grand Rapids: Eerdmans, 1980), p. 46.
5. Dominique Zahan, *The Religion, Spirituality and Thought of Traditional Africa* (Chicago: University of Chicago Press, 1980), p. 9.
6. Sir Norman Anderson, 1975 p. 32.
7. John V. Taylor, *Primal Vision* (London: SCM Press, 1963), p. 64 .
8. G. Ernest Wright, *The Old Testament Against Its Environment* (London: SCM Press, 1950), p. 17.
9. *Ibid.*
10. Ninian Smart, *The Religious Experience of Mankind* (New York: Charles Scribner's Sons, 1969), pp. 192, 193.
11. Zahan, 1979, p. 17.
12. *Ibid.*, p. 9, 13. E. A. Nida & W. A. Smalley, 1959, p. 54.

Chapter 6
THE ROLE OF THE
SPIRITS

The animist believes that his world and all that happens in it—whether to himself or to others—is controlled by spirits. Therefore, if every physical event has a a spiritual co-ordinate, it is only logical for him to seek to manipulate the spiritual powers responsible. As with man, so almost every spirit has his price, and somewhere, a key will unlock the mystery and reveal this price. This is contrary to the biblical approach to God, stated so emphatically in Romans 11:34:

> For who has known the mind of the Lord, or who became His counselor? Or who has first given to Him that it might be paid back to Him again? For from Him and through Him and to Him are all things.

CATEGORIES OF SPIRITS

Generally, the animist perceives the spirit world to be a hierarchy, with four categories of supernatural beings potentially available to man. The hierarchy is headed by a supreme God. The next level is usually a pantheon of lesser divinities and superior spirits. Though capricious at times, they are generally good, exercising great power in a wide range of affairs. Next come the lesser spirits of the ancestors, who are more immediately available to man. Lastly, there is the realm of evil spirits. Because of the importance of ancestor's spirits, they will be last in order of discussion.

THE SUPREME GOD

Some researchers claim that contact with Western culture introduced the concept of one high God to animist societies. For example,

Don Richardson maintains that all people have a concept of a high God above others.[1] In animist thought the concept of a high God is at best deistic. His involvement in human affairs is minimal, if it exists. Legends concerning the cause for his departure from the human realm are many and revealing. One African legend explains that God used to fellowship with man. On one occasion He visited a housewife in the process of preparing her husband's evening meal. Having consumed her time on other pursuits, she was late in her preparations. In her haste she became annoyed with God's interference in her already overtaxed schedule, and foolishly poked Him in the eye with the pestal, an instrument used for pounding corn. God left and has ever since maintained a distance from all of mankind. Others say that God is too busy and too wholly other to concern Himself with human affairs. Should He ever be interested, He can only be reached through other spirit beings in the chain of command under Him. God is too high and too holy to allow mere man to approach Him. Many cultures use such mediators to approach God.

In the animist world God is at best remote. He may be respected, but He cannot be thought of in personal terms. He could be accepted as Creator, Sustainer and even Judge, but not as Father; not as One vitally, personally, and intimately involved in man's daily life. For such mundane concerns man needs supernatural beings closer to himself and more directly involved in the affairs of man's world.

LESSER DIVINITIES

Animist man has postulated divinities and spirit helpers other than a supreme God. The New Age Movement, a current source of animist theology in Western culture, postulates helping spirits. A four-day conference sponsored by Marquette University in 1982 sought to introduce participants to a personal spirit helper:

> The audience was told to "fix" on the first image that entered their imagination . . . It was suggested that this image was frequently that of a household pet—a small cuddly rabbit, a song bird, or perhaps a cat . . . the image . . . should be held and addressed as one would address an intimate friend. The inner advisor never lies, they said; it is always correct. At the end of the exercise the audience was told to ask the advisor how and where future contact could be accomplished. It was stated that a patient's need for psychological and emotional therapy could be greatly reduced or even eliminated by introducing them to their inner advisor.[2]

Dokupil adds a rather informative commentary,

> "Familiars," as they are often called, are described by occultists as little demons who appear in the form of a household or small animal. Their purpose is to give aid, guidance, and counsel to the humans who are in touch with them.[3]

Independent, Self-Sufficient Divinities

Some divinities are thought to be self-sufficient and able to act independently of the High God. They have the same attributes as the High God but may be accorded special spheres of concern. Kerry Lovering notes:

> Some tribal divinities are ascribed certain roles and sacrificial preferences. Ogun, the Yoruba god of war and iron, is the traditional patron deity of people such as soldiers, hunters, blacksmiths, and truck drivers. Sacrifices to Ogun ask for protection from knives, guns, road accidents, and tragedies related to machinery. His favorite animal is the dog although he will accept sheep, fowl, smoked yams, kola nuts, and palm oil. If a dog is killed by a vehicle, it is said that Ogun has taken it for a feast.[4]

This tradition is not unlike that which prevails in Hinduism. The goddess Kali is at one and the same time goddess of fertility and goddess of death. In the temple of Kali in Calcutta, blood flows freely from the many daily sacrifices offered to placate or implore this goddess.

The divinities do not necessarily act in concert with one another, and may sometimes act in opposition. They may be played off against each other, so that they respond to requests jealously. The devotee must act with great care lest any other divinities be alienated. These divinities are thought to have full power to act as they please. Man cannot be sure of their responses either, as they seem to act with great caprice. They can bring man success or cause failure. They can act in anger, or be vengeful, downright mean or hardhearted. Man must bear the consequences and seek ways to restore cordial relations. Divinities are thought to have human appetites which must be fed and human passions which must be appeased. They are placated with different kinds of offerings and sacrifices, each prescribed for the occasion.

If man's own efforts prove unsuccessful, he may turn to shamans, spirit mediums, priests, witch doctors or other religious specialists who are considered effective communicators with spirits and other divinities. Should their services not prove successful, there are yet other means to be employed to effect peace. Among the Yoruba, during times of special crisis, a human emissary was chosen to be sacrificed as a special envoy to the deities whose favors were sought. The chosen person was more often a hero than a victim. Lovering observes:

> Accordingly, he was treated with great respect and indulgence until the appointed day. Then he was paraded through the village thronged by suppliants who reached out to touch him and give him messages for the dead . . . After his departure on his momentous errand, his body was buried in a manner appropriate to an ambassador to the spirit world, replete with gifts for the tribal deities . . . Such sacrifices . . . were viewed by the Yorubas as the ultimate attempt at effecting peace with offended spirits.[5]

Tribal and Household Gods

Household gods are another category of lesser divinities. Sometimes the ancestor spirits serve as household gods, but not always. Household gods are either handed down through the family, or else a religious specialist is employed specifically to make one. Technically, household gods are fetishes, because a familiar spirit has been invited to take up abode in them and has been commissioned with a particular task in the household. The fortieth chapter of Isaiah, verses 18 through 20, describe how such a god may be made. In cultures where household deities are found, the household without one is considered a luckless nonentity without any possibility of success, happiness or security in family affairs.

Tribal gods act as both protectors and benefactors. In the Ivory Coast, writes Aldridge:

> Each tribe has a common fetish [god] that protects a given area. It has the power to make rain, to heal diseases and even to prevent epidemics from breaking out among the children. The fetish is the object of group sacrifices for the protection or blessing of all the villagers.[6]

Specifically, concerning household gods, Aldridge adds:

> The family fetishes (gods) are inherited from the ancestors and involve much more of the life of the people. The family fetishes (gods) give good crops and bring good luck (like winning the national lottery). They cause sterile women to have babies and students to pass

their important exams. . . . No animist would ever think of leaving his village without first consulting the fetish [god] to see if the road is good! . . . . The family fetish (god) also acts as a fortune teller or prophet . . . . The fetish (god) reveals what job a person should seek and the favorable time to try for it. It reveals one's enemies and protects him from his enemies' evil spells . . . . The fetish (god) also acts as financial advisor, counseling when to purchase a car, build a house, or make some other financial investment. No animist would do so without his fetish's (god's) consent . . . . If, in the course of events, the animist is summoned into judgment, his fetish will protect him. He is sure the witch doctor can cause the fetish to cast a spell so strong that his enemies can't even open their mouths to testify against him. He has no worries then about court cases.[7]

To lose such a powerful, all-encompassing benefactor is a loss beyond measure. A case in point was Laban's pursuit of Jacob, to retrieve the household god which Rachel had stolen from her ancestral home, and the consternation which followed.[8] A household god guards over the total welfare of the home and the respective family members of that household. It is to be treated like any other divinity, for it has appetites and passions like that of man, and alienation spells disaster.

A Love-Hate Relationship

Animist man has generally developed what can only be called a strange intimacy with these divinities and/or spirits. It is a love-hate relationship that is tinged with fear. The animist devotee does not think it incompatible or reprehensible or even dangerous to trick the divinities. Take the practice of a *couvade*, for example.[9] If the divinities have persistently been malevolent, then the devotee may believe it to be within his rights to trick the spirits in order to change the course of events. Actions which are normally unacceptable may be quite appropriate should the devotee detect malevolent activity on the part of the deities and/or spirits. For example, the spirits may be scolded, "You come in sickness; why did you not tell me and I would have fed you?" The prayers offered may be more of a diatribe than a supplication:

"You, our gods, you . . . so and so . . . here is your offering. Bless this child and make him live and grow. Make him rich, so that when we visit him, he may be able to kill an ox for us . . . . You are useless, you gods! You only give us trouble! Although we give you offerings you do not listen . . . . You are full of hatred. You do not enrich us."[10]

Such seemingly bold address is not unusual because the gods are believed to be there primarily for man's welfare. Should they fail in providing it, they must be held accountable.

The Construction of an Idol

Whether a people enshrine their gods in objects made of stone, metal or wood, they generally do not think of the idol itself as being the god. Whether simple or elaborate, the object is understood to be the husk providing a contact point—a representation of what is spirit in essence. Therefore the vandalization, removal or destruction of an idol does not necessarily affect the god. The god may merely depart for other parts, even though he may have a very strong affinity for the object revered as a representation of his presence. The indwelling spirit of the god retains power and can leave the material habitat and abide elsewhere. Among the Hindus, Brahmin priests are employed to make the husk of the deity. Should an unworthy person touch the husk, the god simply vacates, and a husk made by the right specialist (in this case a Brahmin priest) must be constructed.

A Spirit Double

Some practicing animists believe that each person has a spirit double. Responsibility for the fulfillment of the person's destiny is ascribed to his double, which has all the possibilities, liabilities, and often faults, that good or bad fortune has given to it. Sacrifices, offerings and prayers are made to this protecting spirit. In a very real sense man thus worships an extension of himself.

EVIL SPIRITS

A third category of spirits are those thought to be entirely evil, constantly seeking to distress mankind. There is no clear or uniform explanation of how these spirits become evil. Some animists believe that certain deceased people become evil spirits during the improper dispatch of the body in funerary rites, or through breaking the tribal custom, an abnormal death or improper ritual performances in life. What Idowu mentions about Africans is also true of animists in other parts of the world. He writes:

It is believed by Africans that a person whose dead body is not buried, that is, with due and correct rites, will not be admitted to the abode of the blessed departed ones, and therefore will become a wanderer, living an aimless, haunting existence. This category of wandering spirits includes those who had been wicked while on earth and are therefore excluded from the fellowship of the good.[11]

Among the animists of the Boudoukon area of Ivory Coast, those who kill others by witchcraft and sorcery are considered sinners and end up as evil spirits (This implies that the Boudoukon people use a word that is precisely translated this way, with its Christian connotations.).[12] Apparently the majority of evil spirits—and there are thought to be many— have existed since days of antiquity. They are difficult to locate and placate, and their work is shrouded in mystery. Special precautions must be taken against them. For example:

> The Fulanis of Benin associate a person's name with his or her spirit. In certain situations . . . speaking a person's name is taboo. It may draw the attention of a spirit, perhaps an evil one. It is never spoken in the presence of a stranger lest it provide a means to curse the owner.[13]

More powerful spirits must be enlisted to provide special protection. Should the evil spirits manage to void this as well as the protection of charms, fetishes and magical paraphernalia, then a special offering must be made. In such cases the services of a religious specialist must be procured to locate the spirit, divine the reason for its activity and prescribe the required means to appease or exorcise it. Should offerings be required, they are performed in a way like those brought to good spirits and ancestor spirits.

These spirits are to be feared because of the mischief they create, the terror they spread and the destruction they work. The good spirits are man's helpers; the evil spirits are man's destroyers.

THE ANCESTORS

A fourth category of spirits, the ancestors, are taken to be the most benevolent of all. They are kinfolk to living man. To the animist there is little question that deceased relatives are still a part of the family. The world of the departed is very much a part of the present world. The ancestors figure largely in most religions. Few peoples do not have a cult of the dead. Because of the importance of the ancestor cult we shall discuss it more extensively.

Role of Ancestors

Ancestral preeminence is one of the main tenets of animistic religion. To the animist, survival of the dead is not a matter for argument; it is an axiom of life. The ongoing existence of departed family members is a given, and therefore the intimacy of the extended family includes them as well as living relatives. Death is simply birth into another life.

To the animist the family consists of the unborn living (those about to be reincarnated), the living living, and the living dead (those who are deceased but are still remembered by the living). Life has no meaning apart from ancestral presence and ancestral power. The tie-in with the dead is so much a part of the whole fabric of life that when someone is about to depart this life, they are requested to take greetings or requests to the previously departed. But communication does not end there. The deceased will again communicate with the living in this present life. The goodbyes or farewells of animists are not forever. Soon—for some very soon—they shall again be in communication with the living. The Kasena people of Ghana believe:

> . . . that the spirit of a dead person stays in his or her house. When a meal is prepared they take food into the deceased's room. The spirit in the room will also be informed when sacrifices are made. The way for the spirit to leave the house is opened when the funeral of the deceased (a ceremony which may not take place until months after the burial of the body) is finally performed.[14]

A missionary in Japan reports that prior to the funeral:

> . . . family and friends remain with the corpse as they believe that the spirit of the deceased is still nearby. Anyone is welcome to pay tribute and burn incense before the coffin. Buddhists believe that everyone who dies becomes a *"hotoke,"* (a god). All ancestors have become gods, and have to be worshiped regularly.[15]

For the animist there is much wisdom in the statement that:

> People who are clothed in flesh and blood . . . had better keep peace with those who aren't. Not only can spirits exercise control over people while they are on earth; they also have something to say when death admits those people to the ranks of the spirits.[16]

Patterns of Ancestor Recognition

Ancestor spirits are regularly acknowledged. Some animists would not think of eating or drinking anything without giving a token offering of it to the ancestors. To forget them is to court their displeasure. Various customs have arisen which show appreciation for their presence with and service to the living. These include performing rituals and other spoken tributes, leaving gifts or sending them on and burning tapers and symbols of paper and other materials.

Ancestors, if not worshiped, are at least highly revered. Controversy exists about whether or not recognition of ancestors with sacrifices and offerings is reverence or actual worship. No one can deny that in the ancestor cult the ancestors are supplicated, or implored like parents to act on behalf of the living.

In Folk Islam the deceased *pirs* (holy men) take on the function of the ancestors. Thus:

> ... the followers of a *pir* believe that in death there will be a marriage or union between their guide and god. Hence, the anniversary of the *pir's* death is celebrated with singing, dancing, *dhikr*, and sermonizing. There is a widespread belief that the *pir* in heaven will be extremely displeased unless the anniversary is celebrated with great festivity on the part of the disciples. Cows, goats and fowls ... are slaughtered ... [17]

In *Sufism: Its Saints and Shrines*, Subhan notes, in connection with ancestor worship:

> Devotees of the saints attending the celebrations are believed to acquire merit ... the particular rites ... combine such features as these: Suras 1; 112; 113; and 114 are recited; these are followed by the repetition of certain prayers for the soul of the departed; finally, the worshiper makes some personal requests. As a rule, a vow is made at this time which must be paid at the tomb when the favor is granted. It is a common practice to tie bits of thread or pieces of cloth, etc., in gratings near the tomb, by way of reminding the saint of the favor asked. [18]

Patterns of ancestor recognition vary for different cultures, but all consider spirits associated with culture heroes and leaders to be especially powerful. The three most important ancestors for the immediate family are the deceased father, the grandfather and the great grandfather. And distant forebears are not forgotten but invited only to certain feasts.

Ancestors are respected for their place in society, and for who they are in the family. For example, when the president of Taiwan died, citizens were expected to follow the traditional custom of paying homage to the dead by offering fruit and placing candles and flowers before his portrait.[19] The fruit, flowers and candles all appease and feed the ancestors, as well as ward off evil spirits. The spirits of chiefs are considered to be very powerful and essential to the welfare of the tribe and/or nation. Therefore, as with deceased family members,

> . . . if the living fail to perform the required duties and rituals, the deceased ancestors may inflict trouble and misfortune on their descendants . . . . One of the duties required of living descendants is to bury their departed in an ideal location . . . . A good grave site is not just to please or appease the ancestors but is believed to benefit the descendants . . . . The prosperity of the descendants will ensure the continuous veneration of the ancestors . . . . The relationship is actually a reciprocal one.[20]

Should burial customs be disregarded, the ancestor spirit will linger in the vicinity, haunt the family, take revenge on enemies, and generally make life miserable for the living. The ancestor spirit may also appear in animal or bird form, in which case they are recognized intuitively by the living. The Bokos of Benin, West Africa, believe that if they are not buried in the correct way they will be rejected for entry into the life hereafter and will be left to wander alone forever.[21]

Most animists believe that it is expedient for the living to perform the right dispatching rituals for the dead. There are many of these practices. They vary from people to people and include sobbing loudly, beating the breast, wearing mourning attire and burning candles. Some of these customs have little to do with actual mourning, and are performed out of fear of the consequences should they be ignored. While the corpse is around, the spirit of the deceased is considered to have more power than after it is buried or dispatched according to custom. Should the spirit be dissatisfied with the procedures at any time, it is likely to appear to the living looking like it did while alive. Sightings are common, according to Mbiti, for, "A considerable number of people report seeing . . . the living dead, both alone as individuals and in groups with other men or women."[22]

Some believe that the spirit of the deceased will linger about the grave or place of dispatch until a sacrifice is offered. This may take place a month, 40 days, a year, or some other customary time after the actual burial or dispatch of the body. Among some Asian Indians it is customary to have a memorial feast 40 days after death. The Zulu people of Southern Africa wait a year before killing a white goat to bring back home the departed spirit to be a functioning member of the family. The Sotho of Southern Africa claim that their dead take their place among the family gods immediately upon death. They sacrifice a steer over the grave as an oblation to the deceased, in honor of their new status as divinity. They also sprinkle blood over the grave, and say a prayer: "Repose in peace with the gods; give us tranquil nights." They make sacrifices on other occasions as well, and offer libations of beer while they entreat the ancestor, now a god, to join the other gods in looking after the living.

Function of Ancestors

As pointed out above, the primary function of the ancestors is to facilitate and maintain the tribal welfare of the living.

> Deep down in the minds of thousands of men and women of every level of spiritual or intellectual attainment is the . . . persistent notion that the deceased still have a part to play, for better or worse, in the lives of the living.[23]

The ancestors are expected to take responsibility for the welfare of the living and be active in their affairs. Their activity is directed toward "restoring order and discipline in compliance with the norms of right and duty, enmity or piety, whenever transgressions threaten or occur."[24] Ancestors are believed to offer advice through dreams, visions or ghostly visitations. Among some pastoral peoples, spectral cattle are heard lowing at night and are believed to be ancestors expressing their concern for the living. Everything in life is of importance to the ancestors. Family ancestors are involved in birth, marriage, sickness, relationships, reunions, family needs and numerous other personal, family and household concerns. It is not unusual to find people who have accepted positions in life due to the promptings of the ancestors. I have personally met individuals in Christian ministry who claim that an ancestor prompted them to accept the call.

The ancestors are guardians over family and tribal morality. For example, the Kasenas of Ghana believe that the Supreme God gave their customs and their concept of morality to the tribal ancestors.[25] If anyone should disregard these, God has given the ancestors permission to inflict punishment through disease, misfortune or lack of success in daily pursuits. They are in a very real sense the shapers and maintainers of the people's conscience. Lovering observes that the Kasenas also believe the ancestors to be the agents through whom God works. Sacrifices are offered so that the ancestors will intercede on their behalf before God—God is begged not to withhold His blessings.[26] The ancestors arrange and dispense the blessings of God. They maintain family possessions and approach other spirits and deities to request favorable response to their words. Animist man says,

> We can face life and its chances with confidence, when we know that there are powers, forces and events on which we can rely, but we must submit to the control of our conduct by rules which are imposed.[27]

Tribal ancestors have influence over rain, planting, seed time, first fruits and other matters which affect a wider community. They are the proprietors of the land, and therefore land can never really be sold outright in traditional animistic cultures. To leave the land is to leave the roots of your heritage. "Where we bury our dead is our home." The above functions are not universal—nevertheless the common consensus is that departed family members continue to reside among the living. They are to be acknowledged, respected and extended the intimacy of family members. In turn, the ancestors are expected to reciprocate by maintaining a vital relationship with, and concern for, their living family members.

There are times when ancestors are thought to be rather ambivalent to their living family. On such occasions priests are consulted and divination is employed to discover why. The prescribed cure may involve a sacrifice like the slaughtering of a steer or some lesser animal life. In times past human sacrifices were common, and they are still practiced in some places today.

Priests are also consulted on other occasions, such as when communication between the dead and the living is not clear. The family member may have had a troubling dream, vision or a ghostly visitation. The priest may then interpret the meaning of it or seek the intervention of another spirit through his normal divination paraphernalia.

Specific acts of worship are too many and too diverse to enumerate. They include offerings of food and other material things, sacrifices of animal life and burnings of incense with prayers. All these serve to maintain good relationships with the departed. The animist talks to his ancestors, beseeches them and even reprimands and expostulates with them. He gives them what they desire.

This dependence on the ancestors provides continuity with the past, a reverence for established customs, an intense awareness of the immediacy of the spiritual world and a demonstrable dependence upon unseen powers. Animist man's dominant passion is to maintain a bond with his ancestors or a hero ancestor, because to him they are life. In times of trouble he finds in them strength and courage, knowing that these relatives in the unseen world are there to help him.

As pointed out before, the animist does not confine himself to one source of help. He seeks to cover all possible bases and enlists all the help he can possibly get. But even if he is expert in knowing how to secure help and manipulate spirit sources, if he does not have a power called life force, his pursuits will be to no avail. He will not be able to translate knowledge into success, happiness or security. Animist man needs life force to face the challenges of life.

ENDNOTES

1. Cf. Don Richardson, *Eternity in Their Hearts* (Ventura: Regal Books, 1981).

2. Stanley Dokupil, "Seizing the Power: The Use of Imagination for Healing" in *SCP Newsletter* 8, no. 6 (October-November 1982), p. 3.

3. *Ibid.*

4. Kerry Lovering, "Barrier to the Gospel: The Spirit World" in *SIM Now* (July-August 1987), p. 2.

5. *Ibid.*

6. Jimmy Aldridge, "Animism: Faith of Fear and Fetish" in *Heartbeat* 22, no.2 (Nashville: Free Will Baptist Foreign Missions, March 1982), p. 3.

7. *Ibid.*

8. Genesis 31: 19, 30-37.

9. The *couvade* is the American Indian practice of having the father go through simulated labor pains while the mother gives birth to the child. By so doing, the evil spirits are supposedly drawn to the father —thus protecting the child from the attacks of the evil spirits. See Paul G. Hiebert, *Cultural Anthropology* (Grand Rapids: Baker Book House, 1983), p. 85.

10. W. C. Willoughby, *The Soul of the Bantu* (New York: J. & J. Harper Editions, Harper and Row Publishers, 1969), p. 85.

11. E. B. Idowu, *African Traditional Religions* (London: SCM Press, 1973), pp. 174-175.

12. *Heartbeat* (1982), p. 2.

13. *SIM Now* (1987), p. 3.

14. *Ibid.*

15. Wilma Visser, *Newsletter* (Oita City, Japan: Japan Rural Mission, 8, no. 1, December 1986), p. 4.

16. *SIM Now* (1987), p. 2.

17. Phil Parshall, *Bridges to Islam: A Christian Perspective on Folk Islam* (Grand Rapids: Baker Book House, 1983), p. 87.

18. John A. Subhan, *Sufism: Its Saints and Shrines* (Lucknow: Lucknow Publishing House, 1938), p. 107.

19. *Pretoria News* (Pretoria, South Africa, January 19, 1988), p. 4.

20. Bernard Hwang, "Ancestor Cult Today" in *Missiology*, Volume V. no. 3 (July 1977), p. 349.

21. *SIM Now* (1987), p. 4.

22. John S. Mbiti, *African Religions and Philosophy* (Garden City: Anchor Books, Doubleday & Company, Inc., 1970), p. 111.

23. E.B. Idowu, *African Traditional Religion* (London: SCM Press, 1973), p. 178.

24. M. Fortes and G. Dieterlin, *African Systems of Thought, (Studies presented and discussed at the Third International Seminar in Salisbury, December, 1960)* (London: Oxford University Press, 1965), p. 136.

25. *SIM Now* (1987), p. 2.

26. *Ibid.*

27. Fortes and Dieterlin (1965), p. 136.

Chapter 7
THE CONCEPT OF
LIFE FORCE

Humanity wants to be maker almighty, master of its own fate and captain of its own soul. Somewhere there is power to be gained to deal with the precarious human condition, and every once in a while some very unlikely person comes on the scene and simply confirms this. Under the title: "Girl's Abilities Mysterious," the *Pacific Daily News* reported on an unusual concentration of power which enabled the girl to perform healings:

> The statue of Santo Nino, the Christ child, was placed on the flattened, upturned palms of the young girl. Suddenly, the statue with a wooden bottom began to rock back and forth from side to side. It bounced upon the girl's hands, turned full circle, and even climbed up her arm as almost 100 people watched. The girl's face was expressionless as she watched the doll move around. She seemed as though she was in deep thought. Her hands remained stationary, other than to accept the weight of the doll as it "danced" upon her hands. The two women stood on either side to catch the statue in case it fell off her hands.
>
> There were no strings or gadgets controlling the doll's movement, and as if to prove that that particular doll was not rigged in any way to perform such a feat, the girl was passed at least thirty other religious statues provided by the audience.
>
> All of them moved around on her hands, and the last one bounced violently, dancing to the strains of *"De Colores"* as the audience clapped rhythmically. Even the most skeptical in the crowd knew that they were witnessing something that was out of the ordinary. Was it psychic phenomenon or religious miracle?
>
> The young girl, Maria Jesusa Bunag, 15, believes the latter. She said that her ability to move objects around with no apparent physical initiation by her hands is the result of a gift given to her by God. She

shuns the idea of scientific explanations such as telekinesis. "Santo Nino is me, and I am Santo Nino," she said last night.

Maria discovered her special ability in February, while she was still in the Philippines. She had seen others with the same ability, she said.

The first time the statue moved for her, "I was scared. I couldn't believe it."

But she soon learned to look at her power as a special gift which helps other people. Santo Nino, she said, talks through her. She is only able to move religious dolls and statues, she said. When a can of soda pop was placed on her hands as a test, it remained stationary. She told the reporter she couldn't move it.

Maria moved to Guam in April, and since April 22, her family has been holding nightly faith healings at their Dededo home. The 7 p.m. meetings start with Tagalog Catholic hymns and a rosary. Then Maria and her sister Maxima, 22, massage oil on the afflicted areas of sick people of all ages who line up to be healed. She has helped many people through the healings, Maria said, but only if the afflicted people believe they can be healed.

The healings are followed by the dancing performance of the religious artifacts, and following a break for refreshments and so that Maria may rest, members of the audience may ask Santo Nino questions, which are answered yes or no by the statue when it either rocks back and forth or from side to side. She said that Santo Nino is sometimes unable to move for her if she is ill or tired. They are like one body, she said. "If I'm tired, he's tired too," she said. Maria has always felt close to religion, she said.

She was born on Christmas, and led rosaries and sang in the church choir in the Philippines. Her family does not charge any type of fee for her healing services, and most gifts are not accepted. Maria shunned the idea of using her ability to make money. "Santo Nino would not like that," she said.[1]

If a girl could do this, why can't others? Animist man is keenly aware of his lack of power, and therefore, he is constantly driven to acquire power, i.e., life force.

Reporting on a seminar held at Marquette University in 1982, Stanley Dokupil wrote:

The audience . . . was . . . asked to follow . . . a guided-imaginary excursion. . . . The imaginary tour led us on to the mountain path and we began our ascent to the top. We encountered seemingly insurmountable obstacles along the way, but were persuasively coaxed on to victory by imagining ourselves strong, possessors of boundless inner reservoirs of strength. The excursion came to an end at the top of the mountain. There we discovered a wise old priest or holy man whom we were told could answer all our questions and *grant us power* (emphasis mine). With closed eyes we were next asked to visualize a radiant white light into which all would become blissfully engulfed.[2]

NATURE OF LIFE FORCE

The drive for power is universal; it is only clothed in different cultural and religious garb. Life force is something of very special quality and essence. It is in part personified power. It is found in everything, especially in animal life. It can increase and decrease. One who has much life force is stronger, or smarter or more successful than someone who has less of it. Life force is similar to the Melanesian and Polynesian concept of *mana*:

> *Mana* means a kind of force or power which can be in anything, and which makes that thing better in its own special qualities, such as they are, perhaps to the point of being marvelous ... There is no difference in the *mana* which is in the tool or its owner, or its maker; it simply causes each one to excel in his special way ... *Mana* ... is an explanation for whatever is powerful, or excellent, or just right ... *Mana* is a sort of essence of nature; it is not a spirit, and it has no will or purpose of its own.[3]

Several other terms convey the same concept of this significant, out of the ordinary power. The Iroquois Indians used the term *orenda*, the Algonquins spoke of *manitou*, while the Sioux call it *wakan*. The Muslim term is *baraka*, and according to Edward Westermark, *baraka*:

> ... is a power for many kinds of good, and it is quite general: mountains have it, the sea has it; it lives in the sun, moon and stars, in animals—especially horses, plants, and magic squares. It tends, however, to be personal, associated with people such as brides and bridegrooms, the new mothers of twins and triplets, and children generally. And it is sensitive to pollution and destruction by uncleanness of various kinds, or by unrighteousness, and generally speaking, women and Christians are bad for it, as is fighting or breaking religious laws It is above all the property of two special kinds of people: descendants of the Prophet and "saints"—holy men. Saints use their power mainly for curing, and *baraka* will remain around a saint's tomb, where its influence will also cure or bestow other benefits.[4]

Other associated terms are life essence, vital force and dynamism. All these terms describe the latent power—some form of psychic force which man pursues and secures to work for him, but which he also respects lest it harm him. The nature of this power, herein termed life force, is:

> . . . spiritual, intangible and all-pervasive. It flows through things but is capable of drawing itself onto a "power focus" in certain conspicuous objects. This power has in itself no moral quality, but it can be tapped and turned to good use or bad, according to the intention of the user. Not everyone can manipulate it; it must be fenced in by many precautions, for it is dangerous, just as electricity is dangerous to those who do not know how to use it.[5]

ACQUIRING LIFE FORCE

How does one experience this spiritual, intangible and all-pervasive power? Some believe that they are simply at the mercy of this power flow. Luck may bring it to them, and should they be born into the right family, then it is passed on to them by virtue of social status and heredity. In the case of Jacob and Esau, the animist will claim that Jacob's ultimate position as father of the twelve tribes of Israel was an immediate result of the blessing (baraka) he stole from Esau when Isaac communicated the life force to him, by the laying on of hands. In this case, cunning secured for him heredity power—life force. Romans 9:10-18 gives the biblical perspective on the matter. This is quite different from what the animist believes.

A number of North American Indian tribes and other people groups believe that a heightened awareness of spiritual powers can be acquired and sustained through the tactile senses. Drugs (marijuana/peyote), severe self-discipline (like a vision quest), self-emptying (through different rituals), the discipline of silence, fasting, dancing (at special festivals like the sun dance), the power of music, etc., are means to secure and enhance life force. This force may be experienced as a sensation or as a flow of power from one person to another. Some experience it when touching an object taken from the person or presence of someone considered well endued with power, or when touching an object prayed over or prepared by some ritual.

Ancestor linkage is thought to strengthen life force and prevent death. Proper relationships with ancestors insure the continuation of life force, facilitating circulation of life, resulting in vigor. Close association with ancestors and other especially powerful persons, such as heroes, leaders and warriors, etc., secures a significant measure of life force to the seeker. The closer one is to the source of life force through status, lineage, etc., the greater the force experienced. As an example, an animist might point to the woman who touched the hem of Jesus' garment, as recorded in Luke 8:43-48. Christ's response to her was, "Your faith has made you whole; go in peace."

Man can increase his life force through regular participation in religious celebrations, liturgies and rituals of various kinds. In fact, if these practices are not regularly maintained, life force can decrease. A person may then feel sick or claim to be dying. In such cases life force has to be revived by being transferred through the laying on of hands or some other ritual. If a person senses the absence of life force he may will himself to die. When all of man's personal resources for securing life force have been exhausted, he can resort to a religious specialist who has means to capture it and put it at man's disposal—for a price. Animist man believes that some men have a larger amount of life force than others and that losing it puts man in real jeopardy of death—which means no security, no happiness, no success. Life cannot be lived without a good measure of life force.

As pointed out above in the description of *mana*, life force belongs to all objects in varying amounts. This force can be concentrated in implements of all sorts to provide them with superior effectiveness. Animals are slaughtered and the blood sprinkled in rooms and over windows and doors. The carcass is buried at a door entrance or window. This is all done in the belief that it may protect the residence and guarantee success for the occupant. This ritual may be confused with the practice of sacrificing to ancestors in order to secure their protection of the family's dwelling place. In fact, it may be done for both reasons—to ward off evil and to secure ancestral blessing.

South Sea Islanders claimed that rocks of peculiar character could convey *mana*[6]—and had the ability to provide growing power to gardens, with far superior results than if fertilizer had been used. Boats were instilled with life force to make them safe and successful in their use. The search for and use of life force appears to be endless. It is difficult to separate the concept of life force from the idea of spirit indwelling, or spirit possession of objects. In a world view where the spiritual and the physical know little distinction, life force can easily be seen as either an amoral force void of personality or as a force akin to a spirit being. The word *wakan* (the term used by the Sioux Indians for this mysterious force and power) more nearly captures the concept of life force as understood by most animistic peoples:

When a priest uses any object in performing a ceremony, that object becomes endowed with a spirit, not exactly a spirit, but something like one . . . the priests call it *tonwan* or *ton*. Now anything that thus acquires *ton* is *wakan*, because it is the power of the spirit or quality that has been put into it . . . Anything may be *wakan* if a *wakan* spirit goes into it . . . *Wakan* comes from the *wakan* beings. These beings are greater than mankind in the same way that mankind is greater than animals.[7]

Interestingly, a number of Christo-pagan cults think of the Holy Spirit in terms of life force. As such, during religious rituals one may even snort in the Spirit, or while speaking, use short staccato-like gasps to inhale the Holy Spirit. These are quite audible and communicate mystery and awe to the audience. Some followers of pentecostal denominations demonstrate the same practices, which apparently bring power to religious exercises like worship and preaching. The Holy Spirit is here thought of as less of a person than an influence. When thought of in this way, the Holy Spirit is a power source to be tapped.

Sacred objects, charms, weapons and other paraphernalia are considered to be empowered with a mysterious power which enhances life force—but more on this later. One of the ways in which life force may be secured is ritual. We will discuss this in the next chapter.

ENDNOTES

1. Jamie Kemp, "Girl's Abilities Mysterious" in *Pacific Daily News*, 17, no. 173 (Agana, Guam, July 24, 1986), pp. 1, 4.

2. *SCP Newsletter*, 8, no. 6 (October - November, 1982), p. 3.

3. William Howells, *The Heathens: Primitive Man and His Religions* (Garden City, New York: The Natural History Library, Anchor Books, Doubleday & Company, Inc., 1962), pp. 24, 25.

4. Edward Westermark, *Ritual and Belief in Morocco* (1926). Quoted by Howells (1962), pp. 31, 32.

5. W. T. Harris and E. G. Parrinder, *The Christian Approach to the Animist* (London: Edinburg House Press, 1960), p. 37.

6. Howells (1962), pp. 25.

7. J. R. Walker, "The Sun Dance and Other Ceremonies of the Oglala Division of the Teton Dakota," in *Anthropological Papers of the Museum of Natural History*, 16, (1917). Quoted in Howells (1962), p. 26.

Chapter 8

THE PRACTICE
OF RITUAL

A ritual is a formula for eliciting help from the spirit world and mastering nature to serve man's purposes. It is the means whereby the spirits may be manipulated. Underlying ritual is the conviction that such manipulation can secure control over events, circumstances or people. The rationale is: "If I do this and this, the other source—be it spirit or god, must do that and that." In fact, the spirit is not merely obligated, but rather is coerced into responding according to the practitioner's desire. If the devotee or officiant of the ritual says the right chant or mantra, performs the right sacrifice, or goes through a liturgy in a particular order, then the god or spirit must do such and such.

THE FUNCTION OF RITUAL

Through correct ritual man seeks to tap into a power source which will give him the feeling and experience of omnipotence. Ritual gives the performer confidence that he has power, and this gives him a sense of security, meaning and identity, within the context of the belief system. Effective ritual sustains the sacred in life because it confirms to the devotees that the deities are in authority. The arrangement is reciprocal: belief validates ritual and ritual validates belief.

Religious rituals help the devotee meet specific goals by securing divine intervention. They are thereby a means of grace. For example, Hindus accept that *Kavadi* (the carrying of a symbol of a vow taken for

93

the protection against the illness of children) secures for the child protection against forces which cause illness. The child participates in an annual ceremony, carrying an elaborate marigold-covered wooden contraption. Should he be too young, a parent carries it for him. Other rituals may also accompany this annual ceremony, further securing power to face the exigencies of life. This serves as a means of grace for the performer, guaranteeing well-being for the child.

The interrelationship between belief and ritual is so complete that the ritual act is also an act of worship—a recognition of a superior spiritual power available to man. The ritual act is sacred and efficacious. Regardless of who practices it, says it or uses it, it is in itself the key which unlocks the door to the desired goal. Muslims believe that whoever recites the *Shahada* automatically becomes a Muslim. Among some Christians, baptism, or catechism class or some other ritual makes a person a Christian. The ritual has a self-contained and automatic efficacy if it is performed correctly.

The efficacy of the ritual has nothing to do with the inner disposition or moral character of the officiant or recipient. Definitions of ethics, morality, and integrity vary from culture to culture. But the performance of the religious specialist is what is vitally important, because the use of correct forms is indispensable in securing the desired objectives.

When performing the ritual, the performer feels its efficacy (a feeling inexpressible in words), which further enhances it. Participation in ritual is not only a means to manipulate the spirit world, but also a way to express emotion. Through ritual the devotee enters more fully into his belief system and feels that he has accomplished more than he ever could through words or belief alone. Even where the main focus of the ritual is the use of magic words, the accompanying physical actions add validity and power.

Animist man believes with his heart as well as his head. Rituals provide a necessary channel and occasion to express feelings—feelings which confirm to him that his faith is correctly placed. Rituals may veil as well as reveal the immensities of man's feelings.

They are indispensable to well-being and right belief. Animist religion is not so much thought out as it is acted out—the abundance of rituals is evidence. This is why it is so difficult to separate religion from what is merely sociocultural in a society.

Rituals are not confined to special events dealing with obvious needs. They are found even in daily routines, even insignificant ones, such as the way a person is greeted. For example, Muslims must use the correct salutation when addressing Allah. To do otherwise shows disrespect, and, more significantly, does not accrue merit. At worst it may bring retribution from the deity. The same is true in some forms of Christendom. Improper ritual not only doesn't achieve the desired objectives, it warrants divine retribution. The devotees are not concerned with the holiness of God, but with the efficacy of the ritual.

THE VALUE OF RITUAL

Ritual has value beyond its usefulness in cajoling or manipulating spirits. Ritual acts renew and strengthen beliefs. Ritual is a codified expression of belief and emotion, demonstrating faith. Parrinder perceptively states, "the rites reveal the religious sentiments as well as the doctrines of faith. The rites also help to show the relationship of religion to the structure of society."[1]

In a sense, the more ritualized a religious system is, the less the walking by faith is necessary. The converse is also true. Both approaches are religiously valid because in both cases faith is what sustains the system. However, the more ritualized the religious system is, the more loyal its devotees are. Ritual sustains and generates the myth underlying the belief system, while it also binds people together socially, psychologically and physically as they participate. Shared activities such as dancing, clapping hands, singing, reciting liturgies, praying, carrying burdens (such as *Kavadi*), sacrificing and performing ceremonies of various sorts all serve to reinforce collective sentiments. These activities are accepted as a necessary part of the belief system. They are cathartic and therapeutic experiences, producing a sense of well-being and assuring the participants that their religious faith is correctly placed. As pointed out above, ritual involves the total person. It contributes greatly to psychological well-being, giving life meaning and encouraging participation in it.

Because ritual practice is so significant, conduct such as the reversal of sex roles, sexual license and drunkenness may be condoned and even encouraged during its performance. Sexual license is common in the fertility cults. Drunkenness is believed to bring on the passivity required for spirit possession. Drug use may facilitate the same by putting man in contact with the spirit world. Everyday norms are suspended, as humor, laughter, free speech, glossalalia, and other normally considered aberrant behavior forms are exhibited.

TYPES OF RITUALS

Rituals may be divided into several types. The most important are calendrical and critical rituals.[2] Calendrical rituals involve the whole of a society: they are scheduled for particular times and are ceremonial in nature. Critical rituals are practiced as need dictates. Societies have a repertoire of these with which to deal with emergencies and other events. The former are communal rituals and include rain making, agricultural rites and purification rites.[3] One example is the *Incwala*, an annual purification rite of the Swazi, during which old clothing and utensils are burned and there is a new beginning.[4] In communal sacrifices food is shared with the spirits to confirm a covenant bond between men and the spirit world, thereby guaranteeing that the terms of the relationship will be fulfilled.[5] There are many ritual practices, each with a specific objective. The people of Israel frequently succumbed to the beliefs of the peoples around them, and practiced rituals themselves. In Isaiah 1, God disregards such activity; in fact He scorns their so-called worship because they lack integrity. They performed the ritualized practices instituted for them by God, but did not obey the other commandments God gave them. These commandments, regarding the less privileged and socially disadvantaged in society—the orphans, widows and poor—are of greater concern to the biblical God than the practice of the religious cult. Israel conformed to outward practices, using them as rituals to coerce God to bless them. And so too, rituals are practiced by animist man with a view to manipulating the spirit world into acting on his behalf.

In ritual practice man sits at the console of a computer programmed to coerce positive spirit activity on his behalf. In ritual, the illusion of omnipotence is created more powerfully than in any other religious practice. In ritual, man controls what happens to himself, to others and to his environment. But his confidence is not without misgivings. The performed ritual may not have been the correct one, or it may not have been performed completely without error. Therefore, animist man is constantly in search of a more potent ritual to achieve his purposes. This may be discovered through divination, dreams, visions or vision quests, or it may be found through other shamanic practices such as witchcraft, sorcery, incantations or the esoteric ministrations of religious specialists. Animist man refuses to recognize the limitations of his creatureliness as distinct from God.

Before looking at the different ways in which animist man attempts to control his world, consideration should be given to ceremony. What is the purpose of ceremony?

CEREMONY

A ceremony is a sacred rite, a formal act or series of acts prescribed by ritual. Ceremony is a visual demonstration of a reciprocal affirmation of recognition, responsibility and accountability of deity to devotee, and of devotee to deity (spirit). Spirit beings need living devotees who will give them recognition by worshiping them through various rites. These rites include sacrifices and offerings, incantations and prayers, as well as other little and not so little acts of veneration, like burning incense or feeding the deities. When the spirit beings are neglected, they in turn refuse to perform their responsibilities to their devotees. The spirit beings generally communicate their displeasure through calamities, dreams and/or visions, and refusal to answer prayers. This was the fundamental assumption of Job's comforters.[6]

Devotees or worshipers need spirit beings, be they gods, spirits or ancestors, to meet their needs and minister to their wants. When devotees are in need of security, lack prosperity or desire success, the spirit beings are reminded (either by ceremony or by verbal encounter) that they will not be served unless they favor their devotees.

THE PURPOSE OF CEREMONY

Ceremony serves to renew, strengthen and in some cases restore bonds between devotees or worshipers and spirit beings (deities, spirits, ancestors). Ceremony is therefore not an individual affair. It is a ritual that brings devotees together in common purpose, which excites and maintains filial relations between spirits and devotees. In a very true sense ceremony serves to unite worshiper/devotee and spirit beings in a common bond of reciprocity. Ceremony becomes a very effective means to control the spirit world to look favorably on the devotees. It is believed to be a necessary preventative of trouble, calamity and general distress of the devotee group. Ceremony is doing what the spirit world expects, requires and even demands. It is maintaining proper filial relationships. Participation in ceremony is imperative because in doing so harmony with the spirit world is maintained, and the cooperation of the spirit world in human endeavors and concerns is secured. True to animist motivation, it is a means of manipulation to secure success and victory for the performers.

Involvement in ceremony provides sociopsychological affirmations for the participants. In the first place, it confirms patterns and feelings of loyalty to the deity (spirit, god, ancestor) and establishes common bonds of loyalty among devotees. These bonds affirm for the participants their need for each other and focus the participants on a common goal. Performing the ceremony, and experiencing its effectiveness in soliciting the cooperation of the spirit world, produces psychological well-being in the devotee. Ceremony is thus a morale builder, and it is self-perpetuating.

Ceremony also serves as a social control mechanism in society by establishing patterns of loyalty, and prescribing parameters of acceptable conduct. Ceremony focuses on religious values in keeping with the religious *cultus*, operates within the framework of sociocultural customs and provides the necessary sociopsychological affirmations so essential for man's well-being.

Ceremony is generally associated with particular rites. It sometimes involves dress and public display. It may involve acts of consecration, of celebration and of religious rite relative to man's many felt needs.

TYPES OF CEREMONY

Ceremonial forms vary from culture to culture, even though the purposes may be essentially the same. Ceremonial meals are quite common. Distinctive dance forms are sometimes required. Music plays a very significant part in ceremony as well, both instrumental (drums, rams' horns, trumpets) and vocal (choral groups, antiphonal chants or incantations). Parades, whether in honor of deities and saints, or to recognize or commemorate certain events, are another form of religious ceremony.

Theater, drama, mime, recitation, storytelling, sacrifice and offering may all serve the purpose of ceremony. The forms of ceremony appear well-nigh inexhaustible, each serving to draw people together in a common objective. And while ceremonies frequently appear to have no apparent objective, careful investigation will reveal the actual purpose. Directly or indirectly, this will relate back to the spirit world and its potential influence on human affairs.

In this respect ceremonies are held at the consecration of armies, at weddings and the accompanying festivities, at births, and at deaths (or sometimes after deaths if dictated by custom). They are held at times of sowing and harvesting, at times of catastrophe, in seeking for a particular blessing, in desire for cleansing and on many other like occasions. Ceremony plays a very large part in all religions. Animist man believes he knows how to use it for his benefit. Christian man will want to avoid communicating through his ceremony the idea that it is a way to manipulate God. Ceremony in a Christian context ought to celebrate the blessing, grace and mercy of God, simply because He is God and deserves the praise of men.

If we are to understand the animist's approach to life, we should seek to understand the various means he has discovered to deal with his world. One of those ways is the use of words.

ENDNOTES

1. Edward Geoffrey Parrinder, *African Traditional Religion* (Westport: Greenwood Press, 1976), p. 79.

2. Quentin Nordyke, *Animistic Aymaras and Church Growth* (Newburg: Barclay Press, 1972), pp. 52-56.

3. Parrinder (1976), pp. 79-90.

4. Hilda Kuper, *The Swazi, A South African Kingdom* (New York: Holt, Rinehart & Winston, Inc., 1963), pp. 68-72.

5. J. Omosade Awolawu, *Yoruba Beliefs and Sacrificial Rites* (London: Longman Group, Ltd., 1979), pp. 138-141.

6. Job 4:7-9, 18; 8:6, 20; 22:2-5.

Chapter 9
WAYS TO EXERCISE CONTROL

Among the most dramatic features of the practice of animism are the means it uses to exercise control over the spirit world. The most common of these are incantations, symbolism, witchcraft, sorcery, charms fetishes and white and black magic.

THE POWER OF WORDS

One of the ways the animist seeks to control his world—a world that is both spiritual and physical simultaneously—is through words. There is a vital connection between life force, magic and words. Words are thought to have power beyond just communicating ideas. In the film *Bedazzled*, Dudley Moore sells his soul to Satan for seven wishes. His only wish is to be loved, but each time he makes that wish, he says the wrong words and the wish fails. He wishes for a pure and innocent woman to love and a nun appears. Each wish is defeated by some misquote of the magic formula. He just cannot get the formula recited the right way and loses his chance to be loved. The use of the power words outwits him.

Words are believed to have force. Ray Benjamin observes that

... through the power of ritual language, the masters ... command the agents of illness to "separate" themselves from the sick person and to take possession of the sacrificial animal . . . the act of invocation transfers to it the malevolent spirits of illness and destruction. In effect the words of the invocation create an exchange of the life of the animal for the life of the patient . . . the most important part has been already accomplished by speech.[1]

The above description may leave one in doubt as to whether power resides in the words or in obedience to command. In animism both concepts are certainly true, but the concept of words with innate power will be the focus of this section.

Words are thought to be like darts which may be directed toward very specific targets. The power of words is direct and need not be mediated by any other agency. "Just speak the word and my servant will be healed"[2] was the request of the centurion to Jesus Christ. The only person Scripture refers to as having such powerful words is God, Who by the power of His Word created the universe out of nothing. The ability to use words in this way is a direct attribute of the Godhead. Whether the centurion's faith was in Jesus Christ or in the efficacy of the word spoken is not sure, but Jesus commended him for his faith and so credited Himself with the healing, not the words spoken.

The animist thinks of power in a spoken word as distinct from the speaker. As with rituals, the effective use of words does not depend on the user or on his disposition. Words have a magic power all their own. Using the proper words correctly will produce the desired result. Therefore certain power words must be handled with great caution.

Some believe that for words to have their strongest efficacy they must be pronounced by a religious specialist. An example of this is the story of King Barak, who sought to have Balaam curse the people of Israel.[3] Though Balaam sought to speak evil, he could only speak good because God controlled his speech. However, Barak had faith in the power of words to accomplish their intended purpose, and so persisted in seeking to have Balaam pronounce the curse.

Words are thought to have inherent power to deal with all realms of life. Some practitioners believe their power is impersonal—similar to *mana*. Others associate spirit powers with the words. In the latter case, words have power to deal with the invisible realm. Using the spirit words can secure exorcisms, call up spirits, and deal with situations requiring drastic action.[4]

Words are indispensable in controlling and propitiating the spirit world, whether they be soothing words, lively, spirited words, or repeated words or phrases such as "hail Mary, the Lord is with thee and blessed be the fruit of thy womb" and "Jesus." Also prevalent are prescribed intonations or cadences (rhythms), like in chants, repetitious singing, droning recitations or other special worship forms.

Words are also believed to have potency when used in prayers, prayer wheels, blessings, curses and rosaries. The King James English used in the Bible is thought especially efficacious, and Arabic is considered the only valid language for the Koran. Euphemisms are sometimes substituted for powerful words, words which might kill if spoken. This association of magic power with language covers numerous events and is widespread in all religions.

The Navaho, famous for their long chants, firmly believe in the efficacy of the proper words. They are extremely careful in speaking their chants. These chants "must be repeated letter perfect, else the entire chant is invalidated. Doing it badly could cause disease."[5]

Malinowski, who documented many spells and charms in the South Pacific, reports that a New Guinea tribe used a magic formula involving alliteration. He observed, "Such play on words . . . shows that the purely phonetic handling of words must be associated with the idea or feeling of their power."[6] In another magic formula, "The opening words are always intoned with a strong, melodious cadence which is not permanently fixed, but varies with the magician." And in another section of the formula the words "are recited slowly and ponderously but not repeated."[7] In one part of the formula the key word is repeated over and over, "as if to fix or rub it (the spell) well in."[8] Sometimes, as in a formula used for the expulsion of a wood sprite, the technique is different: "It is an invocation, and it is to be spoken in a low, persuasive voice."[9] Malinowski concludes that when words are used like this as magic, "a word will often be used in a shape quite different from those in which it is used in ordinary speech . . . it will show notable changes in form and sound,"[10] adding to its magical power.

Because the words are used with a different cadence and form according to their ascribed magic, it is unnecessary to know what they mean. In fact, in some instances, foreign or gibberish words are more efficacious. Malinowski, in analyzing the text of a magic formula, found

> . . . a considerable proportion of the words . . . in magic do not belong to ordinary speech, but are archaisms, mythical names and strange compounds, formed according to unusual linguistic rules.[11]

While trying to analyze the text, Malinowski discovered that not everyone knew what the spells meant. "There are some unintelligent old men . . . who rattle off a formula, and who evidently never were interested about its significance or else forgot it."[12] Nevertheless, they believed the words were powerful, even if they had no idea what they meant. This is not unlike prayer forms used in other religions, including Christianity.

The kinds of words that are thought to be powerful vary. Ancient Egyptian magicians used foreign words like *"Tharthar, thamara, thatha, mommon, thanaboth,* and *abrnazukhel."*[13] In Europe in the Middle Ages, power words were common: "The magicians and sorcerers of the Middle Ages likewise employed gibberish of a similar kind."[14] In addition to gibberish, the names of deity were used magically. In medieval Christianity and frequently in present-day Christianity, power words were often associated with the names of God. In Islam, numbers are used to represent those names.

In the Middle Ages,

> The distinction between a charm and a prayer was subtle, especially since . . . charms incorporated holy names, used Latin phrases similar to those of the liturgy and based their efficacy on the power of the Christian God.[15]

Even more specifically, people used the name of Jesus. However, there are those who

> . . . condemned charms using the name of Jesus to drive away the devil or prevent witchcraft because the ignorant people think that Christ is a conjuror, and that there is virtue in naming of His name to do some strange thing.[16]

Even the Jewish people of the first century of the Church were not immune from this kind of thinking. In Acts 19:13-16, the seven sons of Sceva tried to exorcise demons by "using the name which Paul preached"—"Jesus of Nazareth." They mistook the authority God gave to his servant for a power inherent in his servant's words. The demon did not recognize the supposed inherent power in the magical formula—"the name of Jesus," as the sons of Sceva had perceived.

Likewise, in Folk or popular Islam, words are frequently used to drive away devils and "certain formulas compel God to do what is requested and it is especially the use of the names of God that produce these results."[17] In Islam, as in animistic cultures, the purposes of power words vary from controlling nature, to controlling people, to controlling the spirit world. Verses of the Koran are most powerful against the jinn (evil spirits). Sometimes the *Suras* of the Koran are read, and the person then blows in all directions toward the sky and earth in order to gain protection from calamity or the enemy. Some Muslims also believe in *Qarina* (an opposite sex twin of the individual, who is a progeny of Satan) who comes into the world from *A'alam al Barzakhiya* (Hades) at the time the child is conceived. It is imperative therefore, that the word *bismallah* be pronounced during the act of intercourse, to prevent the child from being overcome by its devil and turned into an infidel. Magic power found in words is indispensable to maintaining welfare.

Practitioners of Folk Islam in Turkey attempt to send away scorpions by stating a prayer or a religious belief. A prayer that is neither Arabic nor Persian will normally paralyze the scorpion. So too, it is believed that demons are controlled by words:

> . . .we had to cross a narrow channel where dirty water was running to the drains. We could not cross this, however, until we had all solemnly spit three times into the dirty water and said, *"Destur bismillah"* to appease the evil spirits that always lurk in dirty places . . . If one did not say, *"Destur bismillah,"* meaning "Go away in the name of God," the evil spirits . . . might . . . feel insulted by the lack of respect shown toward them and give one a push in the back guaranteed to land one face downward in the channel of dirty water.[18]

Words may help one reach the place of rest after death, or so the Egyptians hoped when they took words of power to the grave with them: "The dead man . . . would have passed out of existence at his death but for the words of power provided by the writings that were buried with him."[19] Even the Judgment Day may be made easier because of these magic words:

> In the Judgment Scene it is Thoth who reports to the gods the result of the weighing of the heart in the balance, and who has supplied its owner with the words he has uttered in his supplications, and whatever can be done for him he does.[20]

These beliefs have persisted in many folk religions, including Folk Islam. Throughout life and even in death, animistic man relies on power words to help him succeed.

Use of words falls into several categories. Amulets are probably the most popular way to use words magically.

Tibetan amulets are frequently pieces of paper inscribed with sentences to Buddha, while those of Ethiopia . . . contain legends, spells, secret signs, words of power . . . Japanese amulets against lightning dangers, etc. are usually roughly printed sacred texts or rude woodcuts of the divinity appealed to . . . enclosed in an envelope. These are sold at temples, are not taken out and read, but are renewed annually.[21]

In this latter example, words may be powerful on their own, but it is not a power that lasts forever. Islam also employs amulets with the names of God or the creed. Jews have worn phylacteries as amulets as well, and Scripture has often been recited with the assumption that it is accompanied by magical powers.

Curses directed towards people or things are considered powerful as well. Islam has rules for cursing, and swearing has power according to what is sworn by. Swearing by one's own life is binding, but it is forbidden to swear by the fig or olive trees or by Mt. Sinai. Spells, like curses, are also powerful because of the words used. Lewis Spence explains that spells are thought to work through sympathetic magic because "there is some natural and intimate connection between words and the things signified by them. Things that have once been in contact continue to act on each other even after the contact has been removed."[22] For example, if a drowning man cries "the *suyusaya* fish shall lift me up,"[23] he shall be saved from drowning. Malinowski says this spell in the second person indicates that the "result is verbally anticipated, proving that the spell is to act through the direct force of the words and not as an appeal to the animal."[24]

Nothing is excluded from the realm of words. Longevity can even be attained through muttering verses, according to the Hindu *Rgvidhana*. Says Stutley:

Muttering verses which contain the word *sam* (which means to appease, pacify or calm), and mantras which include the word *svasti*, and the *trivrt* verses, i.e., the nine verses of RV. 1X. 11 addressed to Soma Pavamana. The suppliant immerses himself in water and mutters stanzas containing the words *suddha* (cleansed, pure) and water, and recites the sin effacing *sukta*.[25]

The use of such magical words has special efficacy in producing circumstances within and without a person which issue in long life. These words are essentially mantras, and work as mantras, putting man in contact with supernatural powers. For example, the use of the mantra in the meditation preparatory for engagement in the martial arts guarantees to the user special ability and beyond-normal physical strength and endurance.

Words are powerful instruments to an animist; he uses them every day as a protection against the exigencies of life brought about by the spirit world. The Christian who tries to teach the animist otherwise will have a twofold problem. In the first place it will be hard to convince him that words themselves are not powerful. In the second place—and very importantly—when the animist reads the Bible, he may feel that the missionary is a liar, or ignorant, and that his own animist system is reinforced by the Bible's use of words. For example, God spoke the world into creation (Psalm 33:6,9). By word He controls nature (Psalm 104:7; 106:9) and by word He heals (Psalm 107:20). Isaac blessed Jacob, not Esau, and the blessing could not be revoked, and in Matthew 8:8, as pointed out previously, Jesus healed by a word alone. The animist is bound to say, "See there! The Bible affirms the animist use of words."

Another means of control closely associated with the power of words, is symbolism. The basic premise here is essentially the same—there is power in the symbol.

SYMBOLISM

It seems that man has no lack of means to control everyone and everything. In individual terms, control means that one can keep from suffering, loss or failure. One such means very closely associated with the power of words is the power of symbols. Symbols serve to secure and protect places, people and times from the attacks of evil spirits, and to invite the benevolent spirits to exercise their good offices on behalf of the supplicants. Under the protection of the symbol, devotees feel secure, endued with power and confident.

Traditionally symbols were prepared very much like a fetish and should rightfully be classified with charms and fetishes. A symbol is invested with invisible or intangible capacities. By reason of a relationship or association with spirits, or persons of superior status, symbols are objects of power. As objects of power they excite respect and fear. Like power words, they must be handled with great care and caution. They have a definite identification with, and recognition of, both good and evil. For these reasons symbols are frequently used as charms to either ward off evil or invite good luck.

As indicated, symbols serve primarily to ward off evil. In European and some other cultures, wearing a black dress or black arm bands upon the death of a relative, or when attending a funeral, was thought to make mourners invulnerable to assaults of demons attracted to the corpse. Evil powers are thought to respect some very powerful symbols, such as the cross, the Islamic crescent, Fatima's hand with a picture of an eye in the palm, or certain colors. Other symbols variously acclaimed to be especially powerful, are the: eight-spoke wheel of Buddha, the swastika, the ankh, the goat's horn, the horned hand, the evil eye, the phallus and the sword.[26] Hex signs, tattoos, embroidery on cloth(es), flags and other such symbols are also claimed to be effective. The purpose might not only be to ward off evil, but to draw blessing and secure success to the user. The inherent power of the symbol is a sentry on guard in the interest of its owner, watching over the welfare of his goods.

One area of symbols which is even closer to the concept of power words, is that of gestures. The outstretched hand toward a person in certain parts of Pakistan instantly communicates a curse, though no word may be spoken. The same gesture in other areas would convey a special blessing. The sign of the cross serves to protect from evil and to draw blessing. Only within the context of a culture and a particular religion will gestures be understood and the symbolism be meaningful. Gestures play a significant part in religious expression.

The Bible, too, has symbolism, such as blood on the door posts as a protection from the angel of death; the serpent on the post as a symbol of healing; the vine on the Temple doors as a symbol of life. Each of these will have to be interpreted biblically lest the animist mind associate them with the animist concept of symbolism—an object having power within itself.

Symbolism is just another means of control, and underlying the acceptance of these means as efficacious is the understanding of what is involved in magic. White and black magic are indispensable means for an animist.

MAGIC

Terming magic black or white is strictly a matter of perspective. White magic suggests that the art is being used to achieve good ends and black magic evil ends. But good or evil are merely value judgments made by the practitioners. Nevertheless, these two are thought to differ in intent.

Magic is a means of bringing about good or evil, involving supernatural powers. Magic is thus the art of bringing about results beyond man's own power by cooperation with superhuman agencies. As such, magic may be thought of as a self-help program whereby a person employs means to manipulate supernatural agencies to serve desired goals.

Although magic cannot be separated from any of the previous practices thus far mentioned, the way it will be described here is that it is generally used to further an individual's own purposes. But not exclusively so. Magic may then be used to have a circumstance, person or event act beneficially toward self and/or malevolently toward an enemy. The practice of magic as here described is for personal, selfish and sometimes antisocial objectives, depending on which type of magic is being practiced.

While Malinowski proposed that "the integral cultural function of magic . . . consists in the bridging-over of gaps and inadequacies . . . not yet mastered by man,"[27] and that no great danger is present and success is relatively assured, all evidence from practicing animists would lead us to believe differently. The purpose of magic is first and foremost to gratify desires, whether they are good or bad. It is a selfish way of attaining the unreachable or forbidden. It is a means to control objects, circumstances or people in order to achieve success in the pursuits of life—especially those which will enable one to subjugate opposing forces and gain the upper hand without fear of retribution. It is the ability to do things with stealth—and yet with confidence, because the end result is well-nigh assured.

Malinowski and others[28] have sought to establish a connection between the development of religion and its supposed early associations with magic. They posit that religion has evolved. But having said that, there are similarities in the practice of each religion, and the simple reason may be that man wants to be in control. Because of his sense of powerlessness, the lure of power in magic becomes an intrinsic part in the practice of religion. Both religion and magic claim supernatural agencies upon which they can depend to achieve their objectives.

Some claim that religion is primarily supplicative and magic is manipulative. However, it is difficult to know where the one leaves off and the other begins. Among other approaches to the supernatural, religion beseeches, requests and prays. This is done through sacrifices and offerings or other forms of worship. Magic uses rituals, words and objects such as charms or amulets.

Through proper use these means achieve goals. It is relatively easy to confuse religious practices with manipulative magical means, especially when the motivation in both appears to be personal objectives.

There is a private or personal and a public magic, as will be seen later, along with several other categories of magic.

Divine Magic

The way the miraculous in religious practice is sometimes defined adds to the confusion between what is religion and what is magic. Divine magic is said to occur when God Himself enters the human context and permits a miracle. Says Carroll:

> Because of its [divine magic] workings, Moses can part the Red Sea, Christ will raise the dead, Joshua is able to stop the sun and moon in the sky. This Divine magic . . . is rarely seen on earth, and even a superficial insight into its mechanics is beyond the power of ordinary comprehension.[29]

Even if it should be granted that this is but one of the several categories of magic, the biblical account does not indicate any manipulative means in any of the cases mentioned above. Wherever God intervened in a miraculous way in the human milieu, he did so directly. Furthermore, what man terms the miraculous is quite normative with God—"is anything too hard for God?"[30] This is certainly not the way God is defined in the Christian Scriptures.[31]

Natural Magic

Natural magic is defined as the art of dealing with impartial energies. Here the power is simply cause and effect. This is also referred to as thaumaturgy, the ability to so manipulate means that produce miraculous results. Supposedly no other means is involved, or so says Carroll:

> The magician wishes only to initiate the magic transition to bring his initial energy to bear upon it. Higher nature then takes over and propels the process to its inevitable finale. No heavenly or diabolical intelligence is invited. The practice is totally within the realm of mechanics.[32]

Natural magic is further separated into two divisions. One is conscious natural magic. In this instance a magic ritual (speaking words or bringing together two elements) precipitates a psychic push which makes the magic energy flow. This could possibly be a prayer offered in the name of someone, such as "Jesus' Name," or "Allah, the merci-ful." In unconscious natural magic there is no psychic power involved. In this case the performance of a ritual will induce the flow of magic energy. The same ritual formula will produce the same result every time. When the necessary ingredients come together the desired result is produced.

White Magic

White magic, the art claimed by good witches, invokes good pow-ers and/or spirits to accomplish good purposes. It is also called Theurgy, the aim of which is to "bring man into contact with beings more spiritual than himself to bring virtue down to this lower world."[33] Such involvement with occult powers is considered beneficent because of the good achieved on behalf of the supplicants.

> The good or white protective medicines are prepared by qualified medicine men. They are made by an expert who knows how to manipulate the forces that make them effective.[34]

The practitioner of white magic serves mankind in those difficult-to-resolve problems in human experience. Where man does not suc-ceed by himself, the specialist seeks to secure those things which may not normally be part of ordinary man's experience due to social or economic limitations.

Black Magic

Black magic, as its designation implies, deals with those dark areas of life which are antisocial. Self-interest and self-centeredness motivate it. Man's evil intention "evokes the individual ego at the expense of all other creation." It is "full of self-interest and self-esteem."[35] In fact, the more self-interested one becomes, the more readily he aligns himself with the powers of evil, believing that he will have more control over a situation.

The purpose of black magic is malevolent, and the kind of special-ists sought after are usually sorcerers, wizards or shamans. They claim to know the ritual means to bring evil on others. For example, by making an effigy of an intended victim, they claim to use magic words or objects to inflict suffering. A pin may be thrust into the leg, arm or heart of an effigy of the victim to produce the intended results in his body.

Black magic is a very common concern of animists, and they take all kinds of precautions against it.

> Offensive or black magic is much feared, and many charms are worn with the object of defeating it by use of a stronger power. Babies are loaded with bracelets and charms to protect them from evil influences and witchcraft. Lovers protect themselves against their rivals or jealous husbands. Farmers and blacksmiths arm themselves against accidents with their tools, which may have been caused by sorcerers. Rings are worn against snakes sent by evil men.[36]

Any perceptive observer will know this to be true of all world religions. Magic's effectiveness comes from either homeopathy or previous contact with the victim.

Homeopathic Magic

Homeopathic magic is effective because it operates on the law of similarity—what is done to one will affect the other similarly. Like produces like. Through use of an effigy or some similar means, the desired result can be effected through homeopathic magic. In this way curses and blessings may be placed upon people and places. By proxy one may receive the blessing on behalf of another. The blessing may be transferred because of the law of similarity. Specially prepared potions made of animal parts, plants or other materials, may be scattered on a pathway, around a dwelling, at the entrance to a building or wherever else an intended victim may go. By homeopathic magic these effect a spell or a curse. Some symbols are used this way. Water may be used to bring about cleansing to counter evil magic. Sickness may be carried away by the same means. If the sick person is washed and the soiled water emptied on a pathway, the first animal or human to walk over it will carry the disease away from the sufferer. Naaman's seven dips in the River Jordan to be released from leprosy[37] could be misconstrued as homeopathic magic. Parrinder illustrates from African life.

> In rain making rites water is spewed into the air to make rain fall by imitation, or clouds of smoke are made to rise to help the clouds gather round. A woman may wear a doll in the hope of reproducing a child she has lost . . . In sickness, spots may be pasted on the skin of a sufferer from a rash, and then washed off again.[38]

Magic by Contagion

Unlike homeopathic magic, magic by contagion operates by the law of contact, which means that once things have been in contact (conjoined), they are forever thereafter conjoined. Therefore what is done to the one must similarly affect the other. In magic by contagion, any human part, clothing or other object associated with the intended recipient is used. The prayed-over handkerchiefs the Apostle Paul took to the sick is an example of this. They were effective,[39] but it would be difficult to convince an animist that magic by contagion was not involved.

To avoid evil magic by contagion, many animistic peoples take special care with the birth of a child to properly dispose of the placenta lest it be used to practice magic on the child. Although magic is practiced primarily for personal reasons, a distinction can be made between private and public magic.

In private magic man seeks help from various paraphernalia for specific needs. Charms made of all sorts of materials may be worn:

> [These materials include] mixtures of leaves stuffed into horns, gourds or leather packets and worn by the owner. Men wear teeth of animals, magic miniature scissors and knives, caps to make them invisible or safe against attacks of animals . . . Men wear charms in their hair, armlets of iron or leather, bracelets of tinkling metal girdles laden with leather pouches, anklets of metal. Most common are rings against snakes and scorpions. Finger rings and earrings have frequently magical value. Many of the leather packets worn by modern Africans contain texts from the Koran or the Bible.[40]

All of the above serve to protect animist man from black magic. On the other hand, public magic affects a larger group. Public magic seeks to provide protection for houses, villages, towns, fields, vehicles and other places and things available to the public at large. For example, in Pakistan the characteristic black flag or evil eye painted on vehicles serves to protect both vehicle and occupants from evil onslaught.

Among animistic peoples,

> One sees bundles of feathers, bunches of leaves, packets wrapped in cotton thread, or great parcels hanging from the ceilings of rooms to protect their occupants. Shops have packages or magic brooms nailed above the door, to repel burglars or attract trade.[41]

Similar practices occur among animistic peoples worldwide and are not unknown among many Westerners who claim to no longer adhere to such practices. Even the most educated resort to the practice of magic to achieve desired goals. A Middle-Eastern newspaper carried the following:

> A Bahraini woman who claims to be a genie queen, and her fiancee, have rekindled an ages old controversy, by announcing one free wish per mortal on the occasion of their wedding . . . The wish has to be reasonable and immortality is excluded . . . Non-believers, especially those who make fun of the occasion, will be jinxed within nineteen days . . . For those willing to try their luck, the advertisement says "the wish should be made at 7 p.m. any local time after the subject dons a neck bracelet with the name of the genie royal couple, Queen Bilqas and King Bargan . . . If a total of 19,000 non-believers make fun of us over an area of 19,000 kilometers, they will be hit by an earthquake within a minimum of 19 days and a maximum of 51 days," the announcement warns.

> "Magic does exist, and magicians and sorcerers often employ genies," Al-Qabas was told by Sheik Badr Abdul-Baset, the counselor of state owned Kuwaiti Islamic Finance House. "To deal with genies is to play with fire," cautioned Sheik Muawwad Awad Ibrahim, the director of guidance at the Kuwaiti Ministry of Religious Affairs.[42]

Few peoples, if any, are free from the belief that magic is a necessary part of life and that there are magic means available to deal with problem areas in life. Reference has already been made to the magic associated with charms. More should be said about charms and fetishes, so we now turn our attention to these as a means of control over the eventualities of life.

CHARMS

Charms, amulets and talismans are essentially the same, serve the same purpose and are among the everyday techniques used to influence the outcome of events. Charms enhance the possibility of things turning out well. Charms are the poor man's way to gain control over the many challenges he faces in life. The animist believes that charms guarantee security and provide the possibility of success whenever the caprice of other spirit powers allows him to flounder in time of need. Charms add a needed dimension of certainty to life, enabling him to act with confidence in its exigencies. If this was not so, fear and uncertainty could make life unbearable. Charms are believed to be effective because of their previous associations or derivation. Charms are objects endowed with power, most often *mana*, and are generally worn on the person of the owner. This power makes the charm effective in warding off evil and drawing good fortune to the wearer. A charm is a visible presence of special powers which gives its owner a sense of control in life. Some animists believe that charms can guarantee security to the point that they are completely invulnerable in the face of unusual challenges, even when life itself is at stake.

Charms are so common that among some animistic people markets have stalls selling charms. Newspapers and magazines worldwide carry advertisements offering charms for sale to meet whatever need or desire one may have regarding courtship, business or family matters, or to counter intended evil from both known and unknown sources. Writing on the past use of charms in Hinduism, Stutley observes:

> The two main classes of charms used in women's rites are first, those to ensure a suitable husband and children; second, those relating to demonic forces, counteracting the effects of curses, eliminating rivals and fulfilling individual wishes and ambitions. Though many charms were employed by or on behalf of women, some were used by men seeking to gain some advantage in affairs of the heart.[43]

These practices are still common, not only in Hinduism, but among all animists. Stutley also maintains that

> Fragrant plants and sweet smelling substances are frequently used in love spells and potions . . . Recently, in the U.S.A., the dragon's blood (a gum used in wood staining) love potion has been revived . . . Navajo love beads are also being sold in many American cities.[44]

Charms made of gold have long been thought to bestow on the wearer longevity and other coveted abilities. Gold, it is commonly believed, especially among Hindus, symbolizes immortality, because it was believed to come from immortal fire. "Thus the one who views gold will never die prematurely."[45]

> Legend states that the Daksayanas, the descendants of Daksa, bound a golden amulet on a man called Satanika, who desired long life. The amulet, called the first born force of the gods, not only protects the wearer from demons, but bestows splendor and strength on him.[46]

Such beliefs are quite widespread among animistic peoples. The metal may not always be gold, but the belief is the same.

Charms also serve other purposes. In the Carolina Island group of Micronesia, charms not only make the wearer invulnerable in the face of unusual challenges and ward off evil, they also serve as a point of telepathic and telekinetic contact between persons desiring close contact. In one such case a chief's daughter's activity was known to her father, and she in turn maintained a psychic and clairvoyant contact with him, though they were separated by an ocean expanse of more than two thousand miles.[47] This practice extends to the deceased, who may communicate with the living through special charms.

Although charms are thought to be powerful in and of themselves, they are exceedingly so when treated by ritual specialists. Charms that are specially prepared by specialists or that have been used with sacred objects sometimes become family heirlooms. They are believed to play special roles in family welfare and success. In such cases the charms just about take the place of family gods. Usually they supplement the gods and the many other spirit powers thought essential for dealing with the human condition.

What May Serve as Charms

The kinds of objects which serve as charms are beyond number. However, some objects are considered more potent than others and are much sought after. Among these, some of the most coveted charms are objects formerly used by ritual and/or religious specialists, objects associated with sacred paraphernalia, parts of animals or human beings, sacred cords, animal claws, precious and semiprecious stones, pieces of leather, special metal objects, religious symbols, sacred Scripture texts, the proverbial rabbit's foot, ivory and elephant's hair. Elephant's hair is made into bracelets, sometimes wrapped in gold wire, or made into rings and worn to give superior strength, attract success and overcome problems. Among some animistic peoples a charm ointment or salve is ritually employed to ensure protection against witchcraft, sorcery and the dreaded evil eye.

Charms form an integral part of a society that trusts a great deal of life to luck. But luck is not in question when power objects such as charms, amulets and talismans are used. Power objects dispel uncertainty and produce expectation and the confidence that all will be well. Such power objects are worn in bead form as necklaces, bracelets and rings, or tied as a sacred cord around the body. They are hidden in

115

homes, buildings and other busy places, or carried in pouches and pockets. Concerning the Aymaras of South America, Nordyke observes that they:

> . . . have many objects that are used to control luck, utilized by the layman and the professional. Some of these objects are closely associated with spirit beings, while others apparently have no connection with the spirit realm but are merely instruments of good luck. For instance, in this latter group, the Aymara likes to keep in his house a good luck charm such as a fox skin, armadillo skin or a small stuffed vicuna. These objects are not necessarily on public display; actually they are dumped in a corner, buried under other objects and apparently forgotten. Nevertheless, the fact of their presence seems to be quite important.[48]

Such belief in the power of charm objects is quite common among animistic peoples of all religious persuasions. Life is tenuous at best and would be unbearable without some measure of assurance that man need not be totally helpless in the face of the human condition. Charms serve to lessen the harsh reality of life. But should they prove ineffective, man has access to something more powerful, namely the fetish.

FETISHES

Whereas a charm may or may not be prepared by a ritual specialist, a fetish is generally prepared with a specific purpose in view. A fetish is, therefore, an object endowed with supernatural spirit power, specifically invited by a ritual specialist to indwell the concocted object. The spirit is thus localized and comes under the control of the specialist, becoming subservient to the wishes of the possessor of the object in which it is confined.

A fetish is a spirit shrine which exercises an occult influence according to the possessor's wishes. The fabled genie's lamp in the story of Aladdin was in fact a fetish which served the purposes of the owner.

Although some fetishes are ascribed many different roles, generally the role of the fetish is highly specialized. The localized captured spirit's activities are only efficacious for a particular purpose. Each purpose would therefore require another fetish with its own captured spirit.

Fetishes serve in the emergencies of life. When charms seem to be powerless, the captured spirit, it is thought, will bring the desired results. Fetishes can be prepared for success in work, trade, love-making, changing someone's mind, bringing evil on another, causing sterile women to have babies or bringing students good marks in important examinations.

Because a fetish is made to be a spirit shrine, it is treated with great respect, as if it were a close relative. It is thought to be a coveted friend. Whereas a charm is treated like a powerful object, the fetish has a relationship with its possessor. It is talked to and given offerings, and it is present in times of loneliness. Because a fetish has a very specific function, it tends to be dormant between times of need. At such times it is thought to rest, and to be effective it must be awakened to its task. This awakening takes different forms, ranging from shouting to offerings and other rituals. The localized spirit can at times be very capricious, and it may need to be appeased before it will act.

Unlike charms, which normally consist of only one element, fetishes must be constructed. One fetish in the Cameroons was placed at the intersection of two main roads. The construction involved a whiskey bottle, a dead chicken, some shrubbery and various minor objects. In Asia some fetishes look like a harmless doll or buddha or other such religious articles. Some incorporate sacred scriptures, even the Bible. With proper preparation by a ritual specialist, these are claimed to be exceptionally effective. There are early references to the use of the Bible in this manner. One such awakening ceremony involved binding the Bible with cords and swinging it around. In the other a candle was burned on its pages.

Fetishes made of relics of the dead, especially those of high social, religious and political stature, are considered to be of superior value. The power is not in the fetish object, however, but in the spirit or being that has taken up residence in it. The presence of the spirit assures the possessor that his dear friend the fetish will never leave him nor forsake him in the possessor's intention. His desires will be achieved because he has a specific power available to meet a specific goal. Again the spirit world is there to serve man—man the self-styled and self-proclaimed master of the universe.

Should all the aforementioned means prove to be unsatisfactory, animist man is still undaunted. There are yet other means available—powerful means which do not permit any form of altruism or integrity. The objective is to accomplish a desired result without the dictates of morality. The means are witchcraft and sorcery.

WITCHCRAFT AND SORCERY

Numerous volumes have been written on both of these subjects. Parrinder's *European and African Witchcraft* is probably one of the best known, so a brief overview here will suffice. Witchcraft and sorcery refer to systems of belief centered on the idea that certain persons in a community will resort to means to bring harm to their fellows, to accomplish desired goals, by the use of nefarious supernatural means. Those who engage in such practices are believed to be witches and sorcerers, and looked upon as agents of evil and misfortune.

In spite of the fact that witches and sorcerers are feared, their services are sought for those extreme situations which require drastic action. Animist man may be thought to be fatalistic in his approach to life, but such an evaluation is not consistent with the multifaceted motivation he manifests in seeking to deal with issues which affect his life. It appears that only stronger medicine than his will call a halt to his manipulation of power sources.

Although witchcraft and sorcery are frequently thought to be one and the same thing, and in some ways they are, there are differences, as well as similarities, between the two. One need only recall the trials of the Salem witches in New England in 1680. Apparently some innocent victims were sent to their death. Some doubted whether they were actually witches or practiced sorcery or simply behaved unconventionally.

Witchcraft

A witch possesses an inner supernatural power which can be concentrated to work malice on an unsuspecting victim. This power may be innate or it may be the presence of a familiar spirit. This ability is thought to be hereditary or may have been specially communicated from a known or unknown source as a gift. The propensity to witchcraft is attributed to hereditary or dispositional factors. It can be caught or gotten by desire. The person to whom the gift may be ascribed is totally unaware of the fact that he is responsible for working evil, but his victims seem to have no doubt as to the source of their difficulty. However, when witchcraft is practiced, the user is thought to have a mystical and innate power to effect desired goals which generally augur evil for the intended victim. In witchcraft the techniques of the witch are considered to be supernatural and beyond the comprehension of ordinary folk. The motive in witchcraft is to work deliberate aberrations to bring about fear. The practice is an obvious addiction to evil.

Some more contemporary witches who seek justification and approval for their activities claim that they only use witchcraft to effect good. They maintain that their mysterious activities are simply consistent with age-old practices which have had man's welfare at heart. They seek to project an attitude of altruism, thereby creating an atmosphere of acceptance of their practices. A review of their practices and what they charge for them, however, quickly confirms that these practitioners are just as self-serving as their more traditional cousins who do not deny the use of evil forces to achieve their desired goals.

Whereas witchcraft is a mystical innate power used to bring about evil, sorcery is evil magic in which the practitioner deliberately resorts to maleficent substances or rituals to bring about deliberate harm.

Sorcery

In sorcery a practitioner uses medicines derived from plants, roots, human waste or animal parts. The plant forms may have druglike properties, while human and animal parts are used in connection with homeopathic magic.[49]

In sorcery the techniques of the sorcerer are acts of destructive magic. These are generally accessible to most members of a community. Sorcery demands no special personal attributes and may be practiced by anyone who can acquire the necessary magical substances or learn the spells. The motivation behind the practice of sorcery is generally revenge in the face of injustices, inequities, human interference, envy or downright malice. The practice of sorcery gives man a sense of being able to intervene successfully in the difficult-to-predict elements of life, so that he can control the behavior of man.

Witchcraft and sorcery instill within society some of the greatest fears known to man. While the sorcerer seeks to control the hard-to-predict nature and behavior of man, his own caprice and unpredictable behavior, more frequently than not accompanied by his own selfish ambition, make him an object of fear himself, to the point of tyranny, panic and even death. An article in the *Times of Zambia* illustrates:

> Residents of Kitwe's St. Anthony's township have collected K.110 to hire a witchfinder to identify the person believed to be responsible for several deaths which have occurred in the past three months. And in

Mumbwa, villagers have agreed to call a witch doctor to flush out a sorcerer allegedly terrorizing teachers at Munyati Primary School . . . . At St. Anthony township, adjacent to Mukuba Secondary School, Party Chairman, Mr. Ackwell Bwalya, confirmed four children and two women had died mysteriously . . . One woman had died mysteriously after she refused to lend a pot to another. The woman woke up sick and told her that she had dreamt of fighting with the woman who had asked for the pot. She was taken to the hospital and died the following morning . . . In the Mumbwa affair . . . the teachers said they wanted a remedy as the alleged witchcraft was a threat to their lives. Headmaster Mr. Bernard Luputa said, when he woke up one morning he found a dog chopped to pieces and its parts scattered around his house. Deputy Headmaster Mr. Joseph Mulanga and his family of six have since deserted their house and are sleeping in the headmaster's office. Another teacher . . . said since he came to the school that his wife was having miscarriages. All the teachers have paid K.5 each for a witchdoctor to cut protective marks on their bodies.[50]

Witchcraft and sorcery thus account for many catastrophes, diseases, tragedies, deviant practices and deaths. They also serve as mechanisms of social control, psychological manipulation and enslavement. On the one hand, deviant behavior may attract the attention of a practitioner of sorcery or witchcraft, and on the other, deviancy may make one a suspect of being a practitioner of either practice. In the Boudoukou area of Ivory Coast,

When a person dies, his fingernails and toenails are removed. A tuft of his hair is cut off and attached with fingernails and toenails. This packet represents the dead person and is carried on a stretcher between two young men. The dead man's spirit is questioned to see why he died and especially to find out if he was a sorcerer. If he was a good man they want to know why he died and who killed him.[51]

The power of witchcraft and sorcery extends from the illiterate and uninformed to the sophisticated and educated, as the articles above confirm.

The reality and power of both practices lie in their actual association with spirit power. There are biblical injunctions against these practices because of their association with deliberate and personalized evil as well as demonic powers.[52]

Whatever means of control animist man has devised, in each case he seeks to compensate for and sublimate his sense of helplessness and powerlessness. He denies or refuses to accept the human condition, believing that somewhere and somehow he can re-establish his omnipotence over his world. To animist man, the concept of a loving father, concerned for his welfare and intervening in the human condition to effect blessing, is very foreign. Man alone is the master strategist. Should he not use means of control, he would be overwhelmed by fear.

Along with the means he has devised to control life, man has also discovered ways by which he can receive messages which would help him in his exercise of control. We shall now describe these.

ENDNOTES

1. Benjamin C. Ray, *African Religions* (Englewood Cliffs, N. J.: Prentice Hall, 1976), p. 88.

2. Matthew 8:8.

3. Numbers 22-24.

4. Cf. Hosea 6:5. What would the animist's interpretation be of: "I have slain them by the words of my mouth"?

5. Maria Leach, editor, *Funk and Wagnall's Standard Dictionary of Folklore, Mythology and Legend* (New York: Funk and Wagnall, 1949), p. 210.

6. Bronislaw Malinowski, *Argonauts of the Western Pacific* (New York: E. P. Dutton and Co., 1953), p. 441.

7. *Ibid.*, p. 436.

8. *Ibid.*, p. 437.

9. *Ibid.*, p. 443.

10. *Ibid.*, p. 452.

11. *Ibid.*, p. 432.

12. *Ibid.*, p. 433.

13. Lewis Spence, *An Encyclopaedia of Occultism* (New York: University Books, 1960), p. 377.

14. *Ibid.*

15. Russell Hope Robbins, *The Encyclopaedia of Witchcraft and Demonology* (New York: Crown Publishers, 1959), p. 85.

16. *Ibid.*, p. 86.

17. Bill Musk, "Popular Islam: The Hunger of the Heart," in ed. Don McCurry, *The Gospel and Islam: A 1978 Compendium* (Monrovia, CA: MARC, 1979), p. 210.

18. Irfan Orga, *Portraits of a Turkish Family* (New York: McMillan, 1930), p. 22.

19. Spence (1960), p. 377.

20. *Ibid.*, pp. 377, 378.

21. Leach (1949), p. 51, 52.

22. Spence (1960), p. 377.

23. Malinowski (1953), p. 451.

24. *Ibid.*

25. Margaret Stutley, *Ancient Indian Magic and Folklore* (Boston: Shambhala Publications, Inc., 1980), p. 41.

26. Richard Swiderski, "Italian-Americans From Folk to Popular: Plastic Evil Eye Charms" in *The Evil Eye,* ed. Clarence Maloney (New York: Columbia University Press, New York, 1976), pp. 28-41.

27. Bronislaw Malinowski, *Magic, Science and Religion* (Garden City, New York: Doubleday Anchor Books, Doubleday & Company, Inc., 1954), p. 140.

28. *Ibid.*, pp. 19, 140.

29. David Carroll, *The Magic Makers* (New York: Arbor House, 1974), pp. 67-68.

30. Genesis 18:14.

31. Exodus 34:6-9.

32. Carroll (1974), p. 77.

33. *Ibid.*, p. 69.

34. E. G. Parrinder, *African Traditional Religions* (Westport: Greenwood Press, 1976), p. 117.

35. Carroll (1974), p. 84.

36. Parrinder (1976), pp. 116, 117.

37. II Kings 5:10.

38. Parrinder (1976), p. 113, 114.

39. Acts 19:12

40. Parrinder (1976), p. 114.

41. *Ibid.*, p. 115.

42. Deutsche Press, *Agentur* (March 19, 1987).

43. Stutley (1980), p. 49.

44. *Ibid.*, p. 53.

45. *Ibid.*, p. 43.

46. *Ibid.*

47. Personal account of Palauan student enrolled at the Micronesian Institute of Biblical Studies, Truk, East Caroline Islands, June 1977.

48. Quentin Nordyke, *Animistic Aymaras and Church Growth* (Newburg: Barclay Press, 1972), p. 36, 37.

49. William Howells, *The Heathens: Primitive Man and His Religions* (Garden City, New York: The Natural History Library, Anchor Books, Doubleday & Company, Inc., 1962), pp. 49-52.

50. *Times of Zambia* (Lusaka, Zambia, July 27, 1981).

51. Jimmy Aldridge, "Faith of Fear and Fetish" in *Heartbeat* 22, no. 2, (Nashville: Free Will Baptist Foreign Missions, March 1982), p. 3.

52. Exodus 22:18; Deuteronomy 18:10; 1 Samuel 15:23; 2 Chronicles 33:6, etc.

Chapter 10
WAYS TO RECEIVE
MESSAGES

When the world of man is thought to be spiritual in essence, life can hardly be static. The animist believes he lives in a dynamic world. It is alive and it is constantly communicating within itself. Only non-animist man fails to read his surroundings and receive the messages.

Animist man believes that the spirit world wants to communicate with him and that there are means by which he can know its thoughts and desires. This gives life meaning, but it also provokes a large measure of apprehension, because animist man knows the spirit world as one of caprice and excess. The floods which hit Natal, South Africa, in September 1987, and again in February 1988, are a case in point. Dr. Sam Maila, a Zulu tribal healer and seventh generation *isangoma*[1] and herbalist who claims 6.5 million followers worldwide, interpreted the floods as a message from a nineteenth century king. Dr. Maila wrote:

The devastating Natal floods and their consequent exposing of graves, were caused by the wrath of Shaka Zulu and his ancestors—and there can be no long term relief in sight until Shaka's anger has been appeased. . . . Shaka Zulu's anger was unleashed in September last year when tradition was not followed and Chief Mangosuthu Buthelezi called all the tribes together . . . beside the Zulu king's grave, on the 159th anniversary of his death. The permission to do so from his direct successor, King Zwelithini Goodwill of the Zulus, was not sought, nor was the king asked to be the main speaker as he should have been. They touched the king's grave and sacrificed his cattle without his children being there. No one can talk to Shaka without his royal blood being present. The rains began the very next day. Dr. Maila predicts that the floods will continue until the "right" person from Shaka's family apologizes to the grave. We are being punished for something done wrongly in Zululand. The tribes must be brought together again and the mistakes must be revealed. If Buthelezi does not do so, there are very dark shadows ahead in both his future and the future of his people.[2]

To the animist the message is very clear. When man deliberately breaks custom or refuses to observe taboos, the spirit world responds with drastic consequences. But man is not totally helpless in the face of such judgment. There are ways in which he can restore harmony to his world, but he must first discern what went awry.

Among the ways man may receive messages are dreams, visions and vision quests and—most significantly—divination. The latter includes reading the stars, discovering the significance of omens and interpreting dreams and visions.

DREAMS

Western man, as a product of the Age of Enlightenment and rationalism, is apparently the only one who has lost the means of dreams as valid communication with the unknown and/or spirit world. Freud sought to ameliorate the situation by claiming that dreams do indeed communicate, but that the communication relates to man's suppressed desires. Whether this is true or not, animist man thinks any communication which comes during sleep is as valid, if not more so, as that received during waking hours. It's interesting that the biblical accounts of Jacob's, Joseph's and Daniel's dreams confirm that this belief has foundation in reality.

Animists take their dreams very seriously. To them a dream is a sleep occurrence in which a person is released from physical and other limitations to facilitate communication with the spirit world. Dreams serve as one of the chief sources of revelation from the spirit world to man. Even among religions which claim written revelation, dreams supersede such encoded truth. Dreams serve as the channel of fresh revelation and keep men in constant potential touch with beings who are thought to be omniscient. Animist man expects his dreams to be meaningful.

Dreams are accepted as a means of two-way communication

between the living and the dead and the living and the gods. They are considered a normative way to receive guidance. In Pakistan a Muslim woman believed her dream to be God's way of telling her to convert to Christianity. On several occasions she dreamed of a shepherd who allowed sheep to enter a beautiful meadow. In her dream she approached the shepherd to request entry into such a beautiful place, only to be turned back and to be told that she was not worthy and needed to prepare herself properly. This dream came to her repeatedly and deeply disturbed her. Eventually her husband suggested she consult the missionary, who read to her John 10. Finally she and her whole family were converted to the Christian faith.[3] She was drawn to Jesus Christ through several dreams.[4]

Dreams can bring warnings. In parts of Nigeria, as well as in other countries, dreams involving animals such as cats, owls or goats are especially disturbing. It is accepted that dreams of such a nature augur ill for someone closely related to the dreamer. They are evil omens. A missionary to Nigeria observed that

> A girl who dreamed of a cat falling down a well would be hysterical until allowed to travel to her village to see that no one in her family had died. Sometimes those dreams are genuine premonitions that should be taken seriously.[5]

Examples of such experiences are so common that to explain them, researchers have done in-depth studies investigating the connection between the physical and psychical.

Dreams also communicate important commands. It is not unusual to meet former animists who claim that they entered the Christian ministry in obedience to a specific command from an ancestor who appeared in a dream. Others equate such dreams as prophetic words to be communicated to others. And through such dreams some are motivated to engage in pilgrimages or missions of various sorts.

Dreams may be harbingers of good, confirming promises of blessings. Joseph's dreams prior to his enslavement in Egypt and subsequent elevation to rulership are well understood by the animist.[6] In his capacity for the supernatural, he too knows how to receive a prophetic word of blessing through his dream life. As already pointed out, in dreams man may actually commune with spirit beings and send messages to others distant from him. Whether spirits act as mediums, or the soul of man leaves the body and travels to distant places is a matter of opinion.

Most animists believe that the soul is as real as the body, and that it fulfills its role on nocturnal visits, engaging in astral travel during dreams. According to the cosmology of the people, the soul has the ability to descend or ascend to the abode of the spirits or elsewhere, even to distant planets. Some animists and contemporary practitioners of the occult claim that they can travel in this manner at anytime by entering a trance. This enables them to interview spirit beings and other souls. Man's orbit of friends and power beings is thus significantly enlarged. In his dreams he meets a vast host of power sources which he believes can only serve his best interests. Whether sleeping or awake, man is in contact with the spirit world of which he is a part. Dreams restore to man's waking hours a sense of well-being. Maintaining contact with a supernatural world which centers on his welfare gives man a measure of confidence to face daily reality. Should the waking hours' trials be unbearable, the sleeping hours will again allow him to consult with spiritual powers.

The animist adage is "to live well is to dream well, and to dream well is to live well." Nighttime experiences are assumed to be at least as meaningful as day ones. No distinction is made between dreams (the ideal) and waking thoughts (the real).

Dreams are firsthand experiences that only occasionally need the interpretation of specialists. They are accepted as a very necessary part of life because they bring to man messages which normally come through diviners.[7]

VISIONS

Visions are another way in which man may receive messages. Whereas dreams may be two-way communications, visions generally are not. Visions may come in either waking or sleeping moments. They are thought to have their source outside of the person, whereas a dream it is believed takes place within. In visions, people perceive an event as external to their own senses, something which imposes itself upon the mind. Visions are less common than dreams, but like dreams, visions generally bring guidance, warnings and promises of blessing. There are numerous examples in the Christian Scriptures as well as in the experience of followers of other religions.[8]

VISION QUEST

One kind of vision, the vision quest, is often sought after and may be self-induced. As practiced by many American Indian tribes, a person seeks out a spirit who serves as a familiar contact with the spirit world. But while spirit possession is thought deviant in Western society, it is considered normal in animistic society.

A vision quest enables man to communicate with a host of spiritual powers. He acquires a spirit helper to help him through life and equip him to be a good and successful community member. He is introduced to the spirit world through various rituals and ascetic practices and actually becomes possessed by a spirit being. This inhabitation gives him confidence that he has ability to handle difficult situations. He has earned the right (the power) to make his voice heard in community affairs because of his daring exploits and extraordinary accomplishments. Being possessed, he also belongs to an elite which claims to be the retainer of tribal and religious mysteries.

The indwelling spirit is also thought to be the personal guardian of the possessed. This protector spirit is usually associated with an animal, and in fact, may have so appeared in a vision to the searcher. This animal spirit is also accepted as the totem of the person's family, and actual animals of that type are sacred to that family.

The indwelling spirit gives the possessed ecstatic experiences, *glossalalia*, unusual visions and dreams. These experiences all confirm to the possessed that he has entered the mysteries of life and is in communication with spirit beings. He thus feels that he has attained a measure of control, if not omnipotence, in life. Through his own familiar spirit he also has access to other spirits, who may have their own messages for him.

Some vision quests are quiet and contemplative. Yoga is an example. The objective here is to identify with the spirit within through exercise and meditation. Transcendental meditation is of like nature. When contact has been made with the spirit, rapturous sight and feeling is experienced. In the practice of martial arts there is a time of meditation and preparation. Sometimes a *mantra* is used to contact the spirit within. The *mantra* is the power word which calls the spirit into consciousness. The diverse rapturous experiences found in various religions are all essentially forms of vision quests. The presence and indwelling of the spirit earns the one in contact with them acceptance and standing in his community.

In other vision quests seekers commit violence against themselves. Examples of self-inflicted tortures include jumping from heights, walking on burning coals, thrusting skewers into cheeks and tongue, using drugs, and dancing and drumming and chanting and singing oneself into a frenzy. All facilitate spirit possession. Sometimes spirit possession precedes some of the behavior listed. Either way, the spirit is claimed to ride the seeker, after which the vision is experienced.

DIVINATION

Divination is a technique with which to interpret phenomena of nature and consult spirits. In so doing one discerns messages from occurrences that would not normally be considered meaningful. Animist man believes that the universe is not mute, but charged with meanings and laden with messages.[9] An example from the Maguindanao of the Philippines will illustrate:

> The man groaned, clasping his hands over his gut. With slow seriousness an old woman took an egg and rolled it over his stomach. She held it over the smoky fire in the hut and then carefully cracked it into a bowl. Observing how the yolk ran out, she pronounced the cure: "Sacrifice a chicken and you will be well in two days."[10]

The universe is partner with man—man has a kinship with nature. By entering into dialogue with his surroundings, man can be informed about himself. In fact, to know oneself it's necessary to know the messages which are constantly being sent by nature. Through these messages one interprets one's own destiny and the destiny of mankind in general. But all too frequently the messages come in code form and are not readily understood by the average man. The diviner is proficient in interpreting them.

The Diviner

Not all diviners are altruistic but generally they do seek to be of service to the community. At times they serve as the local fortune-teller, shaman or medicine man. Performance of any of these roles requires an ability to understand the situation at hand and come to an acceptable agreement. This service has a price, however. As the one who holds the code which deciphers the messages, the diviner is free to set whatever price he desires or the market will allow. Because of this, and because of his association with the spirit world, he is frequently feared and despised, and his clients maintain a love-hate relationship with him.

As the official decoder of messages, the diviner makes it his business to know the members of the community (which is one of the reasons they suspect him of evil intentions). He is a student of human psychology and social interactions and uses this knowledge as he meets his client's needs. But the diviner is more than a good psychologist; he is also a discerner of spiritual forces. He has developed techniques with which to engage in spiritual encounter. The diviner must know how to interpret natural phenomena such as fire, water, heavenly bodies. He must have the ability to manipulate and decode the tools of his trade (e.g., cards, bones, dice, etc.). He ought to understand the messages being sent in sacrificial rituals. He needs to understand *haruspication*—the study of animal entrails and such like. He must also know spirit possession, and be a medium himself, able to enter trancelike states or clairvoyant states. His value as a diviner is his ability to penetrate the universe of signs and clarify what they mean in any given circumstance.

The mode of divination is not important, but the preparation of the diviner is. The profession of divination is a skilled one, requiring a lengthy apprenticeship. Says Zahan:

> The function of diviner does not tolerate improvisation; on the contrary, to become a seer it is indispensable to follow a long and hard apprenticeship. It is often even necessary to undergo a veritable initiation, a transformation similar to those which lead man to sources of religious life, to God.[11]

Preparation for this skill will vary from people to people, but there are commonalities, including an above average intellectual capacity, an innate sense of intuition and a facility to probe the universe and to decode its many and varied messages. Specific rituals are followed to become a qualified diviner.

Generally, the potential diviner starts by practicing divination for himself and his friends. This shows his potential ability and serves to confirm his call to himself and the community. He then either apprentices himself to an experienced master diviner or begins a self-study program.

The diviner leads an ascetic and exemplary life, observing strict taboos in order to maintain psychic and intellectual lucidity. He appears so different and unusual that frequently he is thought to be a holy man. Divination is not the sole domain of males; female diviners exhibit these same unusual qualities.

Somewhere in the training process, or even before entering upon the apprenticeship, the diviner secures a double. Upon qualification, the diviner is more than a clairvoyant. He has secured a double which allows him mobility apart from his own physical travel.[12] He secures his double by going through some form of vision quest. The actual process is determined by local custom, but a good diviner needs a double. This double can detach itself from the body of the diviner and consult with the spirit world. When the double is absent the diviner is thought to be dead. He is then unable to divine. He may be in a trance while the double journeys to the spirit world to get the message, or else he may simply sense that his power or life force is drained or absent, and he cannot function properly. The diviner, using his human skills of discernment and judgment, works in tandem with his double or familiar spirit to decipher and interpret the circumstances. Many of them are masters of their trade, having become indispensable functionaries in many communities. This is true as well in some Western communities which pride themselves on their rationalism and enlightenment.

The diviner is not only consulted on all of life's important occasions but in minor ones as well. Some can tell what is physically wrong with a person through a mere handshake.[13] Many people who rely on diviners become one themselves and will give themselves to reading messages in many of their daily encounters. Astrology functions this way. If the world is not mute, and if man's destiny is indicated by natural and supernatural phenomena, then he is arrogant and foolish not to consult the diviner about the future.

Divination is widespread. It is even found in Christian traditions, as the following indicates:

Marta was frightened. She had been losing weight and feeling unwell. Tests indicated nothing wrong. A friend, half jokingly said, "Somebody must have put a spell on you." Marta casually mentioned this to her mother, a Sunday School superintendent and life-long member of a Protestant church in La Paz, Bolivia's most modern city. Marta never dreamed that her mother would approach the *curandero* (maker of spells but also a diviner). The *curandero* cast coca leaves and read Marta's past in the pattern they made. A former girlfriend of her husband, he concluded, had used another *curandero* to put a spell on her. The only cure, he insisted, was to rub a live guinea pig over Marta's body and then take it, dead, to her enemy's town and burn it. This would cause the death of the other woman, he said, and free Marta from her problems. Marta is a well-educated, articulate woman. Her children go to one of the better schools in La Paz. She has attended a Protestant church for years.[14]

In an article entitled "Poor Man's X-Ray," Marjory Koop writes of evangelical church leaders in Bolivia and Peru who are concerned about "this manifestation of residual witchcraft in the church." A videotape they have produced clearly highlights the function of divination and the role of the diviner as a medicine man.[15] The drama opens with Maria saying to her husband,"Nothing we do seems to make you better. Let's go to Jose, the witch doctor. He can do a poor man's X-ray on you." Pedro replies that this isn't right . . . "The guinea pig test is not the work of God's Holy Spirit." "But you're no good to God or to your family if you die," Maria answers. "Other Christians go to witch doctors (diviners) at such times. It's the way of our people." Pedro begins to waver. "God will forgive you," Maria insists. "We can repent after you become well. I will never forgive myself if you die and I have not said that we should visit Jose." Pedro consents. They make their way to Jose's house. Slowly Jose passes the guinea pig over Pedro's prostrate form. "The illness is being transferred to the guinea pig," he announces. "It will show us what is causing your trouble." As he dissects the guinea pig he explains, "It is your liver. See how large and pale it is?" "Yes," they agree. "It is the liver." Jose gives Pedro a concoction. Then he mumbles incantations, takes up the pieces of the guinea pig, and buries them deep in the woods."[16]

The article shows that syncretism will persist until its practitioners are shown the biblical way.

Because the art of divination is considered a very necessary skill in animist society, the diviner in his role as decoder of messages, exercises enormous control over a community. His power and subsequent control induces great fear of his person and of his skill. But there is also the fear of the possibility that error may cloud his judgment and that personal prejudice and malice may influence his diagnosis.

Nevertheless, animist man is not about to surrender his

omnipotence. He may be fearful but he still hopes that his skills and contacts in the spirit world will serve his interests. He has great faith in his own ability, or that of a specialist, to triumph over his human limitations. In his world, messages are not an end in themselves. They come to give guidance and instruction, and so they are deciphered in order to restore harmony and revitalize the human environment.

ORDEALS

An ordeal is a way of receiving messages from the spirit world that is similar to divination. It is a test used to determine the guilt or innocence of someone who is suspected of some violation of custom or taboo. Essentially, the practice of ordeal assumes guilt. It is assumed that because the spirit world is on the side of truth, a person who is innocent will be granted supernatural power to supersede any dangerous or painful test. Even if the test is not dangerous or painful in itself, if the suspect is guilty, supernatural power will supposedly bring the required judgment to bear. In some cases it is assumed that the inward life will validate the outward behavior. Therefore the innocent have nothing to fear, but the guilty will not escape the punishment due them.

In the animist world innocence or guilt is very difficult to establish for several reasons. In the first place a person may be bewitched without knowing it. He may thus have caused harm and be unaware of having done so. It is believed that the ordeal will reveal whether he is the offending party. There is also the possibility that a person may have acted in his sleep. His spirit may have travelled while dreaming and thus have been the culprit in the offense. Another problem in discovering the guilty is that the party may have acted involuntarily under a curse. Though he carried out the act being investigated, someone else may actually have been responsible.

Animist man seldom, if ever, believes that he is actually responsible for his own actions. His failures are caused by spirits, improperly performed rituals and other people. Ordeal will reveal who actually is responsible. Ritual means can be acquired which will cover the guilt of the person undergoing the ordeal from the eyes of the investigators. Justice can be thwarted by ritual means, and the guilty will not be discovered. Then there is always the possibility that an overly sensitive conscience will admit to wrongdoing and yet be guiltless.

Apart from the actual objective of the ordeal, the practice serves to discourage deviancy. Animist man believes that members of society must walk circumspectly. Customs and regulations are necessary for harmonious living. Should a person find a way to circumvent the law and not be caught, he remains a member of society in good standing. In fact, he comes to believe that his superior life force and magic make him superior to the average.

Ordeals take on many forms. Some appear exceedingly harsh and inhuman, except that supernatural help is available. It is available to the innocent because of his innocence, and to the guilty through superior rituals, Innocence may be established by placing a red-hot coal on the tongue or hand of the accused (in which case he will not be burned). Or the accused may be required to pick seeds out of a pot of boiling oil, or submit to having a hot pepper placed under his eyelid, without suffering any burns.

There are references to the use of ordeals in the Old Testament. In Numbers 5:11-31 a woman suspected of infidelity was given water tainted with dust from off the temple floor. If she was innocent, the water of bitterness would do her no harm, but if she was guilty, the water of bitterness would curse her, make her abdomen swell, and her inward parts dry up—a reference either to a miscarriage or sterility. Other references which may relate to ordeals[17], in which poison was used are: Jeremiah 8:14 "Because the Lord our God has doomed us and given us poisoned water to drink, for we have sinned . . .", Jeremiah 9:15 "Behold, I will feed them, this people, with wormwood and give them poisoned water to drink", and Jeremiah 23:15, where exactly the same judgment is expressed.

Ordeals have been thought to be a form of psychological manipulation. Guilt may become apparent as the witch-finder plays on the emotions of the accused. The diviner is generally a perceptive discerner of human personality. Fear of the impending test may produce nervousness, fear and other physical responses in the guilty. The interpretation is up to the diviner. But there is always the possibility of misjudgment. For example, vomiting up poison indicates innocence, as does surviving a weak dose. Should he die his guilt is proved, however. The belief that innocence is accompanied by superhuman ability to endure the trial is supported by widespread evidence.

Receiving and interpreting messages is an essential practice for animist man. But messages are not ends in themselves. They are decoded in order to restore harmony and equilibrium to human society and its environment. Sacrifice and offerings made on the basis of these messages serve to keep the blessings flowing from the spirit world.

ENDNOTES

1. An *isangoma* is a Zulu ritual specialist especially involved in divination. See B.G.M. Sundkler, *Bantu Prophets in South Africa* (London: Oxford University Press, 1970), p. 22.

2. "The Wrath of Shaka...and then the rains came" in *Weekend Argus* (Capetown, February 20, 1988), p. 21.

3. Told to the author by the missionary concerned.

4. Bilquis Sheikh, *I Dared To Call Him Father* (Lincoln: Chosen Books, 1978).

5. Dorrie Poland, *Animist Journal* (Columbia Graduate School of Bible and Missions, Columbia, S. C.: unpublished manuscript, 1985), p. 5.

6. Genesis 37:5-10.

7. Consulting a diviner, such as Nebuchadnezzar did in Daniel 4:6-7. See Sundkler (1970), pp. 265-275.

8. Bilquis Sheikh (1978).

9. Zahan (1979), p. 81.

10. Maria Leydon, "In the Grip of Evil" in *World Christian* (September-October 1984), p. 40.

11. Zahan(1979), p. 88.

12. *Ibid.*, p. 88.

13. "Powerful Belief" in *The Columbia Record* (Columbia, S.C., June 3 1982), p. 4-C.

14. Marjory Koop, "Poor Man's X-Ray" in *SIM Now* 34 (July-August, 1987), p. 6.

15. *Ibid.*, p. 7.

16. *Ibid.*

17. W. McKane, "Poison, Trial by Ordeal and the Cup of Wrath" in *Vetus Testamentum Old Testament Studies in Honour of P. A. H. Boer*, by E. J. Brill (Amsterdam: E. J. Brill, 1980), pp. 478-491.

Chapter 11
WAYS TO
RESTORATION

Animist man has long since discovered that his world does not function well without the principle of *quid pro quo*. If he wants the supernatural to give him blessings such as children, good health, abundant crops and safety from his enemies, he must remain in fellowship with his god and/or his ancestors. All too frequently however, he discovers that his world goes awry. Either his sins of omission or commission have brought alienation to this relationship, or the spirit world, for reasons known only to itself, simply remains unresponsive to his needs and desires. Somehow and somewhere reconciliation must be effected.

MAINTAINING HARMONY

The idea of reconciliation—the need to restore harmony or bring balance or equilibrium back to man's experience of his world—is very much a part of man's religious experience. Writes Alan Tippett:

In . . . Malaita I talked with an old heathen priest at his tribal sacred place. I asked him the meaning of a sacrificial stone that stood before us, which he called the Stone of Reconciliation. Two alienated members of the tribe, or representatives of two alienated segments of the tribe, would make a sacrifice before this stone to the tribal deity, requesting forgiveness for disrupting the tribal cohesion, and registering their desire for reconciliation with each other. Such reconciliation mechanisms are not uncommon . . . they may almost be universal in animist societies. . . .[1]

135

The concern for reconciliation does not arise out of a sense of guilt or even shame, but rather that of fear and the knowledge that disharmony plugs the conduit of blessing. Says Nida:

A sense of guilt expresses itself as an inner feeling of failure for not having lived up to what the society or the deity expects, irrespective of whether one is caught or seen. This sentiment of guilt is far less common than might be supposed . . . regarding oneself as guilty is not in keeping with man's egocentric way of life. Fear and shame are much more convenient attitudes for self-centered people.[2]

Animist man is strongly motivated by expediency as well as fear. Even though he may tip the scale in his favor by his many and varied ways of exercising control over his environment, he does seem to have an innate sense that life can't be all take. There must be some give, even if it's niggardly. It is quite obvious that animist man's giving is not motivated by altruism or generosity. Animist giving is a subtle way of inducing his world to reciprocate by blessing him with the fulfillment of his desires. Omosade Awolawu says "Whatever the purpose may be, it is obvious that something is renounced in order that a certain end may be achieved."[3] The only reason the animist gives is to open and keep open the channels of receiving. Even some notions of hospitality fit into this mode.

Writing in the context of sacrifice, Awolawu observes:

These divinities and spirits are higher and more powerful than men, they can be of great help to those who are loyal worshipers and who observe the family taboos and the ethics of the community; but can be detrimental to those who are negligent . . . In consequence . . . sacrifice . . . has its positive as well as its negative side. On the positive side . . . there is a strong desire . . . to maintain communion with them (beings which have power to sustain or destroy life). They know that they depend upon these spiritual powers for material prosperity, for good health, increase in crops, in cattle and in the family; they consider it expedient to show their gratitude to the giver of good things. . . . On the negative side, sacrifice is offered to counteract the powers of destruction . . . who hate seeing men make progress in life.[4]

Restoration is essentially a way of exercising control. Without it the spirit world will not respond to other rituals of manipulation. Some of the most universal ways of seeking or maintaining restoration are sacrifices and offerings. Sacrifices and offerings are universal religious practices. Says Ringgren:

All over the world, and throughout history, whenever mankind has worshipped divine being, we encounter the practice of sacrifice. The Babylonian sufferer gives a lamb to the gods to ransom himself from the sin he supposes to be the cause of his suffering. The Mexican Aztec kills a young man and offers his heart to the sun god in order to secure the vital forces of the sun for his land. The Moabite king Mesha, offers his son to his national god in order to win a victory over the attacking Israel (2 Kings 3:27). There are thousands of other examples like these of the world-wide religious practice we refer to as sacrifice.[5]

BENEFITS OF HARMONY

Sacrifices and offerings serve numerous purposes. E. B. Tylor says that sacrifice serves as a means of bribing the gods or of paying homage to them in the same way men pay homage to their overlords.[6] Van der Leeuw sees sacrifice and offerings as a gift to the gods in order to have them act favorably to the donors.[7] Robertson Smith sees these practices as a means of maintaining communion between giver and receiver.[8] Westermarck believes it is a way to feed the gods, who in turn will bless man and safeguard him.[9]

The purposes of sacrifices and offerings may vary from occasion to occasion and from people to people. The rituals of sacrifice and offering may be practiced to establish and maintain communication with the spirit world, appease it, seek its help in time of need or even blind it to some taboo infraction. They may also serve to remove guilt—not guilt arising out of conviction of a wrong done, but guilt arising out of fear lest insufficient recognition has been given or appeasement made to the spirit world.

Sacrifices and offerings are frequently involved in removing sickness if the sickness is discerned to be the result of the judgment of the spirit world. Both rituals may be used when sending off the dead or the welcoming of them to a place of honor in the family or at a shrine. Sacrifices and offerings may be made to restore relationships among opposing individuals, families and tribes. Normally, broken relationships and the disruption of peace are attributed to the disenchantment of the spirit world, specifically the ancestors or some regional deity. Only appropriate offerings and sacrifices can restore fellowship with the spirit world, and fellowship will then effect peace between the opposing parties. Among some peoples, sacrifice may be performed to effect purification or cleansing, with a view to re-establishing communion with a deity, although such occasions are rare. They are generally associated with acts of consecration whose aim is either to get the deity to respond to the sacrificer or protect him from evil attacks, or to secure some special favor from the spirit world. The latter will concern buildings, lands or other property which may be possessed by evil spirits. Ultimately, all sacrifices and offerings relate to the well-being of the offerer and/or sacrificer which issues in his success in life. "Something is renounced in order that a certain end may be achieved."[10]

TYPES OF SACRIFICES AND OFFERINGS

Sacrifices and offerings are generally made of those things with which man maintains fairly close relationships. There is a bond with the object of sacrifice or offering. Without such an affinity the ritual would be both meaningless and valueless. Although there may be differences between the secular and religious meanings of sacrifice and offerings, the intent is the same in both cases, namely, the giving up of one thing for the sake of another. In this respect, whatever a man gives—his time, food, clothes, money, animals or life—is a part of himself.

In making sacrifices and offerings, the person may therefore offer cereals or other vegetable life, prepared food and/or drink, animal victims, sometimes human life and other objects. Generally, the occasion specifies the type of offerings or sacrifices suitable. A suitable offering or an appropriate sacrifice also will vary from religion to religion and according to the custom of the people.

Thus far we have considered some commonalities in sacrifices and offerings. They may be used interchangeably at times, yet they differ markedly in quality, quantity and degree.

Character of Offerings

Offerings are usually gifts brought as presents. They are performed with undue restraint. Undue restraint must be understood relatively because the motive of the offerer cannot always be accurately assessed. In animism, nothing is done without a view to receiving something in return. Acts of hospitality are frequently tied to expectations of goodwill from the deity or spirit to the offerer and/or his family. Not to be hospitable and entertain strangers may incur the wrath of the spirit world. Offerings and sacrifices may be a form of hospitality. Offerings are, however, made with less restraint than sacrifices. An offering is usually something the deity or spirit being would appreciate if he were here. In offerings—whether the burning of paper money, the presentation of fruit or other foods, or the pouring out of a libation—the deity or spirit being takes the essence of the matter as the gift of the offerer. On occasion the offerer may, in time, reclaim the husk since the essence has already been absorbed and then put the offerings to customary use.

Character of Sacrifice

By contrast, a sacrifice differs in nature from an offering in that it is normally offered under constraint. It is a required ritual atoning for previous infractions, or an attempt to elicit the special attention of the spirit world. Usually a ritual specialist, be he a shaman, a medicine man or some other specialist, determines what reparations have to be made to restore harmony and balance or effect reconciliation with the spirit world. The nature of sacrifice by comparison with offering is that the owner has no choice as to what is given to the spirits. Custom or divination determines what is appropriate under the circumstances. The object of sacrifice is transferred to the spirit world by destruction. This destruction could be in the form of sending away the victim. (In the Old Testament scapegoating is a description of the atonement.)[11] The sacrifice may also be consumed by burning or partial burning and partial consumption, by someone other than the donor. Although offerings may involve the giving of an animal, in sacrifice it is the spilling of the blood of the victim that makes the ritual efficacious. The shedding of blood serves some very important functions in the animist sacrificial system. In the ritual sacrifice the donor and the victim bond together, but so does the recipient—the god or spirit bonds with the sacrifice. Said Hubert and Maus, in their interesting study on the nature and function of sacrifice,

> This contact (with the victim) is obtained in Semitic ritual, by laying on of hands, and in others by equivalent rites. Through this proximity the victim, who already represents the gods, comes to represent the sacrificer also. Indeed, it is not enough to say that it represents him: it is merged in him. The two personalities are fused together. At least in the Hindu ritual this identification . . . becomes so complete that from then onwards the future fate of the victim . . . has a kind of reverse effect upon the sacrificer.[12]

Through shedding blood in sacrifice, the sacrificer becomes inextricably tied to the deity or spirit being. The blood covenant is established, with mutual obligations which are mandatory at all times. Mutual ownership is established, in which the sacrificer is claimed by the spirit and the spirit stands in special relationship to the sacrificer. Some animists also claim that the shedding of blood revives the spirit, thus awakening it to respond more vigorously to the sacrificer's desires. In turn, the sacrificer is also revived. Faith and confidence in the spirit being is restored, as reciprocal relationships are re-affirmed in and through the sacrifice. Some animists believe that special power is released in the shedding of blood. Say Hubert and Maus, "the act of slaughter released an ambiguous force—or rather a blind one, terrible by the very fact that it was a force."[13] The power could work ill, but if the proper rituals were practiced the effects could be to the advantage of the sacrificer in effecting the desired objectives.

Sacrifice, as practiced above, is generally a voluntary act performed for the sake of benefits.[14] Although restoration or reconciliation may also take place, the intent is to awaken the deity or spirit to meet a need or desire. And it is believed that a blood sacrifice is the most effective way to do this.

The more animism is probed, the more one discovers the apparently inexhaustible resources man claims to have in the face of his finite human condition. In each case man demonstrates his refusal to succumb to his environment and his determination to be his own god in dealing with life's issues. Although sacrifices and offerings are the means to effect reconciliation and restoration, there are other means to help man maintain a state of harmony with his environment. One is the practice of taboo.

PRACTICE OF TABOO

Taboo is the place where the spirit world meets social and religious custom. Taboo enforces the concept of the sacred. It is a prohibition against touching, saying, being or doing something, for fear of harm being inflicted by "the mystic dangerousness of a particular object,"[15] or supernatural power. Certain objects, persons, places and times are forbidden because they are associated with supernatural powers.

Character of Taboo

Taboo is a scheme of systematized fear that excites, and promotes awe and respect, as well as a sense of "awe-fulness." It is one of the strongest checks on man's behavior in both traditional and contemporary society, motivating him to maintain harmony and balance with his environment. Its many rules and regulations encourage him to keep on the narrow path of custom. In a very real sense, taboo is a prohibition imposed by social and religious custom, as a protective measure against deviancy. Not to observe taboo issues in a judgment involving dire consequences, even death. By proscribing behavior on certain occasions, and respecting certain objects and people—what to see, what to touch, with whom to associate, where and what to attend or avoid or use—taboo safeguards and protects a people's accepted physical, social and metaphysical systems. Taboo confirms and supports their world view.

Taboo is a legal system which dictates how life shall be lived in order to realize salvation and blessing. Observes Webster:

> A particular taboo once well established, tends to multiply endlessly ... Thus prohibition is piled upon prohibition ... to anticipate every single possibility of danger in the perilous maze of a world where all things are potentially dangerous.[16]

It is an all encompassing system calling on the spirit world to either validate, restrict or censure human behavior. It was well-taught and practiced by the New Testament Pharisees.

Scope of Taboo

Having come to know the spirit world as one of caprice, and yet of inexhaustible potential for blessing, taboo prescribes the way to maintain harmony with it. Three areas are especially of concern to the animist in the practice of taboo. Sacred places associated with the spirits, or places out of the protective range of certain spirits or deities, are proscribed. The use of land, the celebration of festivals, the observation of new moons or other moon phases or holy days are also taboo concerns. And in vision quests taboos may be extended to what plants and animals are fit or approved for consumption. Animist belief in the power of the spirit world in man's environment is described in Colossians 2:21 as "touch not, taste not, handle not ... after the commandments and doctrines of men, which things have indeed a show of wisdom."[17]

Since the concept of eternal life is so important in animist society, with children maintaining ancestors and ancestors maintaining their offspring, taboo also prescribes and proscribes behavior concerning fertility and continuation of life. Customs regarding marriage are therefore another taboo concern. Therefore religious restrictions and/ or permissions on marriages and approved mates are taboo concerns.

Since sin is thought of as broken relationships, the family being such an important basic social structure requires special proscriptions. The family functions to safeguard reproduction, to nurture children, to perpetuate custom and to see to the transmission and dispatch of the dead through proper funerary rites. The function of the family is a basic tribal and societal concern. Taboo prescribes and regulates such adult responsibilities in society, especially in regards to male and female family roles and behavior. Taboo also establishes restrictions on specific and general social behavior, on social and religious status and on patterns of recognition and respect. The social fabric of society and its religious strength depend on the strength of the family. This is an accepted fact among traditional animists and in most other societies.

Function of Taboo

Some authors claim that "the origin of most taboos is involved in the same Cimmerian darkness that veils the origin of primitive customs generally."[18] Still, the careful observer will note some very valuable functions of taboo. Taboo gives society a sense of the sacred and acknowledges the spirit world as a valid entity which is concerned about human behavior. It recognizes the unity of spiritual, physical and human welfare. Furthermore, it brings social behavior and custom into the realm of the sacred, giving society a measure of law and order by keeping man concerned for the spiritual consequences of his actions.

From the above description it may be deduced that the objects associated with the proscriptions of taboo

> . . . are as numerous and varied as human experiences, for any persons, things, acts or situations may be considered so dangerous that meddling with them recoils upon the meddler.[19]

Some taboo proscriptions require total avoidance—an object is never to be touched, approached or seen. Others are partial taboos, applying only to certain times, particular uses, or ceremonial occasions. Whatever their type may be, it is well to note that

> . . . the authority of a taboo is unmatched by that of any other prohibition. There is no reflection on it, no reasoning about it, no discussion of it. A taboo amounts simply to an imperative thou-shalt-not in the presence of the danger apprehended. That any breach of the

prohibition was unintentional or well-intentioned matters nothing; no allowance is made for either the ignorance or the praiseworthy purpose of the taboo-breaker.[20]

Nevertheless, animist man has found ways to circumvent even the dire consequences of breaking taboo. For example, someone superior in social and/or religious status may supersede the taboos of an inferior. One with more life force or other source of power may cancel out the effect of a taboo of another. Also, the effects of breaking a taboo may be avoided by observation of ritual precautions.

Therefore, although the system of taboos seems to be such a rigid and incontrovertible form of control, animist man is not at a loss at what to do should he transgress in this matter. There is a key to restore harmony and equilibrium to his environment. He may not have it, but someone does, and somewhere it can be found if he will only persist. Animist man has great hope and much faith in his ability to deal with life.

When taboos have been disregarded, or when sorcery or witchcraft have been practiced, animist man can always resort to divination or ordeals or some related means to find the culprit. To do so he seeks out the right specialist, be he diviner or sorcerer, to satisfy his sense of justice.

ENDNOTES

1. Alan R. Tippett, "Possessing the Philosophy of Animism for Christ" in *Crucial Issues in Missions Tomorrow* ed. Donald A. McGavran (Chicago: Moody Press, 1972), pp. 138-139.

2. Eugene Nida, *Customs and Cultures* (New York: Harper Row, 1954), p. 150.

3. Omosade Awolawu, *Yoruba Beliefs and Sacrificial Rites* (London: Longman Group, Ltd., 1979), p. 135.

4. *Ibid.*, p. 137.

5. H. Ringgren, *Sacrifice in the Bible* (London: Lutterworth Press, 1962), p. 7.

6. E. B. Tylor, *Religion in Primitive Culture*, 2 (New York: Harper, 1958), pp. 461ff.

7. Van der Leeuw, *Religion in Essence and Manifestation*, 2 (New York: Harper & Row, 1963), pp. 351ff.

8. F. B. Jevons, *Introduction to the History of Religion* (London, 1921), p. 154. Cf. R. Money-Kyrle, *The Meaning of Sacrifice* (London, 1965), p. 169.

9. E. A. Westermarck, *Early Beliefs and Their Social Influence* (London: MacMillan, 1932), pp. 98f.

10. Awolalu (1979), p. 135.

11. Leviticus 16:7-11.

12. Henri Hubert and Marcel Mauss, *Sacrifice: Its Nature and Function* translated by W. D. Halls (Chicago: University of Chicago Press, 1964), p. 32.

13. *Ibid.,* p. 34.

14. Nida (1954), p. 153.

15. Hutton Webster, *Taboo: A Sociological Study* (Stanford University Press, 1942), p. 2.

16. *Ibid.,* p. 1.

17. Colossians 2:21.

18. Webster (1942), p. 1.

19. *Ibid.*

20. *Ibid.,* p. 4.

Chapter 12

THE ROLE OF THE SPECIALISTS

The animist lives in a world of many powers. Many of them he believes to be responsive to him; others simply need more coercion. Confronted by powers not always kindly disposed, he finds himself at times a victim. He knows all too well that counter powers are seeking to thwart him in his pursuit for self-glorification, preservation and gratification. He also knows that there are three participants in the practice of his religion. There is a manipulator, be it a shaman, witch doctor, prophet, priest, medicine man or any such functionary. There is the victim, who is the object of black magic or some other evil machination. And there is the benefactor, the one who can change matters—a spirit being.

To accomplish his purpose, man must stand in the good graces of this spirit. Through his own practice of ritual he succeeds at times in coercing the deity or spirit being "to come to earth to renew his closeness to man; to descend to him in order to divinize him."[1] But just as frequently, if not more so, he lacks the power, the secrets, the key with which to realize his desires. He needs someone with more professional skill and life force, who can safely transgress areas that are taboo to him and tap effectively into power sources, or tell him how to do it for himself.

SIGNIFICANCE OF THE SPECIALIST

The belief that religious specialists have extraordinary skills with which they contact the spirit world and affect it positively on behalf of supplicants extends to all religions. Large numbers of Christians

145

assume that the prayer of a pastor is more effective than the prayer of an ordinary member. Bogota, Colombia, alone has 8,000 witches, seers, mystics and magic vendors. Should one wish to recover a lost lover, the rapidity of success depends on the specialist one retains. It is reported that

> Lucas guarantees a reunion in four days, 'no matter how far away.' Mariela, the parapsychological mentalist, takes seven but will throw in a cure for sexual impotence. Indio-Amazonico, an amiable mystic with a feather through his nose, promises results in a mere 72 hours.[2]

The right specialist can and does deal with the gamut of man's problems. For example:

> A man breaks up with his girlfriend and swears his body was covered with bite marks as he slept, the result of a hex. Cows are rid of parasites by a witch's incantations. Dying patients are cured by a long-dead Venezuelan doctor who performs surgery on them during the night.[3]

It is not only those whom society considers marginal, gullible and superstitious who seek the services of supposedly magical specialists. Their clients span all social strata and all educational levels, as reported from Bogota:

> Several years ago, the wealthy owner of a bookstore was huddling with Regina Vives—a clairvoyant who says she is advised by her dead mother—when the seer suddenly ordered her client out, to make way for a more esteemed visitor. Surrounded by security men, then-President Alfonso Lopez Michelson passed her on his way in for a consultation.[4]

All religions have specialists. Some are professionals and serve full time in the area of their specialty; some have other roles in society as well. Some specialists have several religious roles while others are limited to one or two functions at the most. It is sometimes very difficult to discern whether the practitioner is only a priest, or a diviner and medicine man as well. In some societies the distinctions are so minimal that they hardly exist and the main function of the specialist may never be recognized.

Generally, specialists are considered to be indispensable to society, because they know and understand the sources of help available to man. They procure the means to deal with problems. The generally high regard in which specialists are held in most societies does not arise out of their moral integrity or exemplary lifestyle. Rather they are sought after for their effectiveness. Because of his abilities the specialist is accorded prestige, reverence and honor. The specialist stands apart because of his craft and skill, regardless of his character. There are few exceptions. Even in Christendom, most devotees seek out specialists for their office rather than their integrity.

> The dealer in the supernatural is understandably viewed as tinged or imbued with the supernatural; he stands apart by reason of the fear, respect and reverence which the qualities of mystery and sanctity about him invoke. In societies with strongly ethical religions he may also stand apart as a paragon and guardian of virtue and as the symbol of divine jural authority .... [5]

Religious specialists are believed to know the secrets and mysteries belonging to the gods. They know how to penetrate these secrets and reveal to their clients the truths which relate to their area of concern. They are also the repositories of the tribal mysteries—those secrets long ago discovered which relate to the success, security and happiness of the people. If they should not know a secret or mystery, they know how to discover it. They are well-schooled in the social and religious customs which relate to personal and tribal welfare and which make for unity and purpose in life. They know the rituals, the formulae which will secure the desired blessings and keep the channels of communication open, maintaining effective contact between spirit world and people.

Specialists in animist society have a holistic approach to life. For example, prescribing medicine for a physical ailment without meeting the psychical need of a client by accompanying incantations or some such practice simply is not done. Therefore, specialists are expected to know the correct incantations and how to use them to arouse the gods to action. They must also know the liturgies with which to express proper respect to the spirit world. More significantly, they are acquainted with the supernatural. They know what to do in the face of caprice or ambivalence, but they also know what is pleasing or displeasing to them and what should be done to bring about reconciliation between the gods and their devotees. To know the way of the gods is to deal effectively with life, because every physical event has a spiritual coordinate. Specialists are attributed superhuman power and skill. They are thought to be well nigh omniscient if not omnipotent, and like animist man in general, they aspire to manipulate their environment. Given time and the right means, nothing is impossible to the specialist.

QUALIFICATIONS OF SPECIALISTS

A number of researchers seek to cast aspersions on the role of the specialist, claiming it tends to be a psychopathological condition. Writes Radin:

> . . . the formulations with which he . . . operates and the techniques he uses are fundamentally rooted in the projections and behavior of individuals carefully selected on the bases of their neurotic-epileptoid mental constitution and that, however normalized these, in the course of time, may have become through the influence of the more normal individuals who entered the profession, their origin in a neurotic mentality is still clearly patent.[6]

Norbeck claims that the presence of normal individuals attracted by monetary awards mitigates somewhat against the quality of neurosis among specialists.[7] He adds,

> No doubt the nervously unstable are selected for religious duties in some societies. Available accounts seem to describe a wide range of kinds of behavior among those candidates which at its extreme includes clinical psychosis . . . Trance and hysterical seizures . . . It seems entirely warranted . . . to say that psychological states which would be regarded as pathological if found among members of our own contemporary society are a common element of primitive religious complexes.[8]

And of course the same could be said for specialists in all religions, including contemporary Western Christianity, especially among Pentecostalism and the charismatic movement. However, both Radin's and Norbeck's evaluations, as well as those of others, appear to arise out of ignorance of the spirit world and its mysterious manifestations in human experience. Though some religious specialists may belong to a lunatic fringe, the majority do not and never have been selected on the basis of psychopathological inclinations. It is more correct to say that they are generally

> . . . mentally agile, resourceful, self-reliant, and assured; (they) must appear secure in order to inspire confidence in others; he must assume responsibility, and most important of all, he must be a leader.[9]

148

Zahan describes the diviner as one characterized by

> . . . great intellectual capacities, his intuition, and his facility for probing the universe and translating its messages . . . his aptitude for entering into contact with others by his keen sense of human relations, by a kind of gift for penetrating the soul . . . [10]

Specialists are generally above average individuals. For example:

> The Aymara needs practitioners to deal with . . . 1) disease and illness . . . 2) the future . . . 3) past misfortune—they want an explanation of why things have happened; 4) bad experiences with nature, such as hail or lightning storms—they want explanations and relief; 5) the ambivalent gods and spirits—so that they will be benevolent toward them; 6) the malevolent demons or spirits—so they will not cause more harm; 7) souls—either their own if it is lost, or someone else's; 8) ghosts—they want professional help to ward off their influence; and 9) omens that they do not understand. [11]

To effectively alleviate the many points of anxiety, the specialist must have attained special skill. He must be able to placate the spirits. Where man's sin has brought a breach in the covenant relationship with the deity, the religious specialist must prescribe the means of reconciliation and/or restoration, and if need be, effect the process. He must be an astute discerner of power sources. He must know where the power sources are and also what counter-powers are available to handle negative powers and/or spiritual or physical matters. He must be a perceptive determiner of taboo infractions. He must be able to divine who and what is responsible for a given disaster or catastrophe. He must at all times be able to discern what the gods or spirits require, what warning they are giving, and what will reestablish harmony and balance to man's human condition. The specialist is therefore the master technician in animist society. Without his services man's tensions and anxieties will totally cripple his ability to deal with the realities of life. Nordyke, in evaluating the Aymara specialists, correctly observes what is also true of animist religious practitioners in general. He writes:

> There are several things that all these roles have in common. First of all, they all employ magical techniques in one way or another; that is, they all try to manipulate some type of supernatural spirit or force for their purposes. Secondly, they all employ one or more divinatory techniques . . . . Thirdly, they all are consulted professionally in some

connection with illnesses and are employed in either causing, divining, or curing sicknesses.[12]

These commonalities make them a force to be reckoned with. Their powers are impressively strong. Their strength is rooted in the belief that they are accomplices of the spirit world, and their accomplishments attest to their relationships with powers beyond anything available to man through ordinary means. They will be in demand because they know that animist man takes his religion with him in all walks of life.[13]

TYPES OF SPECIALISTS

Tschopik's study of the Chucuito of Peru uncovered "six professional categories of practitioners who employ magical techniques."[14] They are: (1) magician, (2) *laika* (sorcerer), (3) *kollasiri* (doctor), (4) *yatiri* (diviner), (5) *t'alari* (chiropractor), (6) *usuiri* (midwife).[15] Harris and Parrinder, primarily concerned with parts of Africa, highlight four:

> . . . there are specialists or medicine men who are expert in the manipulation of magical power . . . priest is best used of those officials who serve in temples and officiate at sacrifices. Most of the great gods have priests at their shrines . . . . In ancestral ceremonies, which concern the family, the chief officiant and sacrificer is often the oldest man or head of the family. The medicine man is concerned with magical medicine, though he may be a priest as well. He is sometimes called a witch doctor. . . . this word strictly applies to those who seek to cure people of witchcraft. . . . Many medicine men are also diviners. They are like our fortune tellers and use stones, sand or some other method of divining. . . . Many of them prepare horoscopes.[16]

Some animist societies have ten or more distinct categories of specialists. Some overlap in their activities, and yet for their clients they "do not duplicate one another; they are rather interlocked and geared in an intricate manner." [17]

We may safely conclude that the majority of animist societies will recognize at least four categories of specialists—sorcerers and related practitioners, priests, medicine men and Shamans. Some perform both benevolent and malevolent services. Some unashamedly practice evil. Some are herbalists and some are masters of liturgy and ritual. Each has a religious and social function.

Priests

The function of a priest is usually to perform rituals, recite liturgies, and chant incantations which only he can properly use. Priests are the guardians and perpetuators of doctrinal orthodoxy, customs and laws. They teach the religious beliefs, either formally or by example. They model effective living. Norbeck writes of the specialist:

> The demands and nature of his office set him off . . . He is often a highly intelligent and learned man, and much of his lore is unknown to others. He must often be serious when others laugh. He observes many dietary and sexual taboos followed less strictly or not at all by others, and he alone might spend long periods in solitude and self-imposed pain and privation.[18]

Priests are in demand as the mediators between the spirit world and people. They are believed to know how to communicate with the spirit world, using words, rituals, correct posture, and clairvoyance. The priest is more efficacious than the lay person in his prayers and ritual performances. He brings to religious function a sense of factuality and efficaciousness.

Priests are generally appointed by the people or their representatives. They are available to anyone. Because of their expertise they are generally accorded prestige and allowed to exercise significant control in society. The priest has no authority in himself however. He stands under the authority of the people or their representatives and of the spirits. He must be commissioned by both if he is to serve effectively and speak with authority.

In some animist societies, depending on their social structure, the head of the family or the oldest member of the family (i.e., grandparent, father, oldest brother) is ascribed the role of the priest. Without him nothing may be done religiously or socially. Religious duties performed in his absence are not efficacious. To seek to supplant or bypass him brings the wrath of the spirit world to bear upon the disobedient, and may even lead to death.

In addition to their priestly functions, priests usually carry out psychomagical practices.

Medicine Men

The second category of specialist is the medicine man. The distinction between the magical (occultism) and the medical is most difficult to discern. The medicine man's treatment may be efficacious because of the curative medical properties inherent in his various concoctions. These may be made of leaves, barks, roots, fibers and even animal parts. Some of the touted cures border on the magical, suggesting involvement with supernatural powers. A sign outside the offices of a Nigerian medicine man reads:

> Children's illness; Convulsions; Stomach, Muscle and many others. Rheumatism; Jaundice; Eye troubles; Chest pain; Backache; Worms; Dysentery Purge; Cough; Gonorrhea; Spleen and other stomach disorders. Treatments are given to pregnant and unpregnant women. Miscarriages for quick and sure relief. Remember that Specialist Native doctor cures many kinds of sickness which English medicine cannot cure.[19]

The advertisement testifies to the amazing abilities claimed by medicine men. But their successes are accomplished in association with supernatural powers, and not by natural medicine alone.

In the practice of contemporary holistic medicine Harner observes that:

> . . . the burgeoning field of holistic medicine shows a tremendous amount of experimentation involving the re-invention of many techniques long practiced in Shamanism, such as visualization, altered states of consciousness, aspects of psychoanalysis, hypnotherapy, meditation, positive attitude, stress reduction and mental and emotional expression of personal will for health and healing. In a sense, Shamanism is being re-invented in the West precisely because it is needed.[20]

When a medicine man confines his practice to pharmacology and/ or herbalism, having learned the medical properties of certain potions through years of training, he functions as the equivalent of a Western medical doctor. Says Lovering,

> In some countries such practitioners are gaining recognition as valuable health care agents. Medical authorities in Peru recently sanctioned the opening of that country's first native medicine hospital. The UN's World Health Organization includes traditional healers as resource people in attaining its goal of "Health for all by the year 2000."[21]

But the traditional healer is more than a prescriber and distributor of herbal and other medicines. Those whom Norbeck refers to as "men who know the leaves"[22] are also psychologists. Animists are firm believers that all of life is part of the whole. The medicine man knows that for a treatment to be effective he must treat the whole person. The physical has a vital relationship with the spiritual. Distress in one sphere has a commensurate effect on the other. In his diagnosis and prescription, the medicine man must relate to two worlds. One is reminded of Jesus Christ making clay with his spittle, applying it to the eyes of the blind man, then instructing him to go and wash in the pool of Siloam.[23] How would the animist medicine man interpret this incident? Was Jesus accommodating himself to the commonly understood holistic healing practices of His day?

The traditional healer will include a ritual in his prescription, such as a bathing, a sacrifice, an offering, an incantation or a body massage. The patient will know that his whole being has been ministered unto.

Occultic practices frequently accompany the practice of medicine, and it is difficult to distinguish between cures brought on by medical properties alone (i.e., herbs and other such medicines) and those effected by Shamanism. There is an element of magic in both traditional healing and much contemporary holistic medicine (such as psychic-surgery).[24]

Shamans

The third kind of specialist is the shaman. Shamanism is seldom found alone. It is not confined to Siberian, Eskimo and North American Indian tribes, but is in vogue in the governmental sphere, the business world and the congregating places of the up and coming, as well as the huts of so called "primitive" people. As David Blundy reports in an article in the *East London Daily Dispatch*, entitled "Weird and Wonderful—Keeping in touch with the dead in today's California":

It was a Hollywood party, 1988-style. The house was, like most houses in California, an imitation—in this case of a late 19th-century Scottish mansion. The drive was cluttered with the playthings of the Hollywood young—Porsches, Mercedes and BMW's bristling with the latest electronic equipment . . . . Inside was a clutter of young actors and actresses, producers, directors, budding movie moguls, writers, and the psychic, a pale, blonde woman who communicated regularly with a dead Chinese and passed his advice on to her friends . . . They were all slim, fit, good-looking, dressed casually but with chic . . . They exuded success. Their optimism was almost aggressive. Their lives were "great," their businesses and films were going "great," their health was "great," their marriages and relationships were no less than "great" .... Californians are finding spiritual succor in the latest west coast cult, the New Age, and mediums have been around for centuries. In California, however, they know how to market spiritualism. The channellers have radio shows, give public performances and private consultations . . . (they) can channel over the telephone.[25]

Shamanism and spiritualism are essentially the same. Shamans are thought to be in direct contact with the spirits. They are expert in using rituals to manipulate supernatural powers, using magic words, incantations and music (usually drumming) to get the spirit's attention. They act as mediums by going into trances, or use others as mediums to channel messages. They are said to be able to make the deceased reappear. They are also adept at producing powerful charms and preparing effective fetishes. They know how to invite a spirit to inhabit fetishes.

It seems as if shamanism cannot be practiced without some form of divination. A shaman can divine the source of a difficulty, whether it be sickness, sorcery, witchcraft or any other malevolent source. He will frequently prescribe how to ward off the attacks of evil spirits or placate the alienated spirits. He knows how to track down sorcerers and witches and overcome their magic with more powerful magic.

It is not difficult to see why the shaman is such an important and powerful member of society. He is thought to be in direct contact with the spirits, to such a degree that his voice can be taken over by a spirit. In the truest sense, the Shaman is a spiritist. Being so closely related to the spirits, he is thought to speak for the spirit world and to it. He not only mediates messages, but unlocks power. His clients experience success, health and good relationships. He is thought to be able to put man in touch with himself, his world, the gods and unleash man's supposed latent power.

The shaman is believed to be able to transfigure himself into an animal, bird, insect, person or other apparition. There are amazing accounts of such happenings.[26] Shamans are thought to have the ability to descend into the netherworld or ascend to the place of the gods. They are reputed to have supernatural ability to bring on catastrophe or remove it and to secure blessing. Balak called on Balaam to bring catastrophe to Israel through a curse.[27] As diviner, seer, magician, medicine man, witch finder, witchdoctor and sometimes even sorcerer, his supposed abilities are indeed super-human, even god like.

Shamans have different names in different societies. All are willing to do just about anything in the supernatural world to meet man's desires. They limit their activity only according to their client's wishes and ability to pay.

Neither ethics, integrity nor morality matter to a typical shaman. With few exceptions, he is quite ambivalent in his morality, condoning almost any practice if it benefits him. Should he be asked to work ill, as in Balaam's case, he will not hesitate to do so. He will cast a spell and so act the part of sorcerer. Or he will divine an illness, prescribing a cure, and so be a good medicine man. At best, good or evil are relative terms in animist morality. Gaining advantage over another is of paramount importance, whether through human or supernatural means.

The above description covers most of the specialists in animist societies. But a fourth category stands on its own, yet overlaps with the office of shaman. This category covers all those specialists who are feared as deliberate agents of evil. The shaman is thought of more as an opportunist, a relativist, and a schemer. He is an entrepreneur who will use any and every opportunity for his advantage. But, strange as it seems in the light of this, he is sufficiently altruistic to serve his clients.

Workers of Evil

The fourth category covers specialists such as sorcerers, witches and wizards—they are workers of evil. Sorcery and witchcraft have already been discussed. Those who practice in these areas are thought to have close links with evil powers and may be possessed by evil spirits. Their machinations are determinately evil and are a detriment to society at large. If a person can dupe the spirits or get away with practicing evil, it is not judged as wrong. But even though animist societies have no clear categories of good and evil, some have such an abhorrence for sorcery that they assign sorcerers, witches and wizards to a place of punishment in the hereafter, rather than the heaven of the ancestors. In the Boudoukou area of Ivory Coast, Aldridge observes:

> Those who kill others by witchcraft are called sorcerers and are deprived of all funeral honors . . . Sorcerers are automatically excluded from going "to be with the ancestors". . . . They are the sinners in animistic culture and God will make them burn since they have been rejected by the ancestors."[28]

Supposedly, being possessed by alien evil spirits, they are believed to have extraordinary powers to perform their nefarious activities. These powers even reach across tribal boundaries. Clients will deliberately seek out sorcerers to get them to cast spells, utter curses, take revenge upon and remove foes, and bring death to their enemies. Their occultic associations make them feared and formidable opponents. They are shunned by all—until a time of need.

They are both feared and hated, yet serve to effect social control and curb deviancy. To draw undue attention to oneself by breaking custom, infringing upon the rights of others, rising to prominence too quickly, or being too successful, may be more than sufficient reason for envy, suspicion and ensuing sorcery. Knowing the effects and results of the sorcerers malevolent power helps to keep community members aware of the need to live in harmony with their fellows and society at large.

Each of these specialists in the animist world has one thing in common—the desire for power. And there is no doubt that they have a lot of it. They are not all fakes. They can deliver on their promises because of their involvement in the spirit world. Like the magicians in Moses' day, they can duplicate the miracles of others.

It may appear to a cursory observer that animism is a conglomerate of trial and error methods for dealing with the spiritual world. Such is by no means the case. Animism, in all of its varieties, is a denial of the Creator/creature distinction. Each of its practices is an attempt to gain control over nature by supernatural means, and to give man the illusion of omnipotence. Specialists are foremost in perpetuating this illusion. They bind the allegiance of their clients by meeting their needs.

Animism is a scheme which may infect any religion to attract man to an involvement in the spirit world. Man has an enormous capacity and need for the spiritual. He is therefore drawn to religious systems that promise supernatural power sources. In spite of the fears endemic to the practice of animism, it is a powerful way of life that should not be ignored. It is a direct challenge to the biblical message and should therefore be evaluated over against the Bible and its teachings. Although it is powerful and permeates all religions, it has many weaknesses which need to be examined.

ENDNOTES

1. Dominique Zahan, *The Religion, Spirituality and Thought of Traditional Africa* (Chicago: University of Chicago Press, 1979), p. 17.
2. "Columbians turn to Witches to solve life's everyday problems" in *The State* Section A (Columbia, S. C., Wednesday, April 15, 1987), p. 16.
3. *Ibid.*

4. *Ibid.*

5. Edward Norbeck, *Religion in Primitive Society* (New York: Harper & Brothers Publishers, 1961), pp. 107-108.

6. Paul Radin, *Primitive Religion* (New York: Dover Publications, Inc.), 1957, p. 154.

7. Norbeck (1961), p. 107, 108.

8. *Ibid*, pp. 118, 119.

9. Harry Tschopik, Jr., *The Aymara of Chucuito Peru, Anthropological Papers of the American Museum of Natural History*, 44, Pt. 2: 1, Magic (New York: The American Museum of Natural History, 1951), p. 294.

10. Zahan (1979), p. 82.

11. Quentin Nordyke, *Animistic Aymaras and Church Growth* (Newberg, Oregon: Barclay Press, 1972), p. 60.

12. *Ibid.*, p. 59.

13. Kerry Lovering, "Barriers to the Gospel: The Spirit World" in *SIM Now* 34 (July-August 1987), p. 3.

14. Nordyke (1972), p. 58.

15. Harry Tschopik, Jr., *The Aymara of Chucuito Peru, Anthropological Papers of the American Museum of Natural History* 44, Pt. 2: 1, Magic (New York: The American Museum of Natural History, 1951), p. 219.

16. W. T. Harris, and E. G. Parrinder, *The Christian Approach to the Animist* (London: Edinburg House, 1960), p. 42, 43.

17. Tschopik (1951), p. 225.

18. Norbeck (1961), p. 108.

19. *SIM Now*, 34 (July-August 1987), p. 5.

20. Michael Harner, *The Way of the Shaman: A Guide to Power and Healing* (San Francisco: Harper and Row, 1980), p. 136.

21. *SIM Now*, 34 (July-August 1987), p. 5.

22. Norbeck (1961), p. 43.

23. John 9:1-7.

24. See Johanna Michaelsen, *The Beautiful Side of Evil* (Eugene, Oregon: Harvest House Publishers, 1982).

25. *Daily Dispatch* (East London, South Africa, February 6, 1988), p. 3.

26. See Florent D. Toirac, *A Pioneer Missionary in the Twentieth Century* (Winona Lake, Indiana: Florent D. Toirac, P. O. Box 542, Winona Lake, Ind. 46590, n.d.).

27. Numbers 22:5-24:25.

28. Jimmy Aldridge, "Animism, Faith of Fear and Fetish" in *Heartbeat*, 22 (May 1982), p. 3.

29. Exodus 7:11.

Chapter 13

THE MEASURE OF MORALITY AND ETHICS

For a religion to be "pure and undefiled," it should be moral and ethical. Does animism qualify? To answer this it's necessary to repeat some issues covered elsewhere. Any religious system may be fairly judged by observing and evaluating its beliefs and practices.

A COMPREHENSIVE RELIGIOUS SYSTEM

When it comes to addressing man's social and psychological needs, few religions can equal animism. It touches every aspect of man's being. It serves man's interests remarkably well.

The social and psychological functions of a religion have to do with its meaning and usefulness for its adherents, and with what part it plays in the total life of a society. Animism's focus on community gives society order and cohesion. Animism also relates its adherents to a source of power beyond themselves. The animist knows from experience that his power sources work. This removes anxiety and encourages confidence in the face of adversity. Animism has an explanation for all aspects of the human condition. Contact with the spirit world may solve problems encountered in the human condition. The spirit world is literally at man's beck and call to deal with all eventualities.

Animism explains human life fairly adequately by providing satisfactory answers for vexing human problems. Being a spirit-oriented system, the animist relates everyone and everything to their influence. In terms of values, animism lives out what it believes. It acts in accordance with the operation of the spirit world and structures its behavior patterns in keeping with its religious priorities. Values and beliefs are nearly synonymous in animism. Most religions fail tragically in this area, claiming beliefs which are seldom reflected in real life. For example, some Christians claim belief in the imminent return of Jesus Christ, but evidence a lifestyle which contradicts such a belief. Some believe that unbelievers in Jesus Christ are doomed to eternal separation from God but do nothing to bring them to faith in Christ.

Animism addresses the personal welfare of its devotees, reducing their fear and anxiety through its relationship with the spirit world, and providing its adherents with the assurance that their understanding of life is correct. Animism thus provides for man's daily physical needs. It postulates supernatural powers which can be coerced to bring about rain, fertility, health, etc. It substantiates for its practitioners that all of life is sacred because all of life is spiritual. The spirit world must be respected and treated with cautionary ritual, since spirits interpenetrate the total fabric of life. There is no doubt that animism is a distinctive religion. It certainly establishes a particular identity for its devotees which issues in a solidarity in community. Animism produces spiritually oriented people, more so than other religions. It also enables its practitioners to communicate with the supernatural, which brings a greater measure of control over power sources. It holds out the promise of the acquisition of a greater measure of life force and skill, the better to manipulate the spirit world for personal advantage. Animism is to a degree prophetic, but only inasmuch as it postulates correctives for aberrant ways. If it calls man to greater ideals beyond himself, it is with an eye to gain personal advantage and/or secure community welfare. The latter is itself a form of personal advantage, since what benefits the group benefits him personally.

Animism does not claim to be a cognitively oriented system, and that is one reason why it appeals to such a vast number of people in all religious orientations. It is a very existential religion. Its strength lies in the fact that it can be lived out without recourse to esoteric doctrines, strict rules or regulations. It is an experiential religion which is more felt than understood. But the key factor which makes it so attractive is that it is powerful. It does not necessarily require that man change. He can essentially live life as he pleases, and yet have power at his disposal.

A Persistent System

Animism is a very persistent religion. The veneer of other world religions may frequently overlay it and even hide it, but it finds expression in many subtle ways. It may so interpenetrate the belief systems of other religions that only a search of the reasoning behind their orthodox practices and superstitions may reveal its presence.[1] Sometimes its presence is so overt that only the ignorant can fail to notice it. Jewelry, the display of flags on vehicles, the evil eye painted on various modes of transport, rigid conformity to ritual practices and the use of horoscopes may all be seen as harmless practices. But upon investigation they will prove to be charms, symbols, forms of divination or means of manipulation—all associated with spirit beings or the occult.

A Status Quo System

Animism supports the status quo. It undergirds community and custom, controlling them by its ideas about ancestors and/or the spirit world. Animism limits and discourages social change for fear of spirit revenge. Spirits approve wealth and status. Control of others, negative and exploitive attitudes towards outsiders, abuse and mistreatment of the less-privileged are all tolerated if not fully approved, because of henotheistic concepts attributed to spirit beings. It appeals to man's desire for personal advancement in spite of the welfare of others; that is, if one should be able to circumvent custom effectively and deceive spirit powers successfully.

Where sociocultural structures strongly influenced by animism have seen a measure of progress, the beneficiaries of progress have been a small elite who live well at the expense of the masses—an outcome animism readily condones. Its motivations to be successful over and above one's fellow man opens the door to all kinds of exploitive, unjust, unethical and dehumanizing practices. The end always justifies the means. If, in the process of getting ahead one can deceive the spirit world or circumvent customs without undue notice, one is considered an exceptional and valued member of society. Obviously such a one is thought to have special spirit world connections with attendant life force and magical powers, and is to be feared and respected by community members.

A Self-Actualization System

Animism is, as so many of its contemporary devotees claim, one of the most ancient of all religions. In fact, it appears very early in the pages of the Christian Scriptures and the history of man. Its basic appeal is reflected in Genesis 3 where man is challenged to be like God, and by implication, his own god. Its basic ideology is given fuller expression in Genesis 11 where the drive to self fulfillment is displayed in the desire to be in community (collectivism) on man's terms. Man seeks his security in the presence of others (vs.2-4) but wants to be self-sufficient. He is self-centered and seeks recognition. Self must be elevated to receive, give and enjoy—"Let us make a name" (v. 4).

The overarching factor that makes it all so appealing is that the system works. Animism is millennia old and precedes most other religious systems. In spite of the fact that other religions were introduced to provide an alternative to animism, they all largely succumbed to it and ended up being systems of manipulation whereby man can work his way to salvation in a *quid-pro-quo* fashion. This encourages contrast, competition and one-upmanship. Whoever achieves is simply better able to handle the spirit world and is entitled to the rewards, a concept that supports the *status quo* and obviates the need for social concern.

QUESTIONABLE MORALITY

Beyond these broad characteristics are others which contribute to making animism a comprehensive, cohesive and paradoxical religious system. Although there may be some exceptions, one common feature which becomes quite apparent as one encounters animism worldwide is the fact that it provides no fundamental basis for moral action. The pursuit of power would not be sanctioned if behavior was morally informed and ethically practiced.

Animist man's most coveted resource for success is life force. Believing that reality is all of a piece, and that everything has varying degrees of life force, one must seek by all means to retrieve this life force for personal use. Life force assures physical and spiritual power. Without physical and spiritual power, man will not have fame, status, wealth, health, sexual vigor or influence in society. The acquisition of life force unashamedly serves selfish ends, and, therefore, it may be acquired by any means, good or bad. Society will act as a control mechanism to lessen the overt bad means, but will by no means prevent them.

Morality is not the ultimate consideration; the acquisition of life force is. Therefore, any means of securing life force is condoned, if not sanctioned. Magic, ritual means, stealth, robbery, sacrifice and even killing are all accepted. The cosmos is manipulated by whatever means necessary to acquire and guarantee security, happiness and success, without reference to any objective standard of morality. Immorality and unethical activity may always be covered (if not expiated) with impunity by ritual means.

If the concept of morality exists, it is a morality arising out of the discipline of custom. Custom establishes that bearing falsehood against a neighbor may be wrong on some occasions. Neighbor is narrowly defined to include only those in the in-group, while all others may be traduced, deceived and exploited as fair game. Although the concept of adultery exists, sexual relations have few parameters, and even these may be overcome through stealth and deception and subsequently covered by a ritual. Justice is at best meted out when convenient. Furthermore, if justice does apply, it will be confined to the in-group, making the unjust treatment of others a matter of no consequence or of no great importance.

Man's actions are not ultimately his responsibility. If the ritual failed to bring about the desired effect, it was deficient. If the spirit world did not respond positively, it served him a raw deal. The responsibility for what happens or does not happen lies with it and not the one who sought life force through it.

Animism is totally anthropocentric. Everything is done for self-advantage. Man's will is supreme. He wants the goodwill of the spirits, not for their sakes, but for his own. Without their goodwill he will not be accorded respect, and he will not have success in manipulating his religious ritual means which will bring him his desired status symbols. His association with, and successful manipulation of, the spirits guarantee security, and this working relationship is in itself an insurance that will enable him to secure more life force. In the animist world, spirituality is the ability to manipulate the spirit world to one's advantage.

ETHICAL RELATIVISM

Animist man has and seeks to maintain an ethical standard however circumscribed it may be. He practices fidelity in marriage; he extends hospitality to strangers; he evidences a sense of justice; he practices love and respect for relatives and traditions; he has a concern for modesty; he demonstrates attitudes of unselfishness and self-sacrifice, as well as many other behavior patterns which can only be evaluated as virtuous. From an insider's perspective, these are all ethical standards, placing the animist religious system on a par with other ethical religions.[2] From an outsider's perspective these virtuous practices are indeed praiseworthy. In fact, they are very impressive until the motivations are understood. Not to be ethical, as prescribed above, incurs the wrath and reprisal of the spirit world. Not to observe custom in these and related areas induces fear of disruption of harmony or balance in society, and/or in man's pursuits of his own self-centered objectives.

Concepts of propriety do exist and are maintained by fear of spirit world recriminations in the face of default. When the restraints of the spirit world are removed during special rites or celebrations, the resulting ethical conduct is depravity itself. The spirits may be cheated with impunity, bribed to overlook human debauchery or deflected with counter medicines such as indulgences. Because the spirits are believed to be so capricious, the devotee will at times respond to them in kind. What, therefore, appears to be an objective standard of ethics and morality does not arise out of altruism but is rather motivated by fear. However, animist man will break custom if he can get away with it, believing that he can appease the spirit world if he gets caught.

CONCEPT OF SIN

How then does this religious system understand the concept of sin? Sin is not judged by some outward objective standard. In fact, it would be futile to search for such an objective standard, for if it should be found, behavior would not be consistent with it. Relativity is the order of the day in animism. What is wrong in one circumstance is condoned in another. Should a matter actually be considered sin, the blame for the act does not lie with the individual but rather with the community, or as pointed out previously, the ritual or the spirit world.

Man is the measure of all, and everything else, including sin, submits to his judgment. He will decide how a deviant act should be evaluated and who should be blamed for it. The animist concept of wrongdoing relates to ceremonial disruption, nonconformity to custom and broken relationships, but not to ethical integrity.

Holiness is an external modality, involving appearances, abstentions, specific behaviors and withdrawal from the normal concourse of humanity. Holiness cannot be understood apart from legalism. It is totally committed to appearances and specific actions outside of normal human behavior. For the average individual, holiness is associated with the maintaining of custom and ceremony and the observance of taboos. Breaches of ancestral law and custom expose the whole community to the wrath of the spirits, and therefore walking in holiness safeguards community structures and will likely elicit positive responses from the spirit world toward man.

Guilt is motivated by the desire to escape the penalty of ceremonial and/or custom offenses. Breaking custom, not practicing ceremony or ritual, all bring spirit retribution. Guilt is not an offense against a holy God who does not and cannot tolerate sin. Sin has no effect on God. There is no objective standard, so there is no question of transgressing His law. Man alone is the loser when he sins, and yet if he can find and perform the right ritual, he can circumvent all the consequences of his sin. However, the thought of possible spirit retribution if the propitiating ritual is not performed promotes worthy social values, strongly encouraging devotees to conform to custom.

Furthermore, morality or ethical conduct are not prerequisites for being worthy or of being effective in this religious system. The animist considers neither to be necessary for spirituality or for practicing religious rituals. The efficacy of spirituality and the practice of rituals has nothing to do with the morality or ethics of the practitioner. Spirituality consists merely in knowing that the world is spirit-oriented and motivated, that man's whole existence is interpenetrated by these spirit beings, and that man can benefit from their services. Morality and ethics have nothing to do with these potentials. Spirits are amoral. Their response to man is capricious—either good or bad may issue from them. Spirit beings, be they ancestors or gods, respond to correct ritual, not to purity of heart or cleanness of hands. Likewise, the efficacy of rituals depends upon the correct performance of the act, with its prescriptions and proscriptions, and not a right heart relationship.

Morality, goodness and virtue have no bearing on being a worthy practitioner of the faith. The most immoral person is totally capable of giving good religious counsel and performing the rituals required for positive spirit response. The key to wisdom is not the fear of God, but rather knowledge of the secrets which spell out how to manipulate the spirit world successfully. One who has mastered these techniques and proved to be successful is revered and honored, apart from moral and ethical considerations. Manipulation is a key concept in animism. A man does not merit anything by being ethical or moral. He acquires everything needed for life by following the correct procedures in the process of manipulation. There is thus no fundamental basis for moral action.

PROBLEM OF FEAR

Although animist man's approach to the spirit world is anthropocentric and amoral, he nevertheless has a high degree of fear motivating his manipulation of the spirits. This is one of the paradoxes that characterize animism. To perform rituals is to work to enlist the spirit world's active involvement in the human sphere. But there is still a nagging fear of not performing the ritual accurately enough to impress and motivate the spirits. That fear is aggravated by the fact that the spirits can never fully be trusted. All too frequently they respond according to whim and fancy. There is a high degree of confidence in the efficacy of the religious system though. Enough positive spirit responses are known of and experienced to support and maintain such confidence. Nevertheless, frequently rituals fail and the spirit world responds negatively. This generates fear. This fear is not always evident in daily life, but it can at times be observed in the commitment to and fervor accompanying daily ritual practices. Fear frequently controls, motivates and is maintained by the harsh realities encountered in daily life events.

On the one hand animism is a powerful religion. On the other hand its practitioners readily succumb to fear. Protective measures to guard man from the onslaughts of the spirit world are essential, for man can never be fully persuaded that the spirits will act favorably toward him. For example, divination can work against the interest of the victim in spite of his innocence. A person may be unjustly accused as a result of faulty divination. Divination has not always served the welfare of the people in decisions which affect community matters. Favorable times for planting or reaping have been incorrectly determined by divination, resulting in great want and even famine. At other times people were told to destroy their goods because divination assured them of new sources of abundance, but they ended up in greater desperation than before. Then there have been times when it was divined that the killing of some would be to the benefit of others, a promise which merely issued in great loss. Again, a person can never be sure that the advice given will be to his benefit. The gods do as they please, yet animist man clings tenaciously to the belief that he can ultimately outwit them. Just give him time and he will find the right ritual for it.

Although no animist would ever admit it, the ramifications of being in relationship with an untrustworthy god or other spirit being have a very negative effect on other aspects of life. What results from animistic beliefs is the exact opposite of communal objectives and desires. Fellow community members are often suspected of being responsible for calamities, catastrophes and the personal misfortunes of others. The presence and practice of magic, witchcraft and sorcery, and the use of other ritual means, are all held responsible for misfortune. Whereas community seeks to bond people together in common cause and concern, animism introduces aberration, division and even destruction.

Animism encourages self-centeredness in spite of its emphasis on interrelatedness, and, therefore, man will not hesitate to blame close kin for trouble. Animism holds that man has the right to exercise power. Should he fail to do so, or not have the ability, someone else is to blame, and should be punished. It is paradoxical that men consider themselves interdependent and responsible for each other, yet often suspect their fellow men of standing in their way.

Not only does the animist deal with untrustworthy gods, but he can never be fully sure of his fellow man's concern for his welfare. It is not unlikely that another may take advantage of him. The system does not necessarily condemn it, and may even encourage it by providing counter-medicine or rituals to counteract such behavior. One cannot even depend on the ritual specialist to be altruistic. He is not beyond putting his own interest above that of his clients.

A System of Bondage

Animism is an enslaving system. Fear of gods, of fellow man, of the environment, of failure and of the inadequacy of rituals all serve to make and keep man a slave to the system. It cannot bring peace, because it is not built on trust and does not deal with guilt and the need for forgiveness. Forgiveness may be sought but cannot be known. Guilt persists but there is no way to remove it.

Animism provides no satisfactory answer to the question of the meaning of life and the significance of history. History as a linear progression is irrelevant. What happens today is what has already happened in the past and will happen again tomorrow. Life simply repeats itself. Man's existence is cyclical. Like the animist's concept of history, it has no objective culminating goal. The only significant meaning in life is the fact that the spirit world enforces customs and deviation will bring reprisals.

The purpose in life is to maintain the status quo. Man must conform to the ways of his ancestors or reap the consequences. According to Willoughby, animism "is blind to the need for harmonious development of the whole man; it insists that all deeds shall be cast in the old moulds."[3] Man is captive to what was, for it will again be, and there is no exit. The only meaning is what he himself will provide through his pursuit of power.

The prophet Isaiah acknowledges that there is power in animism, but he also contends that it is a bankrupt system. It can't save man from himself, his environment or final destruction.

> But these two things shall come on you suddenly in one day; loss of children and widowhood. They shall come on you in full measure in spite of your many sorceries, in spite of the great power of your spells. And you felt secure in your wickedness and said, `No one sees me.' Your wisdom and your knowledge, they have deluded you; for you have said in your heart, `I am, and there is no one besides me.' But evil will come on you which you will not know how to charm away; and disaster will fall on you for which you cannot atone . . . Stand fast now in your spells and in your many sorceries with which you have labored from your youth; perhaps you will be able to profit, perhaps you may cause trembling. You are wearied with your many counsels, let now the astrologers, those who prophecy by the stars, those who predict by the new moons, stand up and save you . . . There is none to save you.[4]

A better and more comprehensive description of animism would be difficult to find. In spite of all its power plays—its sorceries, its spells, its secret knowledge and its use of astrology—it cannot save man from himself, nor can it save him from slavery to the powers of darkness. And the Christian Scriptures don't leave any doubt about this awful reality.

ENDNOTES

1. Isaiah 1:11-15.
2. Judaism, Christianity, and Islam.
3. W. C. Willoughby, *The Soul of the Bantu* (New York: Harper Row, 1928), p. 431.
4. Isaiah 47:9-3, 15.

PART THREE
BIBLICAL
PERSPECTIVES ON
ANIMISM

Chapter 14
THE BIBLICAL
APPROACH
TO ANIMISM

After centuries of missionary activity worldwide, the church has had marked success in establishing itself in most nations. Now the center of Christianity has moved from the Western hemisphere to the Third World. The rapidly growing non-Western church is beginning to assert its own values and beliefs. The resultant developing theologies seek to face issues either ignored by, or not of great consequence to, Western theologians.

INCOMPLETE APPLICATION OF BIBLICAL TRUTH

Western theology primarily occupies itself with historical issues, especially those raised during the Reformation and during the Enlightenment. Of course many of these issues are encountered universally and are valid theological concerns. Periodically, however, some intrepid theologian will seek to deal with current social, economic and political problems in the context of the Scripture. Generally such contributions are considered of much less value than those dealt with by traditional theologians such as Calvin, Hodge and Berkhof. The value of the contributions of these latter theologians are beyond question, but Third World theologians are confronted with issues which seem more relevant to them.

169

A very large percentage of Third World theologians were trained in theologically liberal institutions where allegorical interpretations were common fare. With this theological grid overlaying their own cultural conditioning, they are now seeking to find biblical support for their ideologies. Some of the results are rather interesting.[1] They seem to be asking the right questions about economic exploitation, political oppression and social dehumanization, but frequently their answers have little basis in Scripture. In many instances they interpret the Bible allegorically, so that it appears to support their ideological preference. Other concerns usually overlooked by Westerners are also receiving attention. The value of native spiritual forms, the spirit world, ancestor spirits, nonlinear concepts of time, reincarnation and the equality of world religions are all becoming a part of theological discussions.[2]

These ethnotheologies are generally classed as syncretism by outside theologians, and rightly so, although it is important to ask whether or not the Bible does speak to these issues. A number of these ethnotheologies are so strongly politically influenced[3] that they overlook many crucial questions from the grassroots of society. This is true of Western theologies as well. How does the Bible speak to routine matters? How should a Christian deal with ancestors, sickness, fertility, evil spirits, longings for blessings, relationships, an inhospitable environment, lack of rain and other such issues affecting human welfare?

A sizable segment of Third World Christians still hold their traditional religion in one hand and Christian beliefs in the other. They hold the ideals, values and beliefs of Christianity in high regard, but in times of crisis they know where to find other power sources. Have they tried Christianity and found it wanting, or have they not yet been introduced to biblical Christianity (which responds adequately and powerfully to their needs)?

Perhaps one of the key reasons why syncretism is so rife in all expressions of Christianity—whether it be a traditional Christianity or a modern-day liberalized version—is the concept that the Bible reveals itself in time. Its revelation is not yet complete. As a result theology at any point (but especially in the Old Testament) is still struggling with cultural and religious encumbrances from the surrounding environment. Therefore theology progresses. Little thought seems to be given as to how the gospel and all biblical revelation were not shaped by animist culture but rather revealed it. Biblical revelation was given within the context of animism. Wright more accurately describes the situation prevailing when he points out that

... the ancient polytheisms ... died with the death of civilizations of which they were the buttress. They had no means of interpreting history ... [they] had no hope of earth, but attempt[ed] to climb the ladder of reason or mysticism out of earth's misery. On the other hand, [stands] biblical faith with its firm insight [into] the redemption of God, which is known most fully only in the very events which proved the downfall of the gods. It is Israel which first broke radically with the pagan conceptions of the meaning of life and provided the view of history and the characteristic hope on which the New Testament and the Christian faith so firmly rest.[4]

LEARNING FROM ISRAEL—GOD'S MODEL

Biblical faith stands in marked contrast to all other religious systems. As pointed out previously,[5] and reiterated in the New Testament,[6] the bottom line in animism is that man wants to control his own destiny. He wants to be his own god, and that is exactly the issue to which the Bible responds emphatically and comprehensively. In fact, the Old Testament is a bulwark against animism. For that reason Wright states rather emphatically that

The Church which lacks the Old Testament again becomes easy prey to paganism and cannot provide the answer or the hope for the present desperate dilemma of man ... [It tends] to succumb to man's hope for integration, happiness and security in the world as it is. It has preached the Gospel as a new kind of paganism, the value of which is strictly utilitarian. Religion is good for us; it gives us comfort and peace of mind; it is the only hope for democracy; it alone can support the status quo and make us happy within it. Yet biblical hope and pagan comfort are not the same thing ... biblical hope is based solely upon God, upon his promises, and upon his election. It is known only in the context of judgment and of the Cross, in the acceptance of a severe ethical demand, of cross bearing and cross sharing, and of a calling which one works out with fear and trembling.[7]

Man's search for personal fulfillment and his pursuit of power sources is not characteristic of biblical faith. Biblical faith demands a very different approach to life. It is summed up in the words of Jesus Christ:

If anyone wishes to come after Me, let him deny himself, and take up his cross, and follow Me. For whoever wishes to save his life shall lose it; but whoever loses his life for My sake shall find it.[8]

There is no room for utilitarianism in biblical faith.

Israel, God's Old Testament model people, was given a totally different value system[9] from that of the surrounding nations. She was also given a sociocultural structure[10] mandated by God, which was a unique alternative to that characteristic of other religious systems. As Wright says, without exception the worship in these systems

> . . . is based essentially on the conception of the efficacy of an individual's works, whether of magic, sacrifice [food for the Deity's need], reason, mystical exercise, or the giving of alms.[11]

By contrast, in Israel

> . . . proper worship begins with the proper inner attitude toward God, with fear (holy reverence), faith, trust and love. The sacrificial rites have lost their pagan setting and all thought of God's physical need of food and drink is done away. Sacrifice is instead a means which God provides whereby He may be worshiped, whereby sins may be atoned and communion re-established. Sacrifice has no efficacy in the hands of the pagan or of the hard-hearted sinner who commits his wickedness with premeditation and a high hand. No atoning sacrifice will avail for such a person; he can only humble himself and with repentant heart throw himself directly on the mercy of God . . . The means of worship are efficacious only when properly used "in sincerity and truth". . . in faithful obedience to God's will . . . . The central religious festivals are not rites of sympathetic magic . . . [through which] man takes on the form and identity of a god . . . [to secure] for himself the primal blessings and security of nature . . . . In Israel, the major festivals . . . had at their center historical memory and commemoration in which the saving acts of God were rehearsed.[12]

The difference between biblical faith and other religions, especially animism, is most obvious. The approach to God, the practice of religion and the routine of life are all distinctly different. Response to God is based on faithful obedience to his will, and nothing less.

BIBLICAL FAITH IN CONTRAST TO ANIMISM

Numerous Old Testament passages review the difference between the unique Israelite faith and the animistic practices of the nations. In the face of these practices God instructed Israel:

> You shall utterly destroy all the places where the nations whom you

shall dispossess serve their gods, on the high mountains and on the hills and under every green tree. And you shall tear down their altars and smash their sacred pillars and burn their Asherim [fertility deity and venues for fertility rites] with fire, and you shall cut down the engraved images of their gods, and you shall obliterate their name from that place. You shall not act like this toward the Lord your God.[13]

Why was such drastic action necessary? Again, God answers:

When you enter the land which the Lord your God gives you, you shall not learn to imitate the detestable things of those nations·.... There shall not be found among you anyone who makes his son or his daughter pass through the fire, one who uses divination, one who practices witchcraft, or one who interprets omens, or a sorcerer, or one who casts a spell, or a medium, or a spiritist, or one who calls up the dead .... For whoever does these things is detestable to the Lord; and because of these detestable things the Lord your God will drive them out before you. You shall be blameless before the Lord your God. For those nations, which you shall dispossess, listen to those who practice witchcraft and to diviners, but as for you, the Lord your God has not allowed you to do so.[14]

The above practices characterize animism, and biblical faith breaks radically with them.

Biblical faith rejects a self-centered utilitarian approach to the spirit world. It rejects participation in a socially accepted religious cultus which seeks security, success and happiness, and it rejects a religion which is

... without vigorous historical memory, without understanding of ... sin, without forgiveness, and without renewal in a covenant community which has been founded by the redemptive activity of God.[15]

Because the sociocultural structures of many Third World peoples are so akin to the sociocultural structures evident in the Old Testament, the message is often not understood or is overlooked or ignored. Throughout history man has often looked for some authority to support his practices rather than have them evaluated by divine revelation. But in numerous instances in Scripture, animistic belief and practice is evaluated and judged, and the biblical alternative is offered. Of all the Old Testament books, Deuteronomy and Isaiah deal most specifically with animism. God wants to highlight the wholly otherness of a nation which submits to His mandated approach to life. This is in contrast to paganism or animism, in which man responds to nature's seasons and manipulates spirit beings for selfish ends. Moses describes the people of God in this way:

> For you are a holy people to the Lord your God: the Lord your God has chosen you to be a people for His own possession out of all the peoples who are on the face of the earth. The Lord did not set His love on you nor choose you because you were more in number than any of the peoples, for you were the fewest of all peoples, but because the Lord loved you and kept the oath which He swore to your forefathers, the Lord brought you out by a mighty hand, and redeemed you from the house of slavery, from the hand of Pharaoh King of Egypt. Know therefore that the Lord your God, He is God, the faithful God . . . .[16]

And again:

> And now, Israel, what does the Lord your God require from you, but to fear (reverence) the Lord your God, to walk in all His ways and love Him, and to serve the Lord your God with all your heart and with all your soul, and to keep the Lord's commandments and His statutes which I am commanding you today for your good? Yet on your fathers did the Lord set His affection to love them, and He chose their descendants after them, even you above all peoples, as it is this day. Circumcise then your heart, and stiffen your neck no more. For the Lord your God is the God of gods and the Lord of lords, the great, the mighty, and the awesome God who does not show partiality, nor take a bribe. He executes justice for the orphan and the widow, and shows His love for the alien by giving him food and clothing. So show your love for the alien for you were aliens in the land of Egypt. You shall fear the Lord your God, you shall serve Him and cling to Him, and you shall swear by His name. He is your praise and He is your God, who has done these great and awesome things for you which your eyes have seen. Your fathers went down to Egypt seventy persons in all, and now the Lord your God has made you as numerous as the stars of heaven.[17]

The Wholly Other God

Throughout these two passages the differences between biblical faith and animism are clearly underscored. In the first place, God directly involves Himself in human affairs. He is not a far off God who has to be approached through intermediaries, such as ancestors or lesser gods or spirits. He is not a God who responds to bribes. He cannot be manipulated by ritual or sacrifice. He responds to man on the basis of His own sovereign choice and not because man has induced Him to do so, as in animism. Israel did not discover Him in the process of looking for a more powerful spirit to do their bidding. Rather God chose them, insignificant as they were. By a demonstration of great power superior to that of the Egyptian deities, He delivered them out of slavery. He proved to be an ethical God of superior ability.

God is not capricious like the deities of animism. He is faithful. He is bound by an oath. He is in covenant relationship, operating according to an unchangeable standard structured for the total welfare of people. He is always impartial, just, and loving and concerned for the welfare of all people. Animism's gods and their intermediaries are not. They respond only to a few devotees. God, however, is a holy God, righteous in character and just in his dealings with man. He expects His people to be exactly the same. Though the rite of circumcision symbolized the fidelity which God sought with Israel, He required more than a physical indication of that devotion. He also required a circumcised heart and a continual inward relationship with a person—Himself. He demanded holiness, as well as love for and proper treatment of all people, not only a positive response to the in-group.

People are not a means to an end as in animism, but ends in themselves. They are of great worth to God. Likewise, His people are to execute justice for all, including the less privileged. The God of Israel gives food and clothing even to the alien. He loves man for his own sake and not because man can reciprocate. Not so with the animist. Other nations have their own gods, be they ancestors, or favorite spirits who serve their own interests only, and to whom only the favored few are of value. The God of Israel loves His people and blesses them, providing for their every need and removing even their sicknesses. And He does this all without ritual. And what He did for Israel He will do for all peoples.

God's response to His people is one of love and integrity, and in keeping with His character is one of holiness, love, righteousness, kindness, grace and mercy. These qualities are not found in any other god. He is the God who is Wholly Other. He is the God to be celebrated and not appeased. He is to be enjoyed and worshiped because of His sheer goodness. He is to be trusted, for from of old He has consistently kept His promises. He can be counted upon to operate by His Law and to fulfill His Word. The preceding generations have proved this to be so. The biblical records describe One who is unchanging in His faithfulness, His love and the fulfillment of His promises.

He is not a God of caprice, as thought of by those outside of biblical faith. There is no need for another God who may be more trustworthy, more compassionate, more involved and concerned for His people. Unlike the gods of the nations, the God the Bible describes is unchangeable and is always righteous and just. Because He is *sui generis* He detests anyone who misleads man, and anything which debases, dehumanizes and destroys man. His instructions are therefore specific regarding beliefs and practices which are totally contrary to His character. What are some of these beliefs and practices?

Ancestral Lands

In Deuteronomy[18] we learn that the ancestral lands are a gift of God. Israel did not come to be dwelling there by happenstance or through the exploits of some ancestor, mythical or otherwise. In fact, elsewhere in Scripture the Israelites are reminded that the land is God's, and they are but tenants.[19] God brought them there and gave it to them. God dispossessed the nations, and He could very easily dispossess Israel if she should prove to be faithless in her covenant with Him.[20] In animism, the land and its boundaries relate to the ancestors who, by happenstance or superior life force, had gained access to it.

Treatment of People

We also learn[21] that the God of Israel treats all peoples impartially. He is no respecter of age, social status, economic means, religious office or ethnic background. He does not favor those who claim a close relationship with Him. Neither is he impressed by someone's ability to instill fear in others. Justice is to be applied equally to all, and measured by God's righteous standards—His law and statutes. There is no room for relativity. God's commands are absolute at all times, under all circumstances for all peoples. In animism the will and fancy of the oppressor is quite acceptable. So is the spirit world's caprice, divination, deceit, injustice and bribery. While these are very much a part of the animistic system, they are abominations to the God of Israel. His righteous will is supreme and never swayed by anyone's attempt at manipulation.

A Relationship in Obedience

The God of the Bible demands obedience.[22] The relationship He demands is not based on the use of effective rituals or other forms of manipulation. But it is judged by an objective standard—obedience to His commandments and mandates. He demands not blind obedience, but obedience which is volitional and based on His past faithful actions on behalf of His people. It is an obedience based on promise and fulfillment. When obedience characterizes the relationship, God will intervene in human affairs. Man's welfare is God's concern. He Himself will take up the cause of His people. He will fight for them against all their enemies. He will carry them as a father carries his little son. There is not even a hint of such an intimate, compassionate, tender yet powerful relationship to be found in animism. In animism man is always the initiator and must first perform the required ritual to awaken the deity to his need. He must cajole the deity into action through ritual, and even then he cannot be sure that the deity will respond favorably. The relationship is at best *quid pro quo*. By contrast biblical faith stresses obedience to God's commands in the interest of man's total welfare. God will then act in the interest of His people. God is the initiator and man responds in obedience. God is the focus of adoration and praise and man the recipient of God's blessing.

The God of All Nations

The God of biblical faith is a God who honors His promises, even to those who disregard His statutes. Deuteronomy 2:1-9 points out that He does not take advantage of Israel's enemies but respects their rights. Not even the people of Canaan were treated cavalierly by God.[23] They were given time to turn to Him, but when their sin had reached its climax and they refused to repent, God dispossessed them and gave their land to Israel. He is not a henotheistic God—a tribal deity. He is the God of the nations. Though He has elected to work especially through one nation to get the attention of the others, He remains the God of all peoples. Through Israel the nations will see for themselves how He desires to be a God for all peoples—if only they will walk in obedience to Him. The animist deities have no such consideration for other nations. Their compassion, if it is there at all, extends to national boundaries only. Should it seem to go beyond these boundaries, it becomes in fact coercion, as others are forced by sword or by political and economic means to practice the imposed religion. This is totally unlike the God of Israel who seeks from man a moral volitional response—"Choose you this day whom you will serve."[24]

He is also a jealous God.[25] He is jealous for His people's welfare, and will, therefore, not tolerate any deviation which will lead them into falsehood or submission to other deities. Such deities are at best self-centered, distant and indifferent to human need. Not so the God of Israel—"For what great nation is there that has a god so near to it as is the Lord our God whenever we call on Him?"[26] He is transcendent but also immanent. He is not a regional deity either. His power and control are not confined to certain geographical areas. The whole world is His domain, be it the plains, the mountains, the seas or the heavens. He controls all to accomplish His purposes. His power is not confined to any object, nor are they merely extensions of Him. He is distinct from His creation yet Lord over it—"Know therefore today, and take it to your heart, that the Lord, He is God in heaven above and on the earth below; there is no other."[27]

In contradistinction, the traditional animist thinks of everything as spirit-indwelt, with one thing being an extension of another. He believes that life force indwells all but can be concentrated in one, to be used against another. Spirit beings are regional deities at most. Their control is limited, and they may well be overpowered by a stronger deity. The God of Israel, to prove His power over all powers,[28] took

> ... for Himself a nation from within another nation by trials, by signs and wonders and by war and by a mighty hand and by an outstretched arm and by great terrors .... He personally brought you from Egypt by His great power, driving out from before you nations greater and mightier than you, to bring you in and to give you their land for an inheritance ....[29]

The Imperative of Ethical Behavior

God permits no changes to be made in his statutes and judgments—no additions and no subtractions. Any departure from God as the sole focus of life, or any spiritual deception, will receive its just reward.[30] Graven images of any creature or references to heavenly bodies are not to be the focus of worship. Turning to these creaturely objects, should God's people ever do so, will bring His judgment upon them.[31] Animism—with its focus on the heavens, nature, and multiple deities—brings God's punishment upon peoples, for it departs from the ways and statutes of God. Thus the God of Israel is clearly established as a God over all creation. All serve His purposes. Should any rebel against His authority, their rebellion will issue in judgment, so that they worship and serve the creature rather than the Creator, with all its attendant dehumanization.

Contrary to the practices of animism, so characteristic of the nations surrounding Israel, the God of Israel established specific ethical behavior codes to safeguard the dignity and integrity of people. Exploitive relationships, manipulation and unethical and immoral motives and actions are rigidly and severely censured. By contrast, time, family, life, sex, possessions, speech, destiny are sacred.[32] None of these matters are neutral in God's order of life. They are not subject to man's whim and fancy, as in animism. They all come under God's scrutiny, and any infractions will incur God's judgment, for each proscription is an evidence of God's wisdom focused on man's total welfare—"Oh that they had such a heart in them, that they would fear Me, and keep all My commandments always, that it may be well with them and with their sons forever."[33] In brief, that sums up biblical faith.

THE UNINFORMED CHURCH

The scope of this study does not permit a detailed step by step search through Scripture to expose every aspect of animism. Chapter 15 will, however, seek to highlight some further differences between animism and biblical faith. These differences are beyond question and should stimulate biblical theologians to take a fresh look at the Bible, specifically the Old Testament. The Old Testament is an expose´ of animism in all its forms even when such forms claim to be legitimate expressions of Christianity.

Some of Christianity's contemporary utilitarian expressions should be carefully checked for pagan influence. Wright poignantly describes the situation when he says:

> The Church has preached a Gospel of individual pietism and "spiritual experience," separated almost completely from the common life and from the historical programme of God as revealed in the Bible, while emphasizing prayer and promising the immortality of the soul. It is not that these things in themselves are totally wrong in their proper setting, but here they are separated from their total biblical context. As such, they are a reversion to pagan "normalcy," to an individualistic, self-centered, utilitarian worship . . . . For what purpose is the Scripture read, Christian truth expounded, and the sacraments administered? There would appear to be a great uncertainty in the churches of our day about this question. The average Christian,

however, seems to have little sense of the difference between biblical and pagan worship . . .[34]

If the above assessment is correct, then the kind of Christianity exported worldwide has actually encouraged syncretism. If religion is purely utilitarian, why not use the best available practices of every religious system to produce a superior religion? If any other religion fulfills the utilitarian function better, why confine people to the Christian way of doing things? The doctrine of Universalism is then the proper and loving Christian response. *Or is it?*

Biblical faith claims to be categorically exclusive. Its concept of God, man, man's approach to God, and God's approach to man, is distinctive. It teaches that God is on a mission in this world, that man is called to participate with God in that mission, and that God is not there to support man in his own private mission. That is the biblical position. Special attention should, therefore, be given to specific animistic practices censured by Scripture. They may then be purged, and man's strong motivations to do his own will rather than God's can be better understood.

ENDNOTES

1. Orbis Press, Maryknoll, New York, has published a number of these. Among others: Sergio Torres and Virginia Fabella, editors, *The Emergent Gospel: Theology from The Underside of History* (1978); Kofi Appiah-Kubi and Sergio Torres, editors, *African Theology Enroute* (1979); Virginia Fabella (ed.), *Asia's Struggle for Full Humanity: Towards a Relevant Theology* (1980); Modupe Oduyoye, *The Sons of the Gods and the Daughters of Men: An Afro-Asiatic Interpretation of Genesis 1-11* (1984).

2. Among others: S. J. Samartha, *The Hindu Response to the Unbound Christ* (Madras: CLS, 1974); M. M. Thomas, *The Acknowledged Christ of the Indian Renaissance* (London: SCM Press, 1969); Raymond Pannikar, *The Unknown Christ of Hinduism* (London: Darton, Longman and Todd, 1964); Pablo Richard, et al., *The Idols of Death And The God of Life A Theology* translated from the Spanish by Barbara E. Campbell and Bonnie Shepard, (Maryknoll, N. Y.: Orbis Books, 1983); John Mbiti, *Concepts of God in Africa* (1970), *New Testament Eschatalogy in an African Background* (1971); K. A. Dickson and P. Ellingworth, *Biblical Revelation and African Beliefs* (1969); K. A. Dickson, "Towards a Theologia Africana" in *New Testament Christianity for Africa and the World* eds. M. E. Glasswell and E. W. Fashole-Luke, (1974); "African Theology—Whence, Methodology and Content" in *Journal of Religious Thought* 33 (Fall-Winter 1975); C. Nyamiti, "African Theology: Its Nature, Problems and Methods" in *Gaba Pastoral Papers* 19 (1971); G. Setiloane, "The God of my Fathers and my God" in *South African Outlook* (Oct., 1970); J. H. Cone and G. S. Wilmore, edi-

tors, *Black Theology—A Documentary History* (Maryknoll, New York: Orbis Books, 1979); F. Eboussi Boulaga, *Christianity Without Fetishes: An African Critique and Recapture of Christianity,* translated from the French by Robert R. Barr, (Maryknoll, New York: Orbis Books, 1984).

3. For example, works on Liberation Theology are generally Marxist in political ideology. Cf. Jose Miguez Bonino, *Doing Theology in a Revolutionary Situation* (Philadelphia: Fortress Press, 1975); Jose P. Miranda, *Marx and the Bible: A Critique of the Philosophy of Oppression* (Maryknoll, New York: Orbis Books, 1974); J. Severino Croatto, "Biblical Hermenuetics in the Theologies of Liberation," in Virginia Fabella and Sergio Torres, editors, *Irruption of The Third World Challenge To Theology* (Maryknoll, New York: Orbis Books, 1983), pp. 140 -168.

4. G. Ernest Wright, *God Who Acts* (London: SCM Press, 1972), p. 26.

5. Genesis 3:5.

6. Romans 1:18-32.

7. Wright (1972), p. 26.

8. Matthew 16:24-25.

9. Exodus 20:1-20.

10. Exodus 21, 22, 23.

11. Wright (1972), p. 27.

12. *Ibid.,* pp. 27-28.

13. Deuteronomy 12:2-4.

14. Deuteronomy 18:9-14.

15. Wright, 1972, p., 29.

16. Deuteronomy 7:6-18.

17. Deuteronomy 10:12-22.

18. Deuteronomy 1:1-8.

19. Leviticus 25:23.

20. Deuteronomy 29:22-28.

21. Deuteronomy 1:6-46.

22. Deuteronomy 1:21-31.

23. Genesis 15:16.

24. Joshua 24:15; Cf. Deuteronomy 32:46-47.

25. Deuteronomy 4:24.

26. Deuteronomy 4:7.

27. Deuteronomy 4:39.

28. Deuteronomy 4:35.

29. Deuteronomy 4:34, 37, 38.

30. Deuteronomy 4:25-28.

31. Deuteronomy 4:28.

32. Deuteronomy 5:12-21.

33. Deuteronomy 5:29.

34. Wright (1972), pp. 26-29.

Chapter 15
THE BIBLICAL RESPONSE TO SPECIFIC ANIMISTIC PRACTICES

Animism's chief presupposition is the sovereignty of man. Man plans his world, he directs it, and he is the maker and shaper of things on earth and in heaven. Rushdoony correctly observes,

> The supreme effort of man (is) to command the future, to predestine the world, and to be as God. Lesser efforts, divination, spirit-questing, magic and witchcraft. . . . All represent efforts to have the future on other than God's terms, to have a future apart from and in defiance of God.[1]

Man can be successful in life if he is privy to knowledge—secret, elitist knowledge—to either attain power in the phenomenal realm or have a mystical introduction to power sources in the noumenal realm. Whichever realm man seeks to penetrate and use, the motivation is based on the denial of the Creator/creature distinction.

Man desires to be coequal if not superior to God, and therefore consistently substitutes his own knowledge for God's. By doing so he claims coequality and rejects any notion of judgment for not living by God's statutes and judgments. Having successfully excluded a Sovereign God from his world,[2] man now is free to put his faith in means which will facilitate the achieving of his own objectives—that of transcending his creaturely limitations. The Bible lists many such means which have provided man with a false authority to work out his destiny. Among others, these are: witchcraft, sorcery, necromancy, astrology, prophecies, divination, omens, wizardry, charms, spells, propitious times and fire-walking.

Each of these practices relates to the manipulation of spirit beings to do man's bidding. The previous chapter pointed out that God will not yield to manipulation, and that He alone is the initiator of blessings. We can therefore expect that biblical faith will severely censure these practices, for they are not only contrary to the character and nature of God, they are actually bold contradictions to and substitutes for God's providential dealings with man. What are the biblical responses to these animistic practices?

WITCHCRAFT AND SORCERY

In Scripture, God repeatedly condemns the practices of witchcraft and sorcery in absolute terms. The word used in the Hebrew, *kasaph*, refers in its several variations to sorcery, witchcraft, the practice of magic, and incantations. Witchcraft involves all of these practices and may be the umbrella word for these evil activities. As used in Scripture, the broad overarching term will also include the above practices. Each of these alienate man from God and place him in the driver's seat of his own destiny. In New Testament parlance, man is bewitched[3] when he replaces God for another.

In each case, God's censure is unmistakable. For example:

There shall not be found among you anyone . . . who practices witchcraft, or one who interprets omens, or a sorcerer, or one who casts a spell . . . for whoever does these things is detestable to the Lord; and because of these detestable things the Lord your God will drive them out before you . . . For those nations which you shall dispossess, listen to those who practice witchcraft and to diviners, but as for you, the Lord your God has not allowed you to do so.[4]

It was said of Manasseh, King of Judah, that

. . . he practiced witchcraft, used divination, practiced sorcery, and dealt with mediums and spiritists. He did much evil in the sight of the Lord, provoking Him to anger.[5]

Jezebel, wife of Ahab, King of Israel was known for her "harlotries . . .

and her witchcrafts are so many."[6] Her judgment, as prophesied by
Elijah was:

> ... the dogs shall eat the flesh of Jezebel; and the corpse of Jezebel shall
> be as dung on the face of the field in the property of Jezreel, so they
> cannot say, "This is Jezebel."[7]

Speaking of future judgment coming upon Israel and the nations,
Micah the prophet states:

> I will cut off sorceries [practices of witchcraft] from your hand, and
> you will have fortune tellers no more ... And I will execute vengeance
> in anger and wrath on the nations which have not obeyed.[8]

Of the heartless Assyrian city Nineveh, "the bloody city, completely full of lies,"[9] Nahum the prophet said:

> ... the charming one, the mistress of sorceries [witchcrafts], who sells
> nations by her harlotries and families by her sorceries [witchcrafts].
> Behold I am against you ... I will throw filth on you and make you
> vile, and set you up as a spectacle. And it will come about that all who
> see you will shrink from you and say, Nineveh is devastated.[10]

In Galatians, witchcraft and sorcery, among other practices, are
deeds of the flesh, and "those who practice such things shall not inherit
the Kingdom of God."[11] There are numerous other references to
witchcraft and sorcery, and in each case the judgment of God is
expressed in no uncertain terms.[12]

CONTACT WITH ANCESTORS

Of all animistic practices, contact with the dead (necromancy) is the
most problematic, persistent and widespread. Animists believe that
death is a new birth into a spiritual body, without any change in character. They also believe that the living continue in dialogue with the
dead and that the dead have the capacity to communicate with the living, either directly or through mediums.

Notions of reincarnation are usually associated with this belief in
the living-dead who remain in communication with the living.
Although many seek to justify this practice, and some Third World
theologians include it in their ethnotheologies, the Bible strongly
denounces it.

Necromancy presumes the need of a mediator between God and man. It also assumes that a deceased member of the family has a better understanding of family needs and has more concern and compassion than a distant God. Such assumptions are in total contradiction with the character and person of the God of Israel. They are simply another version of Gnosticism.

Biblical teaching speaks of God as personal, compassionate, merciful and impartial. He is One who untiringly seeks after man. Isaiah the prophet expresses surprise at the fact, therefore, that Israel should turn from the living God to consult with dead ancestors:

> And when they say to you, "Consult the mediums and the wizards who whisper and mutter," should not a people consult their God? Should they consult the dead on behalf of the living?[13]

Because Israel ignored God's law, and rejected His testimony, and sought counsel from the dead, their judgment will be that

> ... they will pass through the land hard-pressed and famished .... Then they will look to the earth, and behold, distress and darkness, the gloom of anguish; and they will be driven away into darkness.[14]

As Isaiah points out, Egypt's resorting to idols and the dead is the result of God's judgment upon them:

> So I will incite Egyptians against Egyptians; and they will each fight against his brother, and each against his neighbor .... Then the spirit of the Egyptians will be demoralized within them; and I will confound their strategy, so that they will resort to idols and ghosts of the dead, and to mediums and spiritists.[15]

Biblical faith does not deny that the dead may be responsive to the living. A case in point is the story of Saul, the medium at Endor, and the appearance of Samuel's spirit.[16] In this case Samuel did appear, to the apparent surprise of the medium. There is no indication that either fraud or demons are at work in this instance. Furthermore, the fact that Scripture warns against this practice presupposes that there must be the possibility of communication between the living and the dead. Moses warns the people of Israel that they must not "imitate the detestable things of those nations .... There shall not be found among you any who ... call up the dead."[17] This was a common practice in Canaan and for that reason, among others, God was driving the

Canaanites out of their homelands. According to the Bible, mediums or spiritists are to be dealt with harshly. The denunciations are clear:

> Now a man or a woman who is a medium or a spiritist shall surely be put to death. They shall be stoned with stones, their bloodguiltiness is upon them.[18]

Not only does Scripture forbid necromancy, it requires death for those who contact the spirits of the dead. Both the practice and the one who can make it a reality lead people away from God, from fellowship with God, from obedience to the statutes and judgments of God. Ancestors become a substitute for God, thus making reconciliation with God, relationship to God and worship of God redundant. Ultimately, as Scripture avows, "there is a way which seems right to a man, but its end is the way of death."[19]

The craft of spiritism is occultic—demonic powers may impersonate an ancestor. Demons know the past history of all, but at best can only guess at the future. Thus, they manipulate man and the future, so that the future becomes a self-fulfilling prophecy. One can never be certain that the demonic is not present in necromancy, and even if it isn't, the practice in itself is a detestable matter in God's evaluation. God will not share His glory with another. He is a jealous God who demands the total loyalty of all His followers, because in living in obedience to Him there is total welfare.

SHAMANISM

Shamanism—the involvement with spirit beings, for whatever reason—is strictly forbidden by Scripture. Seeking out the help of any religious specialist who consorts with spirit beings is condemned. These practitioners were called astrologers,[20] mediums,[21] diviners,[22] magicians,[23] soothsayers,[24] sorcerers,[25] spiritists,[26] and false prophets.[27] Any type of spiritistic practice was severely denounced and condemned:

> "You shall not allow a sorceress to live"[28]; "Do not turn to mediums or spiritists; do not seek them out to be defiled by them"[29]; "As for the person who turns to mediums and to spiritists, to play the harlot after them, I will also set my face against that person and will cut him off from among his people"[30]; "Now a man or a woman who is a medium or a spiritist shall surely be put to death. They shall be stoned with stones, their bloodguiltiness is upon them."[31]

There are many dangers involved in spirit contact, and the toll exacted for blessings received through spirit sources is exceedingly high.[32]

DIVINATION

Another ancient practice is divination. Animist man is no different from others in his curiosity. He seeks to understand the present and divine the future. Like all the other practices, it calls God's Word into question. Man is not satisfied with God's explanation of life. And if this explanation mystifies him, he does not trust God to fulfill His promises. Man believes that if he can enter the world of mystery, he may be able to change circumstances.

Knowing the reason behind events, whether past, present, or future, gives man a sense of omnipotence. He overcomes his finitude and exercises control. It puts him in the driver's seat, and God is consigned to lesser significance in the events of life. God's providence is not considered sufficient. Man must determine his own destiny. Divination is an integral part of witchcraft.

Also associated with the practice of divination are: astrology, fortune-telling, omens, casting the lot and consulting oracles. The Bible does not leave the reader in doubt as to God's evaluation of these practices. These are all part of the detestable religious inventory of the nations who do not know God.

> When you enter the land which the Lord your God gives you, you shall not learn to imitate the detestable things of those nations. There shall not be found among you . . . one who uses divination . . . or one who interprets omens.[33]

Concerning Babylon's use of divination in coming against Israel, Ezekiel the prophet points out:

> For the King of Babylon stands at the parting of the way, at the head of the two ways, to use divination; he shakes the arrows, he consults the household idols, he looks at the liver. Into his right hand came the divination . . . . They see for you false visions, while they divine lies for you . . . . You will be fuel for the fire; your blood will be in the midst of the land. You will not be remembered, for I, the Lord, have spoken.[34]

The false prophets in Israel were wont to use divination along with their false visions and so mislead the people of God:

Thus says the Lord God, "Woe to the foolish prophets who are following their own spirit and have seen nothing . . . They see falsehood and lying divination who are saying, 'The Lord declares' when the Lord has not sent them; yet they hope for the fulfillment of their word . . . So My hand will be against the prophets who see false visions and utter lying divinations. They will have no place in the council of My people, nor will they be written down in the register of the house of Israel, nor will they enter the land of Israel, that you may know that I am the Lord God."[35]

The true prophet of God had no need of divination, because, says God: "I will put My Words in his mouth, and he shall speak . . . all that I command him."[36] On the contrary the false prophet spoke out of his own knowledge, or out of what he had come to know through divination—both transgressions that issue in death. Moses said:

But the prophet who shall speak a word presumptuously in My name which I have not commanded him to speak, or which he shall speak in the name of other gods [usually through the use of oracles, omens, divination, etc.], that prophet shall die.[37]

How was the false prophet to be known from the true prophet of God?

When a prophet speaks in the name of the Lord, if the thing does not come about or come true, that is the thing which the Lord has not spoken.[38]

Of course, the prophet may have spoken in the name of another god, and that in itself should expose him as being an impostor, deserving of God's judgment. God's way of success centers in His Word. It alone can give man direction for life and explain to man how elevating himself[39] and relying on his own knowledge rob him of knowing peace and experiencing the blessing of God.[40] Therefore, God says to the Chaldeans:

Let now the astrologers, those who prophesy by the stars, those who predict by the new moons, stand up and save you from what will come upon you. Behold, they have become like stubble, fire burns them; they cannot deliver themselves from the power of the flame . . . .[41]

However, the Psalmist maintains that those who center their lives in God's Word, "do no unrighteousness; they walk in His Ways."[42] And the reason is that God's "Word is a lamp to [their] feet, and a light to [their] path,"[43] bringing illumination to all of life. Such a resource is not known to the animist. He himself must seek out his own destiny through divination and its many related ritual practices, all denounced by the God of Israel.[44]

RITUALS

Rituals are very important to animists. Rituals, being means of power to manipulate the spirit world, are foundational to animistic belief. Man can accomplish his objectives through them, totally aside from human virtue and character. The Bible, however, deplores and condemns this attitude and practice. When Israel reverted to the pagan practice of seeking to manipulate God through the divinely instituted rituals for worship, God severely censured them:

> "What are your multiplied sacrifices to Me?" says the Lord. "I have had enough of burnt offerings of rams, and the fat of fed cattle. And I take no pleasure in the blood of bulls, lambs, or goats. When you come to appear before Me, who requires of you this trampling of my courts? Bring your worthless offerings no longer, incense is an abomination to Me. New moon and sabbath, the calling of assemblies—I cannot endure iniquity and the solemn assembly . . . . I hate your new moon festivals and your appointed feasts, they have become a burden to Me. I am weary of bearing them. So when you spread out your hands in prayer, I will hide My eyes from you. Yes, even though you multiply prayers, I will not listen. Your hands are full of bloodshed. Everyone loves a bribe, and chases after rewards. They do not defend the orphan, nor does the widow's plea come before them."[45]

And why was God so angered at the performance of these rituals? Because they were performed without a proper heart's relationship with Him. In Deuteronomy God expresses this deep felt longing in respect of His people:

> "Oh that they had such a heart in them, that they would fear Me, and keep all My commandments always, that it may be well with them and with their sons forever!"[46]

A ritual practice, even one instituted by God, is valueless when it is used for purposes of manipulation, and when the practitioners are living in disobedience to the laws and commandments of God. Therefore, Isaiah called the people back to obedience. The people who once were faithful in their obedience to God, who observed justice and did righteously,[47] are again exhorted to:

> Wash yourselves, make yourselves clean; remove the evil of your deeds from My sight. Cease to do evil, learn to do good; seek justice, reprove the ruthless; defend the orphan, plead for the widow . . . . If you consent and obey, you will eat the best of the land; but if you refuse and rebel, you will be devoured by the sword. Truly, the mouth of the Lord has spoken.[48]

Ezekiel refers to the same detestable attitude. The hearts of the elders of Israel were cesspools of idolatry. God says:

> Son of man, these men have set up their idols in their hearts, and have put right before their faces the stumbling block of their iniquity. Should I be consulted by them at all? Therefore speak to them and tell them, 'Thus says the Lord God, "Any man of the house of Israel who sets up his idols in his heart, puts right before his face the stumbling block of his iniquity, and then comes to the prophet, I the Lord will be brought to give him an answer in the matter in view of the multitude of his idols, in order to lay hold of the hearts of the house of Israel who are estranged from Me through all their idols.[49]

God will not yield to manipulation no matter what ritual means are used. God desires their repentance and obedience, but if they will not, then judgment will come. Ezekiel writes:

> Therefore say to the house of Israel, 'Thus says the Lord God, "Repent and turn away from your idols, and turn your faces away from all your abominations . . . And I shall set My face against that man and make him a sign and a proverb, and I shall cut him off from among My people. So you will know that I am the Lord . . . . And they will bear the punishment of their iniquity; as the iniquity of the inquirer is, so the iniquity of the prophet will be, in order that the house of Israel may no longer stray from Me and no longer defile themselves with all their transgressions. Thus they will be My people, and I shall be their God, declares the Lord God."[50]

Unlike animism, biblical faith demands a heart's relationship with God which is evidenced, not only in piety, but righteousness and justice in all one's actions.

CHARMS

One dead giveaway that a person is trusting in some magical means—some power source—for success, security or happiness is the wearing of charms. Charms may be objects blessed by or secured from a religious specialist. These may be rings, arm bands, anklets, necklaces, sacred strings or other objects carried on the body. As in the case of the aforementioned, charms detract from the character of God and call into question His ability to protect, provide, sustain and keep one in the face of the challenges of the human condition. Charms provide a person with a false sense of security and trust, encouraging one to act independently of God and to ignore His provision for life's challenges. God is thereby effectively removed from life and replaced by other gods thought to be more directly involved in man's welfare.

The association of charms with the spirit world leaves one in no doubt as to where and how charms receive their efficacy. God is displaced and spirit beings receive man's allegiance. The God of Israel tolerates no divided allegiance. Charms are an abomination to Him. They are commonly used and claimed to be effective, but when God judges, it is as Jeremiah points out: "For behold, I am sending serpents against you, adders, for which there is no charm, and they will bite you, declares the Lord."[51]

Ezekiel also highlights God's indignation in Israel's trusting in charms. Arm bands were used as magical means of success in life, which God saw as bringing destruction to His people:

> Thus says the Lord God, "Woe to the women who sew magic bands on all wrists . . . . Behold, I am against your magic bands by which you hunt lives there as birds, and I will tear them off your arms; and I will let them go, even those lives whom you hunt as birds."[52]

God's judgment upon all such practices is without question:

> "But as for those whose hearts go after detestable things and abominations, I shall bring their conduct down on their heads,' declares the Lord God."[53]

There are numerous animistic practices referred to in the Bible. Animism cannot possibly bring man into an abundant life,[54] and even if it could, its rewards are short-lived. No one makes an alliance with the spirit world, specifically the powers of darkness, who does not sooner or later discover that Satan is a liar and a murderer who will exact a high price for his services.[55]

FIRE-WALKING AND HUMAN SACRIFICE

There are numerous references to human sacrifices, especially those made in fire to pagan deities.[56] This type of ritual murder is still practiced today. It was fairly widespread in Israel at certain times.[57]

Some of the references to human sacrifice in fire could be translated to refer to fire-walking.[58] For example, "anyone who makes his son or daughter pass through the fire."[59] Again: "cause their sons and their daughters to pass through the fire to Molech."[60] In both cases—sacrifice in fire or fire-walking—God's Word denounces these practices and refers to them as abominations which come under God's judgments.

SPELLS AND CURSES

The casting of spells, sometimes known as "tying a magic knot," is a common animistic practice. The idea is to join with a spirit to become as one against a person or a problem. This practice may also be associated with the ritual of cursing. For example, when Balak called on the diviner Balaam[61] to curse the people of Israel who were about to engulf his kingdom, he said:

> Please come, curse this people for me since they are too mighty for me; perhaps I may be able to defeat them and drive them out of the land. For I know that he whom you bless is blessed, and he whom you curse is cursed.[62]

Isaiah refers to the practice of casting spells, or enchantments: "In spite of the great power of your spells . . . stand fast now in your spells."[63] Scripture recognizes the practice and points out that in the face of God's power and judgment, this presumably powerful practice cannot bring deliverance.

PROPITIOUS TIMES

The Bible mentions the practice of seeking out propitious days for performing desired activities. Stargazers, astrologers and diviners are engaged to determine such lucky days which will augur success for the desired activity. The King James Version in its translation of this practice, distinguishes between observer of times and one who practices witchcraft or divination. Although it is difficult to separate the one from the other, the seeking out of propitious times is a distinct ritual.

There are several biblical passages in the King James Version which refer to this practice[64] and condemn it. Here too man seeks to sidestep God's providence and control of history.

MAGICAL PRACTICES

God denounces all magical practices. The Apostle Paul refers to the practitioners of magic as "full of all deceit and fraud, you son of the devil, you enemy of all righteousness, will you not cease to make crooked the straight ways of the Lord?"[65] Judgment was passed on the magician and he became blind. The Bible condemns in strongest terms those who practice any form of magic.

REINCARNATION

The concept of reincarnation, also present in animism, denies the basic fundamentals of Christian faith and therefore is opposed by God. The differences between Christianity and reincarnation are well presented by Wilson and Weldon. They point out that Christians believe in judgment that issues in eternal consequences upon death; that God judges; that Jesus Christ atones for man's sin; that there is a Hell; that Jesus is God; that there is a personal Satan and demons; the Bible is God's Word; that Heaven is a distinct place; that there will be a personal resurrection and immortality; and that God exists in a trinity. Reincarnation, on the contrary, states that man has many lives in order to perfect himself; that man really judges himself; that man needs no savior; that everyone will return to the divine; that Jesus need not be God—but an incarnation of many before him; that all evil is of man's own making; that all religious writings are of equal value; that there is no heaven, only progressive spirit realms; that there is no resurrection; and that God is a human concept embracing all of life and is life itself.[66] The comparison speaks for itself. Reincarnation is an anti-biblical concept which denies God's sovereign control over His creation and His judgment of man and his sin.

DEMONIC POWERS

The Bible teaches that the devil is behind all false religions and approaches to God, and that he has a great company of followers who assist him in his deception and destruction of men.[67] McDowell and Stewart[68] note the characteristics of demons described in the Bible: they are spirits without bodies;[69] they were originally in fellowship with God;[70] they are numerous;[71] they are organized;[72] they have supernatural power;[73] they are knowledgeable of God;[74] they are allowed to roam the earth and to torment people;[75] they can inflict sickness;[76] they can possess or control animals[77] and human beings;[78] they can cause mental disorders;[79] they know that Jesus Christ is God;[80] they do tremble before God;[81] they do teach false doctrine;[82] they do oppose God's people;[83] they do attempt to destroy Christ's Kingdom;[84] God takes advantage of the actions of demons to accomplish His divine purposes;[85] and God is going to judge demons at the last judgment.[86] The characteristics of the demonic world are evident in the practice of animism. The very fact that animism subscribes to a very different concept of God indicates its subjection to "principalities and powers."[87] Its involvement with the spirit world is nothing other than what is described above.

SUPERSTITIONS

Superstition is also characteristic of all animistic systems. Though it is not based on actual occultic phenomena, superstition is, in itself, an avenue of deception in which man is subject to ignorance and fear. God's providence is not understood or known, and therefore man walks in bondage to fear. Instead of being in dominion over the created world as God intended,[88] man lives in fear of it. Therefore he is constantly having to take precautionary steps lest he break taboo or run afoul of a spirit world that seems to be more opposed to him than for him.

The power of superstition lies in the fact that it is a deception of Satan to keep man in bondage to himself, fearful of submitting to God as a loving heavenly Father who concerns Himself with the welfare of His creation.

ANIMAL SPIRITS

God intended the animal kingdom to be under man's dominion. In animism man sees a spirit world to which he must respond spiritually. Scripture recognized this response and censured it:

They shall no longer sacrifice their sacrifices to the goat demons . . . .
This shall be a permanent statute to them throughout their generations.[89]

This practice could be an apology to the goat spirit, which man feels he must make because of his kinship with nature. It could simply be the recognition of a power source or the object of worship, because of the forceful characteristics of a male goat.

BODY MUTILATION AND TATTOOS

The biblical injunction is clear: "You shall not make cuts in your body for the dead, nor make tattoo marks on yourselves: I am the Lord."[90]

These could be marks of protection to ward off evil. They could be openings to allow good spirits to enter the body to counteract evil ones. Death and evil are generally associated in animist thinking. The animist must therefore have means to ward off evil. Body mutilation may serve to provide empowerment for protection. Everything physical has a spiritual coordinate, therefore, scarification cannot be understood apart from its spiritual dimension.

SPIRIT PROTECTORS

Not knowing the God who concerns Himself with every detail of man's existence, animist man postulates the need for spirit protectors to guard his property and person. Here, too, Scripture has clear instruction: " . . . nor shall you place a figured stone in your land to bow down to it; for I am the Lord your God."[91] It is quite customary to have spirit houses or spirit protectors guard over property or to bring special blessing to a given place.

SIGNS

" . . . to seek omens."[92] Seeking out signs or omens and then adapting the routine of life according to what they portend are common practices. Astrology charts serve in this way. Other signs may be discerned in nature. For example the flight of birds or the appearance of unusual designs, forms or objects in nature could well augur either evil or good. The heavens play a significant role in this respect. Regardless of what these signs may be or where they may appear, Scripture does not allow any other control or providence to replace God. We read,

And beware, lest you lift up your eyes to heaven and see the sun and the moon and the stars, all the host of heaven, and be drawn away and worship them and serve them, those which the Lord your God has allotted to all peoples under the whole heaven.[93]

And the warning follows:

If a prophet or a dreamer of dreams arises among you and gives you a sign or a wonder, and the sign or the wonder comes true, concerning which he spoke to you, saying, 'Let us go after other gods . . . and let us serve them, you shall not listen . . . for the Lord your God is testing you to find out if you love the Lord your God with all your heart and with all your soul.'[94]

Dreams and prophetic words are commonly given much credence, but if these do not align with God's Word they are to be denounced.

PROSTITUTION AND/OR FERTILITY RITES

Fertility rites are an abomination to God. He is the God who blesses families with children, fields with harvest and the endeavors of man's hands with abundant return. Therefore Scripture commands, "None of the daughters of Israel shall be a cult prostitute, nor shall any of the sons of Israel be a cult prostitute."[95] Baalism was upheld by fertility rites. Orgies were considered normative. Israel was not slow in adopting these practices at periods during her history. The biblical accounts are replete with God's abhorrence of this sensual idolatry.

SACRIFICES AND LIBATIONS

Making sacrifices and pouring out libations is part of ancestor and spirit recognition. Scripture recognizes the fact of these practices. God's response to such practices is to denounce them and affirm the fact that there is no god who can compare with Him in His care for people.

And He will say, "Where are their gods, the rock in which they sought refuge, who ate the fat of their sacrifices and drank the wine of their libation? Let them rise up and help you, Let them be your hiding place."[96]

LIFE FORCE

The desire to secure power is strong in animism. God will not share His glory with another, and He therefore demonstrates His power on behalf of those who are in relationship with Him. No amount of life force can accomplish the purposes of God; only the gift of His power can do so. Therefore

> ... the Lord said to Gideon, "The people who are with you are too many for Me to give Midian into their hands, lest Israel become boastful saying 'My own power has delivered me'."[97]

POWER OBJECTS AND/OR FETISHES

The power of fetishes is beyond dispute. There were times when the people of Israel thought of Moses' shepherd's crook—which became the rod of God—as a power object. Why couldn't Moses use it to provide their wants and perform the miraculous apart from God's direction? The ark of the covenant was at times treated as if it were a fetish. The biblical account reveals God's response to this attitude:

> When the people came into the camp, the elders of Israel said, "Why has the Lord defeated us today before the Philistines? Let us take to ourselves from Shiloh the Ark of the Covenant of the Lord, that it may come among us and deliver us from the power of our enemies."[98]

Animistic practices are encountered throughout the history of the people of Israel. The New Testament makes mention of these practices and the resultant behavior. The correctives in both the Old and the New Testaments are clear. God desires those who will respond to Him to have hearts totally focused on His loving grace and mercy. The greatest and foremost commandment is:

> You shall love the Lord your God with all your heart, and with all your soul, and with all your mind ... And a second is like it, You shall love your neighbor as yourself.[99]

How then shall the Church of Jesus Christ overcome and replace religious systems which actually rob God of His Glory? That is the challenge the Church faces. It will be discussed in the next chapter.

ENDNOTES

1. R. J. Rushdoony, *The Institutes of Biblical Law* (Nutley, New Jersey: Craig Press, 1973), p. 32.

2. Gary North, *Unholy Spirits: Occultism And New Age Humanism* (Ft. Worth, Texas: Dominion Press, 1986), p. 151. Cf. Romans 1:18-32.

3. Galatians 3:1.

4. Deuteronomy 18:10,11,12,14.

5. 2 Chronicles 33:6.

6. 2 Kings 9:22.

7. 2 Kings 9:36-37.

8. Micah 5:12,15.

9. Nahum 3:1.

10. Nahum 3:4-7.

11. Galatians 5:19-21.

12. Exodus 22:18; Deuteronomy 18:10; 1 Samuel 15:23; 2 Chronicles 33:6; 2 Kings 5:22; Micah 5:12; Nahum 3:4; Galatians 15:20.

13. Isaiah 8:19.

14. Isaiah 8:21,22.

15. Isaiah 19:2,3.

16. 1 Samuel 28:7-21.

17. Deuteronomy 18:11.

18. Leviticus 20:27.

19. Proverbs 14:12.

20. Isaiah 47:13.

21. Deuteronomy 18:11.

22. Deuteronomy 18:14.

23. Genesis 41:8.

24. Isaiah 2:6.

25. Acts 13:6,8.

26. Deuteronomy 18:11.

27. Jeremiah 14:14.

28. Exodus 22:18.

29. Leviticus 19:31.

30. Leviticus 20:6.

31. Leviticus 20:27.

32. See Kurt Koch, *Christian Counselling and Occultism* (Grand Rapids: Kregel Publications, 1973).

33. Deuteronomy 18:9-10.

34. Ezekiel 21:21,22,29,32.

35. Ezekiel 13:3,6,9.

36. Deuteronomy 18:18.

37. Deuteronomy 18:20.

38. Deuteronomy 18:22.

39. Isaiah 47:10.

40. Joshua 1:8,9.

41. Isaiah 47:13,14.
42. Psalm 119:3.
43. Psalm 119:105.
44. Numbers 23:23; 2 Kings 17:17; Jeremiah 14:14; Ezekiel 13:6; 13:23; 21:21; Acts 16:16.
45. Isaiah 1:11-15, 23b.
46. Deuteronomy 5:29.
47. Isaiah 1:21.
48. Isaiah 1:16,17,19,20.
49. Ezekiel 14:3-5.
50. Ezekiel 14:6,8,10,11.
51. Jeremiah 8:17.
52. Ezekiel 13:18,20.
53. Ezekiel 11:21.
54. John 10:10.
55. John 8:44.
56. Leviticus 18:21;20:1-5; Deuteronomy 12:29-31; 1 Kings 1:7,33; 2 Kings 23:13; Jeremiah 32:35; 49:1,3.
57. 2 Kings 16:3; 17:17; Psalms 106:38; Jeremiah 19:4,5; Ezekiel 16:21.
58. Kurt Koch, *The Devil's Alphabet* (Grand Rapids: Kregel Publishers, 1969), pp. 54, 55.
59. Deuteronomy 18:10.
60. Jeremiah 32:35.
61. Joshua 13:22.
62. Numbers 22:6.
63. Isaiah 47:9,12.
64. Leviticus 19:26; Deuteronomy 18:10,14; 2 Kings 21:6; 2 Chronicles 33:6.
65. Acts 13:10.
66. Clifford Wilson and John Weldon, *Occult Shock and Psychic Forces* (San Diego: Master Books, 1980), pp. 86, 87.
67. 1 Peter 5:8; Ephesians 6:12.
68. Josh McDowell and Don Stewart, *Understanding the Occult* (San Bernardino: Here's Life Publishers, 1982), pp. 47-49.
69. Ephesians 6:12.
70. Jude 6.
71. Mark 5:8,9.
72. Matthew 12:24.
73. Revelation 16:14.
74. Matthew 8:29.
75. Matthew 12:43-45.
76. Matthew 9:32,33.
77. Mark 5:13.
78. Luke 8:2.
79. Mark 5:2,3,5.
80. Mark 1:23,24.

81. James 2:19.
82. 1 Timothy 4:1.
83. Ephesians 6:12.
84. 1 Peter 5:8.
85. Judges 9:23.
86. 2 Peter 2:4.
87. Ephesians 6:12.
88. Psalm 8; Genesis 1:26,28.
89. Leviticus 17:7, cf. Deuteronomy 32:16,17.
90. Leviticus 19:28, cf. Deuteronomy 14:1.
91. Leviticus 26:1.
92. Numbers 24:1.
93. Deuteronomy 4:19.
94. Deuteronomy 13:1-3.
95. Deuteronomy 23:17.
96. Deuteronomy 32:37,38.
97. Judges 7:2, cf. Zechariah 4:6.
98. 1 Samuel 4:3.
99. Matthew 22:37,39.

Chapter 16

THE CHALLENGE
TO THE CHURCH

Herman Williams, a converted Navaho Indian and former missionary to the American Indian community of South Dakota, testifies to the significant powers available to animists. He describes the practice of skin walking as a form of astral travel, in which a person is able to materialize into different animal forms. To gain some greater power to do skin walking, human sacrifice may be performed, after which the sacrificer goes into a trance. While in that state a vapor comes out of his mouth and forms into an image, which then flows into the hide of some animal. This apparition is then sent on its journey to accomplish particular objectives for its owner. Upon return the person concerned can describe the entire experience exactly.

He tells how he and his family saw a beautiful and impressive deer buck. While they were watching it, the deer buck materialized into a wolf. They noticed that around its neck was a Navaho medicine bundle and concluded it was a skin walker. He also told of the time when owls and coyotes spoke to him in his own Navaho tongue, and of how they served as messengers of both good and evil in his Indian cosmology.

While ministering in South Dakota, this same Navaho Christian missionary had a hard time breathing whenever he entered the Indian reservation. He could only sleep sitting upright in bed. But whenever he was off the reservation, his breathing was normal and he could sleep lying down. One night he heard Indian drums and singing which seemed to be coming out of the nearby kitchen. He went to check but found nothing. The drumming and singing persisted for several nights, and he eventually traced them to the inside of the bedroom wall. When he prayed against whatever it was, it immediately stopped. The heaviness in his chest subsided, and he felt well and could lie down and sleep.

Early the next morning he heard a loud, desperate knocking on the front door. It was a distraught Indian woman asking him to come and pray for her sick husband. Upon entering the room, he found a twisted, contorted figure, obviously in great pain and agony. He asked her how long her husband had been that way, and she informed him that it had begun the night before. Upon further inquiry he discovered that the man was a shaman. By using some of the Navaho Christian missionary's hair, the shaman had made medicine with which to kill him, in order to remove the threat that his ministry was to his practice of shamanism. The missionary concluded that by taking authority over the presence in his house—the drumming and singing—he had actually taken authority over the evil perpetuated by the shaman. He did pray for him, but he died a horrible death.[1] The Church is still there though, testifying to the fact that its Lord is above all powers.

Whatever the reader may think of the above account, it is fair to say that Western naturalism has no epistemological category in which to place such mysterious happenings. But the more Western man suppresses the knowledge of truth, the more occult phenomena like that illustrated above will take on new importance.[2] When man substitutes his own knowledge in the place of God's knowledge, he becomes susceptible to occult forces and these occult forces are powerful and able to perform miracles.

Christians should recognize that there is a counter religious system in opposition to biblical Christianity. It is a counterfeit system, devised and maintained by powers of darkness determined to rob God of the glory which is rightfully His—"the glory due His name."

THE OCCULT ALTERNATIVE

There is truth in the saying that men want neither determinative scientific law—such as is commonly subscribed to in most Western countries—nor pure chance or fatalism to rule over them.[3] They also refuse a God that rules, shoving Him out of their world by denying His creation and judgment. Man desires a measure of control over his destiny and has, therefore, come to place his faith in other powers besides God. For Western man these powers may be techno-scientific, but not always. He bows his knees to many other idols which affirm his greed, lust and sensuality. To the less secular mind set—the mind drawn to animism—these powers are known and realized in the practice of witchcraft, necromancy, astrology, divination, wizardry, sorcery, charms, spells and choosing propitious times. In this way man asserts his autonomy from God and deals with powers which he manipulates and which supposedly yield to his will. In actual fact he himself becomes enslaved to these powers, doing their bidding, and robbing God of the praise He rightly deserves. From the day Adam questioned the word of God, man has sought for some voice of authority other than God's. That leaves him open to occult powers which stand under the authority of Satan.[4]

The truth of human bondage to occult powers[5] poses some rather significant challenges to the Christian communicator. What is involved in bringing converts out of "the Kingdom of darkness into the Kingdom of God's dear Son"?[6] Is there a biblical model to follow to accomplish such a formidable task? Does it involve an actual encounter with the power? Will the implementation of this model lessen the tendency of the Church toward syncretism? Will it allow for a greater measure of contextualization? Would it encourage the development of a truly biblical ethnotheology?

All of these obviously rhetorical questions are effectively covered by the strategy entrusted to the Apostle Paul and spelled out in his defense before Agrippa.[7] However, before we attempt to apply this methodology, we ought to understand the basic factors involved in bringing about change which issues in conversion. These factors do not discount the power of God in effecting conversion, and we should recognize that they are quite in keeping with biblical understanding.[8]

CONSIDERATIONS IN EFFECTING CHANGE

Advocates of change must grasp the nature and meaning of animist forms if they are to lead animists into a meaningful and realistic understanding of the changes that will be brought by the Gospel.[9] It is as Willoughby so perceptively states:

> We cannot teach him to fill out his old forms with a fuller meaning, nor show him a more excellent way of expressing or satisfying his aspirations, until we so master his forms and expressions as to become sure of the nature of his cravings and discontents.[10]

The overview of the practices of animism here has been given in an attempt to understand the aspirations, motivations, needs and frustrations of the animist. Beyond these factors, an attempt was also made to

understand how a particular practice served to discourage deviancy—thereby serving as a social control mechanism. Simultaneously,
a particular practice may also serve to foster a measure of respect for
the sacred, and of balance and harmony in relationship. Communicators must therefore be careful of merely rooting them out and
thus leaving people without stabilizing factors.

W. Robertson Smith pointed out[11] that no advocate of change comes
to a people starting, as it were, with a blank page, as if the newly
introduced concepts will stand on their own merits. The new system, in
this case the Christian message, must be in contact all along the line
with the older ideas and practices which it will already find in possession of the people. In fact,

> . . . a convert from [animism] cannot suddenly divest himself of what
> a hundred generations has woven into every strand of his mental and
> moral nature . . . . The seed sown may be of the very best quality, and
> the soil may be suited to the new crop; but old hopes, fears, ideas, and
> impulses spring up—stray seeds of former crops that the field
> carried.[12]

Obviously, the past of any person does not lie behind—but rather
within—the person. Therefore, short of a total rebirth in which the old
is replaced by, or reinterpreted by the new on every level, the convert
will inevitably revert during times of stress to the way of life he knows
as meaningful. Wherever we don't take the existing religious faith of
people seriously and deal with it specifically, they will continue to hang
on to it and find their answers to life in an alternative power source,
other than God.

For Christianity to be more than a formal and cultural religion, it
must be introduced at every level of human existence. The new scheme
of faith must adequately answer to the religious instincts and suscept-
ibilities that already exist in the people. It must, therefore, take into
account the traditional forms in which all religious feeling is expressed.
Furthermore, it must use language[13] which men accustomed to these
old forms can understand.

By evaluating the animist's religious forms, it becomes patently
clear that his approach and involvement with the spirit world is most
unlike the typical Westerner's response to the Christian faith. In fact, it
has been correctly observed that most Western missionaries first seek
to secularize the animist, and then convert him to Christianity.[14] In the
process, the animist's sense of the sacred has, to a large measure, been
destroyed, with a resulting lack of fear for God. Furthermore, the awful

consequences of leading a sinful life are not taken seriously. When people are told by misinformed missionaries that there is no need to fear spirit beings, they then counter, "Why fear God, who so readily forgives?" The mental and spiritual environment of a person cannot be erased without in some way destroying a sense of the sacred, which may never be recaptured.

In approaching the animist, the Western missionary will have to realize that the Christian message must enhance the concept that this world is spiritual, not merely material. Furthermore, the fact that an animist sees his world as integrated, rather than consisting of many discrete parts with no particular relationship to a whole, must be taken into consideration. This is quite unlike that of an individualistic, private Western model.

WORLD VIEWS

To relate to such a world, the Western missionary will have to submit his world view[15] to that of the Bible. What are the differences? Which world view is more nearly correct?

Western World View

In general, a Western world view strongly affirms that all there is in life is what can be seen and experienced with the physical senses. This affirmation has not been all negative. In fact, this belief led men on the course of discovery and has produced a world in which technological and scientific attainments have radically affected the quality of human life for the better. Western man has prided himself in the quality of physical and material life he has achieved. This has resulted in unfortunate ego- and ethnocentrism, that have placed religion on the same level as the material and the physical. Western man has convinced himself that his salvation lies in the realm of the cognitive. He will be saved by knowledge, especially scientific knowledge. Thus Western man has essentially succumbed to the ancient heresy of Gnosticism.[16] The natural consequences are the belief that truth is found in the cognitive and the intellectual realm only and not necessarily, or in association with, the spiritual realm.

Religion, as a result, is only an option at best, and certainly not essential for life. Religion need not have any bearing on man's approach to the rest of life. Man can successfully separate his religious life from his secular life. Furthermore, spirits are not real because they cannot be perceived by man's natural senses. If they are not real, then how can they influence life? Western man is confident that he can be educated to handle every area of life, and that given time he will resolve all of his problems. Marxist thinking is a natural outflow of the Western world view. Man does not need a god to deal with the challenges of life. Man can indeed go it alone, or so he believes and acts.

Animist World View

The animist world view, by contrast, perceives all of life to be spiritual. The material world exists only as it submits and subscribes to the spiritual. Both the physical and the spiritual are of one fabric. This perception has severely limited man's expression and realization of his creativity. It has the propensity to maintain the status quo, if not to give in to fatalism. The spirit world controls everything in life, and should man want to relate to it, and live in its good graces, he must secure spiritual power. Spiritual power can be secured by the fusion of secret knowledge and magic. Both are motivating pursuits in life.

Biblical World View

Both the animist and the Western world view emphasize elements of the biblical world view, but in each case the truth is pushed to an unrealistic extreme.The Western world view recognizes the material and physical world as good and available to man, but claims for it a goodness aside and apart from God. This is contrary to the Bible. The Bible asserts that matter is not evil, that man was made in the image of God, that they are to the glory of God. But it says that sin has afflicted both with unfortunate consequences, and therefore also with limitations.

The animist world view recognizes that the world is under the control of spirits, but it rejects both the authority of God over His creation, and the idea of human accountability. In animist thought man must secure the offices of the spirit world in order to make life meaningful and to attain his own selfish desires. Man is not accountable for his actions, because all of life is subject to the control and caprice of the spirit world. According to Van Til, there is

> . . . a secret treaty between rationalism and irrationalism—a treaty against God. The very ideal of pure factuality or chance is the best guarantee that no true authority, such as that of God as the Creator and Judge of man, will ever confront man.[17]

There, then, is the bottom line for both world views. Both are essentially anti-God. The biblical world view maintains that God, who is in control of the universe, has established both physical and moral laws by which He operates. Man must respond freely or suffer the consequences. However, it is not a closed system. The Bible attests to God's intervention in all of life, in keeping with His compassion and purposes. What man calls miracles are God's interventions on behalf of man's welfare. The biblical world view maintains that spirits other than God do influence life, and that Satan, the usurper of human dominion and authority, is determined to deceive and destroy human life and God's world. However God has created good spirits—angels—to be helpers to man. The biblical world view therefore maintains a balance between the extreme of materialism and the extreme of everything being subject to spirit domination. Neither God nor spirits are absent from the world. Nor is man either autonomous or forced to respond in a particular way.

Both extreme world views—Western and animist—need the corrective of the biblical perspective, but the greater responsibility lies with the Christian communicator because he claims to be informed by the Bible. Then, too, being the advocate of change he should remember that the new information—the biblical perspective—must be embodied in the old if it is to replace the old weakness with a new strength. In other words, the gospel must become incarnated in the frame of reference of the receptors, if it is to bring about change. That being the case, what points of contact are there in animism which may be affirmed by the Bible?

POINTS OF CONTACT WITH ANIMISM

In some respects animism is accurate in its perceptions of life's realities. The Bible and animism both accept the . . .

Spiritual View of Life

As pointed out above, the animist concept is an extreme. Nevertheless there is a significant degree of congruence between it and Christianity. In this regard, God's transcendence, but also His immanence, will have to be stressed. The role of minor divinities and spirits could be relevantly related to the ministry of angels and archangels. The cloud of witnesses of Hebrews 11, could be understood as ancestors, and the concept of evil spirits is well covered in the Bible. However, the biblical constructs must not be misconstrued to be the true counterparts of these spirits, with the exception of evil spirits.

Significant emphasis will have to be placed on the pervasive ministry of the Holy Spirit as the indwelling, guiding, strengthening, affirming, teaching and also convicting One.[18] The person and work of Satan, along with His legions, must be carefully explained with special reference to the triumph of Jesus Christ over Satan, in His death, resurrection and ascension. Jesus Christ is not merely Savior; He is Lord over all, including principalities and powers, and He brings deliverance to man.[19] Spirit encounters are not to be discounted but rather evaluated and submitted to the judgment of the Bible. This introduces the next point of contact, namely that the animist is . . .

Open to the Message of the Bible

The animist understands from his own perceptions of word power that the Bible speaks, and that what it says is creative in itself. To seek to prove that the Bible is God's Word, and to seek to impress the animist with the validity of the text, are misguided endeavors. The animist is already impressed with the fact that what God has said is recorded in a readable volume. He sees in Scripture a realistic, down to earth imagery and treatment of his human problems and therefore sees an accurate picture of his own heart.[20] As far as he is concerned, the signs, wonders and works contained therein attest to the reality of spiritual power, and when the communicators of the Gospel present a Jesus of power—being "witnesses unto Him"—the animist lends a ready ear. To this end, drama and films on the life of Christ have been used with remarkable success.

Apologetics certainly has its place, but more frequently than not, regardless of the religious veneer he seeks to project, the animist has an open ear for the supernatural events recorded in the Bible. Such events are familiar to him. The message of the Word therefore evokes a ready response from him when accompanied by a demonstration of the works of God. This is part of the uniqueness of the Christian message and mission.

Many organizations and religions have been, and continue to be, involved in works of humanitarian compassion. But none can impart new life, nor bring real peace, nor reconcile man to God and his neighbor, nor bring deliverance from demonic oppression. In the words of Adeyemo, African theologian and churchman:

All these remain as divine prerogatives which God in Christ has delegated to the Church via the Holy Spirit. To this end therefore the Lord gives to His Church power to witness . . . What is this Power? In Matthew 10:1 we read: "And when he had called unto himself his twelve disciples he gave them power . . . " Jesus did not give them good advice; nor general principles on evangelism; nor techniques of appropriate technology, good as all these are . . . He knew that he was sending his disciples to the battlefield . . . he gave them an appropriate weapon—power from on high . . . the ability or strength with which one is endued to carry out an operation . . . the power of authority and the right to exercise power. What is the purpose of giving them power? . . . He gave them authority: to drive out evil spirits (10:1); to preach the good news of the Kingdom (10:7); to heal the sick (10:8); to raise the dead (10:8); to cleanse those who have leprosy (10:8); to drive out demons (10:8); and Luke adds: to give peace to those who receive them (Luke 10:5-6).[21]

All of the above are points of contact with the animist, regardless of the religious veneer he uses to hide his true orientation. His drive is for power to handle life, and the message of the Bible is that God is the Source of all power, and that the Church is to mediate that power to deliver men out of all bondage. "If our witness with compassion lacks a demonstration of the Spirit's power, then our uniqueness and distinctiveness is gone."[22] This brings us to the third point of contact. The animist is . . .

Providentially Disposed for Response to the Gospel

He regularly encounters supernatural powers greater than himself. He works to discover ways to effectively and harmoniously respond to those powers. Throughout the Bible God reveals Himself to man as the God who moves powerfully in the history of mankind. He is the God who makes startling promises and then fulfills them. By His Holy Spirit He comes alive within man and empowers him for life and godliness.[23] The animist is also providentially disposed to know the difference between right and wrong, however he may conceive of this concept. He knows that wrong actions bring retribution while right ones issue in rewards. As Tippett observes, his notion of what a sinner is may not be clear, but there is a basis there upon which may be built.[24] Basically, the animist is "salvation oriented,"[25] desiring to escape punishment and attain specific goals. He is also disposed toward effecting reconciliation. He practices action apologies—the giving of gifts to cover wrongdoing. He understands communal meals, sacrifices, giving of gifts and other rituals which serve to remove enmity and induce acceptance and favor.[26] All of these have parallels in the Bible which the missionary can use to communicate the gospel.

The fourth point of contact is the fact that the animist does understand the . . .

Concept of Power Encounter

He knows how one spirit can overcome another and how a superior spirit is called upon to exorcise and take the place of the weaker one. In his world of spirit caprice he knows how to turn from one power to another to achieve his objectives. Thus when he is confronted by the superior power of the Holy Spirit in conversion, and led to "turn from idols, to serve the living God," he has a better perception of who and what has come to indwell him.[27] In fact, Tippett observes: "My experience and research have led me to see that usually conversion is a power encounter and Christ is a Lord of power."[28]

Throughout the history of the Church, she has been engaged in power encounters against the forces of evil. Therefore, to presume that a person can come out of the domain of darkness into God's Kingdom without a power showdown, assumes that Satan will allow transfer of membership without a battle. The Bible doesn't support this notion.[29]

To the animist, anything less than a power encounter in which one not only assents volitionally to cognitive input, but also feels the encounter experientially, is indeed a poor exchange. His motivation in life is to find power; he involves himself with powerful gods. Surely his new found faith is not only objectively true but also subjectively life changing and empowering, enabling him to live in victory over all principalities and powers.[30] The fifth point of contact is the persistence he demonstrates in wanting to establish and maintain . . .

Contact with the Spirit World

He spares no effort to discover the right means to dispose the spirit world to respond to his entreaties on his terms. He understands the practice of prayer. He knows that he lives in a world in which man needs help, and he knows such help is available to man if he can find the right means.

Animist man believes he is the prime mover in initiating spirit contact. This is the exact opposite of what the Bible teaches. Nevertheless, these beliefs can be used to help man understand that God seeks him in Jesus Christ and draws him in the Holy Spirit. He can be brought to know that he can indeed respond to God in realistic and meaningful ways—and vice versa. God desires man to be in fellowship with Himself, to be dependent upon Him and to live in obedience in His presence.[31] God does promise His protection and His abundant blessing to rest upon man.[32] God also desires that man seek His face and that man make his requests known unto Him.[33] Information like this must touch upon the needs the animist feels. The information should therefore be presented as an alternative to his way of enlisting spirit help. Care should be taken so as not to criticize his traditional way, but rather to build on it, or to fill in the gaps in his perception of relationship to the spirit world.[34]

Perhaps the most subtle and yet most promising point of contact relates to the animist's desire for . . .

A Personal Relationship with a Spirit Being

To maintain such an ongoing relationship he orders his life according to custom and observes taboos. He does not, however, follow a code book on ethics and morality. Rather he depends upon experiential knowledge—he feels and acts out what he believes the deity would want and prescribe.

The typical Western communicator, in his desire to convert people, usually seeks to present certain propositional truths as essential preparation for accepting Jesus Christ. This then is understood by the target audience to mean that by doing and not doing certain things, a relationship is established with God. Parroting certain beliefs and avoiding certain practices is understood by the animist to give one a personal relationship with God, because his own religious system is legalistic to the core. Tippett helps clarify the basic issues at stake when he says:

> The Christian way is not a legal code, or a "statement of faith," but a journeying with Christ. Christian ethics cannot be set down in a code book; they spring from a relationship between Master and disciple . . . . Effective mission is more "bringing men to Christ" than teaching the Christian way, for the way cannot be taught to unbelievers; it has to be experienced as men tread it with Christ.[35]

The point is that men and women must be introduced to a living Christ, one who is still alive and at work today in every sphere of life. Therefore Christian communicators are not to present a plan or a program, but rather a person—Jesus Christ. For that reason the Bible is written as a narrative rather than a legal code. It presents a living Christ, still active in all the affairs of men. The animist comprehends this very well. His own concept of the spirit world tells him that spirit beings surround him, interpret everything and are involved in every aspect of his life.

What the Greek searchers asked of the disciples, people everywhere ask of Christ's disciples today: "Sirs, we would see Jesus."[36] We'll learn how to arrive at this point in the next section as we discuss the five-fold method for effective evangelism. But the points of contact are useful in highlighting the animists motives and ways of dealing with his felt needs. Therefore, throughout the application of the fivefold method, these points of contact must be kept in view.

A FIVEFOLD METHOD OF EVANGELISM

The Apostle Paul understood his commission to the nations to be

... to open eyes so that they may turn from darkness to light and from the dominion of Satan unto God, in order that they may receive forgiveness of sins and an inheritance among those who have been sanctified by faith in Me.[37]

Here he sets forth a fivefold method which is invaluable in establishing effective churches in the context of animism. The steps outlined here are both progressive and sequential. Some of these steps may possibly be taken in a fairly short space of time, but a convert who experiences each step will know the basis of his belief and not struggle to know what it means to be a disciple of Christ.

There are several steps in bringing people to Jesus Christ. First, a person must be brought to an awareness of God—His Christ, His Holy Spirit, His Church and His mission. The potential convert must have his eyes opened. Secondly, he must realize that there are two kingdoms vitally interested in his response to life—one of darkness and one of light. Third, he must decide whether or not to turn from the one kingdom to the other, from the dominion of Satan to the dominion of God. Fourth, he must consummate the decision in an actual encounter with the powers of darkness and turning to God in order to accept salvation by receiving forgiveness of sins. Finally, he is to be incorporated into the fellowship of the church—"an inheritance among those who have been sanctified by faith in Me." So what are the applications of this?[38]

CREATE AWARENESS—"OPEN THEIR EYES"

After years of struggling to communicate the Gospel effectively, a group of missionaries came to believe that God's wisdom in placing the Book of Beginnings—Genesis—in the beginning of the Bible should suggest something in terms of evangelism strategy. So they began by teaching the book of Genesis in a way that captured the imagination of the hearers. Throughout the study of Genesis the missionaries said nothing about the need to make a decision for Christ. Rather, they let the hearers anticipate the next installment. They then followed up Genesis with a careful presentation of the Gospel of Matthew. Both studies were done in a narrative style. Needless to say, after such a careful and thorough presentation, they had made their audience aware of God, of His Christ, of His Holy Spirit, of His Church and of her mission. If a person must decide to be a disciple of Jesus Christ, ought he not to know what is involved? What it means? What will be required of him? The problem of meaning must be uppermost in the thinking and teaching of the missionary. Is the message coming across as a philosophy or as life? Is Christianity merely a moral, legal or ethical code, or is it life itself—a power gospel? Is it a message that is directed to the problems of the communicator or to the felt needs of the audience? Are the listeners understanding biblical words, or are they fitting these into their non-biblical world view? In other words, what do they understand by the words used for God, Spirit, Son of God, sin, love, forgive, sacrifice and many others?[39]

It is quite possible that long before the end of the study, the hearer may already have come under strong conviction. But the time for decision is still a few steps off. It is essential to wait until the next steps are covered.

REALIZATION—DARKNESS AND LIGHT

In this step, it's important to make the hearers aware of the fact that there are two kingdoms, not of equal strength, but nevertheless desirous of directing man's destiny. This is the level on which biblical teaching concerning the powers of darkness are studied. Passages like Ezekiel 28 and Isaiah 14 are drawn to the audience's attention. A clear distinction must be made between the two kingdoms and between what's involved in submitting to either. The hearers must realize that the Christian message can bring such a great change that they can be moved from fear to faith. Then, as Nida says, "there can be a definite

213

move away from basic mistrust of an irresponsible spirit world to a confidence in an eternal, loving and just God."[40]

Here we may introduce the ministry of angels, highlighting their beneficent activity on behalf of man as over against the malevolence of demons. In this step potential converts must realize the difference between darkness and light and the effect they have on man's life and destiny.

One's motivation for accepting Christianity must be carefully considered and dealt with. It will affect one's view of Christianity, of the character of the Gospel, of the nature of the Christian ethic and of the concept of Christian responsibility.[41] Christianity is not a quid pro quo religion.

Sometimes in our haste to see people come to Christ as Lord and Savior, we have viewed comprehension as conversion, not having allowed for probable base motivations, nor for the actual process of decision-making, which is the third step.

DECISION-MAKING—FROM THE DOMINION OF SATAN TO GOD

God wants people to respond to Him volitionally. He wants them to know what is involved in becoming His disciple and on what basis they may become a Christian. They are expected to understand first, and then to commit themselves to Him without reservation. This essential third step may take a relatively short time, but it should not be avoided. Rather, on the basis of what the potential convert has come to know about biblical truth, he now volitionally, with all his heart, mind and soul, elects to submit to God and be His disciple. He must decide whether he will deliberately turn away from the Kingdom of darkness and turn toward the Kingdom of God's dear Son. He must understand what the outcome will be of his decision, either for or against God.

The Apostle Paul, writing to the Church in Thessalonica, points out how they turned from idols to serve the living God. This third step is, therefore, the step that leads to repentance. It is a recognition of one's own willful ways, of the sinful tendency of substituting self knowledge for God's knowledge. It is a recognition of one's tendency to yield to sin, and of the awful consequences of not confessing one's sin before a holy and just God.

During this process, additional biblical instruction will be necessary. The potential convert ought to be taught what salvation means, how it was achieved by Jesus Christ, and what happens when a person has turned from Satan to God. He must be introduced to the triumph of Christ over all powers in His death and resurrection. He ought to know what is the ministry of the Holy Spirit and what is involved in being a Christian.

The missionary must take note of the fact that generally animists make decisions communally. Consensus is important because animists derive much of their sense of worth and humanness by interacting as members of society. For this reason family or group evangelism is so important.[42] Upon having reached an informal decision, the person must be brought face to face with the actual encounter.

ENCOUNTER—RECEIVE FORGIVENESS OF SINS

The encounter may be a very quiet event or traumatic one. As Tippett says neither the animist, nor anyone else,

> . . . should be allowed to drift into Christianity. The passage from animism to biblical faith is a definite clear-cut act, a specific change of life, a "coming out of something," and an "entry into something" quite different.[43]

If converts have deliberately been involved in demonic activity, they will have to renounce all Satanic activity and/or relationships. Whatever occultic paraphernalia they used, or wore on the body, such as charms, etc., they must destroy with the help of Christian believers. It is vitally important that the convert, not the discipler, destroy the paraphernalia. In so doing, he learns how to take authority over the powers of darkness with the help of the Living God. Every hidden thing must be exposed, dealt with and done away with. Any hesitation or reticence ensures the failure of the attempt. All Satanic holds must be broken, whether they be personal or ancestral.

In this step the convert must realize that the God presented in the Bible is superior to all powers. He is Sovereign Lord. He must also realize that the Holy Spirit is the Living Christ, indwelling those who have come to know God the Father through Jesus Christ. The convert must himself pray a prayer of renunciation, the so-called sinner's prayer and express his gratitude to God for His gift of salvation. He may be led in this prayer by another, but the principle is that "with the mouth confession is made unto salvation,"[44] and so forgiveness is received.

This step is nothing less than a power encounter, and it is even more dramatic than the power encounters which the animist knows. The convert has come to realize what it means to be translated out of the "kingdom of darkness into the kingdom of God's dear Son." This is nothing less than a supernatural rescue and deliverance. Follow-up is essential, in order to establish the new convert in the faith. And that brings us to the fifth step.

INCORPORATION—AN INHERITANCE AMONG CHRISTIANS

In this step it is essential to help the convert become a functioning member of the Church. He must have a sense of belonging as he shares in a common love for Jesus Christ and as he participates fully in worship, service and witness. He must feel wanted and useable in the cause of the church. He must be able to feel at home with his new brothers and sisters and truly experience life in the Body of Christ. This is not merely an ideal, it is imperative. Some have found cell groups an effective way to accomplish this objective. The evidence to support their claim is the remarkable growth of strong and large Christian churches in many parts of the world.

Incorporation involves getting the convert to participate actively in the total ministry of the church, to commit to being a citizen of God's Kingdom, and to do good works.[45] It involves getting him to testify to Jesus Christ as Lord by both word and deed and to understand that the Church is here to declare the glory of God among all nations.[46] The teaching of the Word of God must focus on God's objectives for all mankind, while also seeking to bring converts to maturity in Christian character.[47] Members must be given a reason for being. Only God's mission in this world, namely world evangelization, qualifies as a large enough purpose and ascribes Him the glory.

The Church is to reclaim from the usurpers—the demonic and their agents—all those held captive. Whatever dehumanizes is an affront to God and therefore must be of vital concern to the Church. However, her most important task is to bring people into a personal relationship with Jesus Christ. Doing anything less than this is a truncation of the purpose of the Church. The Church of Jesus Christ must realize that she is not in a struggle with fellow humans, but with principalities and powers of darkness.[48] She is called to spiritual warfare. Her weapons are not first and foremost economic or political but spiritual and mighty to the pulling down of stongholds.[49] The teaching of God's Word must evoke within the Church a confidence that she is more than conqueror through Jesus Christ,[50] and that Jesus Christ's death on the cross was with the express purpose of destroying the works of the devil.[51]

Not only is effective incorporation necessary to have the convert realize his potential for Christ's cause, but the church must be indigenously structured so that people may participate in their expression of the Christian faith in their own way. They must be linguistically, culturally and functionally a distinctive people of God, and yet not exceed the bounds of what is biblically mandated. No matter what contextualization calls for, the biblical absolutes can never be relativized. In God's wisdom, He revealed Himself within the context of culture. Whatever He made binding in those cultures is still binding today.

Thus, step by step, a person is led from not being a follower of Jesus Christ, to being a well-informed, well-prepared and active member of the Church of Christ. As he is helped from one step to another, the Christian message is contextualized within the person himself and within his cultural frame of reference. Feedback throughout the process enables the convert to apply God's Word to his own peculiar situation and so discover a biblical theology which answers to his world view and speaks within his cultural frame of reference. Syncretism is minimized because his decision to be a disciple of Jesus Christ is based upon steadily progressive and well-informed instruction. It is also likely that his faith will be more dynamic, because it arises out of a knowledge of what it means to be a Christian, along with an actual encounter and showdown with the god of this world, who had previously blinded him to the Gospel.[52]

The possibility of employing acceptable cultural forms through which he may express his Christian faith is likely, because the instruction came to him while he was still very much a part of his own sociocultural structures. If the missionary knows the aspirations and frustrations of the animist, he will seek to answer his questions within the context of that which the animist already knows and understands.

There is a need for such thorough exposure to Christian teaching before a decision is made, because Satan does not willingly or very amiably take leave of the citizens of his domain. Furthermore, should they decide for Christ without such a solid foundation, the level of their Christian faith will make them easy prey to the continuing attacks of Satan. The only way to stand firm against Satan's onslaughts is to put on the whole armor of God,[53] to resist Satan and to expose his evil deeds.[54] To do this a person must know who God is, what He has accomplished for mankind, and how He continues to work purposefully on behalf of man. God's Word is essential—it is the sword of the Spirit—but it is also the source which stimulates and motivates faith in a great God who is Lord over all.

The Scriptures, along with an active prayer life, must evermore be the central focus and motivation in the life of the church member. Christians have to know that they are at war with gods of power. Nowhere are people free from the onslaughts and the deception perpetrated by powers of darkness. Animism in its myriad forms and expressions infects every human structure. It is Satan's master plan to keep people from walking by faith with the God revealed in the Bible. Therefore it will always be essential to submit all religious experience, teaching and methodology to the Bible—God's Word. Short of this Christianity will be less than biblical, and Christians will live in defeat.

In summary, the task of the advocate of change is to bring people to Jesus Christ so that they will be delivered from the powers of darkness and be new creatures in Christ. Then as God's new humanity they can move out in power into enemy territory, and reclaim those who are still children of disobedience. The advocate of change will want to respect people's past and salvage for the expression of Christianity anything and everything that does not contradict the Word of God and use it for God's glory. He will also want to study closely the points of contact which are already there in animism and lead people from the known felt need to the unknown need of salvation in Jesus Christ. He himself will want to be so saturated with God's Word that he can take a person, step by step, into the presence of the living God revealed in the Bible. He will want to pray and labor in such a way that multitudes of animists will bow the knee to Jesus Christ as Lord and Savior.

The Church is being challenged on all fronts, but that is nothing new. The powers of darkness are constantly at work to alienate man from anything and anyone which may bring him into a dynamic relationship with the God of the Bible. Their aim is to dehumanize humanity and ultimately to destroy it. The challenge to the Church is to rise up, to use the weapons placed at its disposal by God Himself, and to expose all powers as non-powers before the Lord of the Church. The gods of power are many but they do not have authority. The Church has a delegated authority to continue the work initiated by Jesus Christ, to call to account all powers, and to declare and demonstrate that Jesus is Lord, to the glory of God.

The mission of our Lord is still the mission of the Church. And so the Church of Jesus Christ also affirms that

The Spirit of the Lord is upon Me, because He anointed Me to preach the Gospel to the poor. He has sent Me to proclaim release to the captives, and recovery of sight to the blind, to set free those who are downtrodden, to proclaim the favorable year of the Lord.[55]

ENDNOTES

1. These accounts were presented in a class session at CBS during the Winter Quarter of 1987, by Rev. Steve Wood of the C&MA concerning a certain Herman Williams of Yuba City, Arizona.

2. Gary North, *Unholy Spirits: Occultism and New Age Humanism* (Ft. Worth, Texas: Dominion Press, 1986), pp. 44-48.

3. *Ibid.*, p. 40.

4. Acts 26:18.

5. Ephesians 2:2; 4:17.

6. Colossians 1:13.

7. Acts 26:18.

8. Acts 17:16-34; John 4:6-30.

9. 2 Corinthians. 5:17.

10. W. C. Willoughby, *The Soul of the Bantu* (New York: Harper & Row, 1969), p. xix.

11. *Ibid.*

12. *Ibid.*, p. xxxiii.

13. What is meant here by "language" includes religious practices. Cf. A. R. Tippett "The Evangelization of Animists," in *Let The Earth Hear His Voice*, ed. J. D. Douglas (Minneapolis: World Wide Publications, 1975), p. 850-51.

14. A. R. Tippett, "Cultural Compulsives," in *God, Man And Church Growth*, ed. A. R. Tippett (Grand Rapids: Wm. B. Eerdmans Publishing Co., 1973), pp. 167-169.

15. Paul G. Hiebert, *Anthropological Insights for Missionaries* (Grand Rapids: Baker Book House, 1985), p. 212.

16. Gary North (1986), p. 27.

17. Cornelius Van Til, *The Defense of the Faith* (rev. ed.) (Philadelphia: Presbyterian & Reformed, 1963), pp. 124-26.

18. John 16:7-15; Acts 1:8; Acts 2:33, 38; 4:31-33; etc.

19. Luke 4:18; Colossians 2:14-15; 1 John 3:8.

20. Eugene A. Nida, *Introducing Animism* (New York: Friendship Press, 1959), p. 61.

21. T. Adeyemo, *Witnessing With Power* (unpublished manuscript, n.d.), pp. 1-2.

22. *Ibid.*, p. 4.

23. 2 Peter 1:3.

24. Alan R. Tippett, "Possessing the Philosophy of Animism for Christ" in *Crucial Issues in Missions Tomorrow*, D. A. McGavran (Chicago: Moody Press, 1972), p. 138.

25. *Ibid.*, p. 137.

26. *Ibid.*, p. 138-39.

27. 1 Thessalonians 1:9.

28. McGavran (1972), p.141.

29. Luke 11:21-22; Ephesians 2:1-4; 4:17-18; 6:10-12; 1 Peter 5:8.

30. Ephesians 1:21.

31. John 15:1-7.

32. Psalms 27; 90; 91.

33. Philippians 4:6; Luke 11:9-13; John 14:14.

34. Acts 17:22-31.

35. McGavran, 1972, p. 141.

36. John 12:21.

37. Acts 26:18. Cf. Alan R. Tippett, "The Evangelization of Animists" in *Let The Earth Hear His Voice*, ed. J. D. Douglas (Minneapolis: World Wide Publications, 1975), p. 847-849.

38. These steps are adaptations of A. Van Gennep *Rites of Passage* (Chicago: Phoenix Books, 1960.)

39. *Ibid.*, p. 850.

40. Nida (1959), p. 63.

41. Douglas (1975), p. 849.

42. Terry C. Hulbert, "Discipling by Families: A New Testament Pattern" in *Discipling through Theological Education by Extension*, ed. Vergil Gerber (Chicago: Moody Press, 1980), pp. 49-62.

43. Douglas (1975), p. 848.

44. Romans 10:10.

45. Ephesians 2:10; Titus 2:7, 14; 3:8, 14.

46. Psalm 96:3, 8.

47. Ephesians 4:12-13.

48. Ephesians 6:12.

49. 2 Corinthians 10:4.

50. Romans 8:37; 2 Cor 2:14.

51. Colossians 2:14-15; 1 John 3:8.

52. 2 Corinthians 4:4.

53. Ephesians 6:10ff.

54. Ephesians 5:8; James 4:7.

55. Luke 4:18.

BIBLIOGRAPHY

Adeyemo, T., "Witnessing With Power." Unpublished manuscript, n.d.
Aldridge, Jimmy. "Faith of Fear and Fetish," in *Heartbeat*. Nashville: Free Will Baptist Foreign Missions, Vol. 22, March, 1982.
Anderson, Sir Norman, ed. *The World's Religions*. ed. by William B. Eerdmans, Grand Rapids: Eerdmans, 3d ed, 1980 (copyrighted by Inter-Varsity Press at present).
Argus, "Weekend," Cape Town, South Africa, February 20, 1988.
Awolawu, J. Omosade. *Yoruba Beliefs and Sacrificial Rites*. London: Longman Group, Ltd, 1979.
Baum, Archie J. *The World's Living Religions*. Carbondale: Southern Illinois University Press, 1964.
Bouisson, Maurice. *Magic: Its Rites and History*. London: Rider and Co., 1960.
Boyd, Bob. *Baal Worship in Old Testament Days and Today*. Scranton, Pa.: Rev. Robert T. Boyd, 1712 Academy Street, Scranton, Pa., 18504, 1979.
Brugge, David M. and Charlotte J. Frisbie, eds. *Navajo Religion and Culture Selected Views*. 1st ed. Sante Fe: Museum of New Mexico Press, 1982.
Buswell, J. O., Jr., *Systematic Theology of the Christian Religion*. Grand Rapids: Zondervan Publishing Company, 1971.
Caquot, Andre, and Sznycer, Maurice. *Ugaritic Religion*. Leiden: B. J. Brill, 1980.
Carroll, David. *The Magic Makers*. New York: Arbor House, 1974.
Cederroth, Sven. *The Spell of the Ancestors and the Power of Mekkah*, Goteborg, Sweden: Acta Universitatis Gothoburgensis, 1981.
Columbia Record, The. Columbia, South Carolina, June 3, 1982.
Courlander, Harold. *The Drum and the Hoe*. Berkeley: University of California Press, 1960.
Daily Dispatch. East London, South Africa, February 6, 1988.
Davies, T.W. *Magic, Divination and Demonology: Among the Hebrews and Their Neighbors*. New York: Ktav Pub. House, 1969.
Deutsche Press. Agentur, March 19, 1987.
Dorson, Richard M. *Folklore in the Modern World*. The Hague: Mouton, 1978.
Driver, Harold E. *Indians of North America*. 2d. ed. Chicago: University of Chicago Press, 1970.
Dundes, Alan, ed. *Varia Folklorica*. The Hague: Mouton, 1978.
Eliade, Mircea. *From Primitive to Zen*. New York: Harper & Row, 1967.
_____. *Shamanism: Archaic Techniques of Ecstasy*. New York: Pantheon Books, 1964; Princeton, N.J.: Princeton University Press, 1951.
_____. *The Sacred and The Profane: The Nature of Religion*. New York: Harper Torchbooks, 1961.
Fernandez, James W. *Briti: An Ethnography of the Religious Imagination in Africa*. Princeton, N.J.: Princeton University Press, 1982.
Ferre, Frederick et al., eds. *The Challenge of Religions*. New York: Seabury Press, 1982.
Ferre, Frederick. *Basic Philosophy of Religion*. New York: Scribners, 1967.
Flornoy, Bertrand. *Jivaro*. London: Elek, 1953.
Fortes, M. and G. Dieterlen. *African Systems of Thought*. London: Oxford University Press, 1965.
Fortune, R. F. *Sorcerers of Dobu*. New York: E. P. Dutton & Co., 1963.
Frost, Garvin. "Church and School of Wicca." A letter of Introduction. New Berne, North Carolina. n.d.
Geertz, Clifford. *The Religion of Java*. New York: The Free Press, 1969.
Gregor, Arthur S. *Witchcraft and Magic*. New York: Charles Scribner's Sons, 1972.
Harner, Michael. *The Way of the Shaman: A Guide to Power and Healing*. San Francisco: Harper & Row, 1980.
Harris, W. T. and E. G. Parrinder. *The Christian Approach to the Animist*. London: Edinburgh House Press, 1960.
Harwood, Alan. *Witchcraft, Sorcery, and Social Categories Among the Safwa*. London: Oxford University Press, published for the International African Institute, 1970.
Hiebert, Paul G. *Cultural Anthropology*. 2nd. ed. Grand Rapids: Baker Book House, 1985.
Hodgson, Janet. *The God of the Xhosa: A Study of the Origins and Development of the Traditional Concepts of the Supreme Being*. New York: Oxford University Press, 1982.
Hoebel, E. Adamson. *Man in the Primitive World*. New York: McGraw-Hill, 1949.
Howells, William. *The Heathens*. New York: Doubleday & Company, 1962.
Howes, Michael. *Amulets*. London: Robert Hale, 1975.

Hubert, Henri and Marcel Mauss. *Sacrifice: Its Nature and Function.* Translated by W. D. Halls. Chicago: University of Chicago Press, 1964.

Hulbert, Terry C. "Discipling by Families: A New Testament Pattern," in *Discipling Through Theological Education by Extension.* ed. Vergil Gerber. Chicago: Moody Press, 1980.

Hultkrantz, Ake. *Belief and Worship in Native North America.* 1st ed. Syracuse, N.Y.: Syracuse University Press, 1981.

Hume, Robert E. *The World's Living Religions.* New York: Charles Scribners Sons. Rev. ed., 1959.

Hwang, Bernard. "Ancestor Cult Today." *Missiology* V, no. 3, 1977.

Idowu, E. B. *African Traditional Religion.* London: S.C.M. 1973.

Jensen, Erik. *The Iban and Their Religion.* Oxford: Clarendon Press, 1974.

Jevons, F. B. *Introduction to the History of Religion.* London, 1921.

Keeler, Clyde E. *Land of the Moon-Children.* Athens, GA: University of Georgia Press, 1956.

Kelsey, Morton T. *Dreams - The Dark Speech of the Spirit.* New York: Doubleday, 1968.

Kemp, Jamie. "Girl's Abilities Mysterious." *Pacific Daily News,* 17. Agana, Guam, July 24, 1986.

King, Noel Q. *Religions of Africa.* New York: Harper & Row, 1970.

Kluckhohn, Clyde. *Navaho Witchcraft.* Boston: Beacon Press, 1967.

Koop, Marjory. "Poor Man's X-Ray," in *SIM Now,* 34, July-August, 1982.

Kraemer, Hendrik. *The Christian Message in a Non-Christian World.* New York: Harper and Brothers, 1938.

Kuper, Hilda. *The Swazi, A South African Kingdom.* New York: Holt, Rinehart & Winston, Inc., 1963.

Leach, Maria. editor. *Funk and Wagnall's Standard Dictionary of Folklore, Mythology and Legend.* New York: Funk and Wagnall, 1949.

Lessa, William A. and Evon Z. Vogt. *Reader in Comparative Religion: An Anthropological Approach.* 4th ed. New York: Harper & Row, 1979.

Levy, Robert I. *Tahitians.* Chicago: Univ. of Chicago Press, 1973.

Leyburn, James E. *The Haitian People.* New Haven: Yale University Press, 1966.

Lovering, Kerry. "Barrier to the Gospel: The Spirit World, " in *SIM Now,* 34, July-August, 1987.

Lowie, Robert H. *Primitive Religion.* New York: Liveright Publishing Corp., 1952.

Mahony, F. *A Trukese Theory of Medicine.* Stanford University, Ph.D. Ann Arbor, Mich: University Microfilms Inc., 1970.

Malefijt, Annemarie de Waal. *Religion and Culture.* London: Collier-MacMillan Ltd., 1968.

Malinowski, Bronislaw. *Argonauts of the Western Pacific.* New York: E. P. Dutton, 1953.

_____ *Magic, Science and Religion.* Garden City, New York: Doubleday Anchor Books, Doubleday & Company, Inc., 1954.

Maloney, Clarence. ed. *The Evil Eye.* New York: Columbia University Press, 1976.

Martello, Leo L. *Black Magic, Satanism and Voodoo.* New York: H. C. Publishers, 1972.

Maurier, Henri. *The Other Covenant: A Theology of Paganism.* New York: Newman Press, 1968.

Mbiti, John S. *African Religions and Philosophy.* Garden City: Anchor Books, Doubleday & Company, Inc., 1970.

McCurry, Don. editor. *The Gospel and Islam: A 1978 Compedium.* Monrovia: MARC., 1978.

McDowell, Josh & Don Stewart. *Understanding Non-Christian Religions.* San Bernardino: Here's Life Publishers, 1982.

McGavran, Donald, ed. *Crucial Issues in Missions Tomorrow.* Chicago: Moody Press, 1972.

McKane, William. "Poison, Trial by Ordeal and the Cup of Wrath (Num. 5:11-31)". *Vestas Testamentum* 30, 474-492, '80 (on microfiche).

Melton, J. Gordon. *Magic, Witchcraft, and Paganism in America: A Bibliography.* Compiled from the files of the Institute for the Study of American Religion. New York: Garland, 1982.

Mendonsa, Eugene L. *The Politics of Divination: A Processual View of Reactions to Illness and Deviance among the Sisala of Northern Ghana.* Berkeley: University of California Press, 1982.

Michaelson, Johanna. *The Beautiful Side of Evil.* Eugene, Oregon: Harvest House Publishers, 1982.

Money, Kyrle, R. *The Meaning of Sacrifice.* London, 1965.

Morgan, Kenneth W., ed. *The Religion of the Hindus.* New York: The Ronald Press Co., 1953.

Munday, J. T. *Witchcraft in Central Africa and Europe.* London: United Society for Christian Literature, Lutterworth Press, 1956.

Musk, Bill A. "Popular Islam: The Hunger of the Heart," in *The Gospel ands Islam: A 1978 Compendium,* ed. Don McCurry. Monrovia: MARC, 1979.

Neill, Stephen. *Christian Faith and Other Faiths.* London: Oxford University Press, 1970.

Newbell, Niles Puckett. *Folk Beliefs of the Southern Negro.* New Jersey: Patterson Smith, 1968.

Newell, William H., editor. *Ancestors.* Paris: Mouton Publishers, n.d.

Newell, William H., ed. *The Hague.* Mouton; Chicago: distributed by Aldine, 1976.

Nida, E. A. *Customs and Cultures.* New York: Harper and Brothers, 1954.

Nida, E. A. and W. A. Smalley. *Introducing Animism.* New York: Friendship Press, 1959.

Norbeck, Edward. *Religion in Primitive Society.* New York: Harper & Brothers, 1961.

Nordyke, Quentin. *Animistic Aymaras and Church Growth.* Newberg, Oregon: Barclay Press, 1972.

North, Gary. *Unholy Spirits, Occultism and New Age Humanism.* Ft. Worth, Texas: Dominion Press, 1986.

Noss, John B. *Man's Religions.* New York: McMillan Company, 1969.

Orga, Irfan. *Portraits of a Turkish Family.* New York: McMillan, 1930.

Onyango, Symons. *Set Free From Demons.* Nairobi, Kenya: Evangel Publishing House, 1979.

Oosterwal, Gottfried. *People of the Tor.* Assen, Netherlands: Royal Van Gorcum Ltd., 1961.

Oosthuizen, G. C. *Post-Christianity in Africa.* Grand Rapids: Eerdmans, 1968.

Otto, Rudolph. *Das Heilege.* Translated as: *The Idea of the Holy,* by John Harvey. New York: Oxford University Press, 1958.

Parrinder, Geoffrey. *African Traditional Religion.* 3d. ed. London: Sheldon Press, 1974.

_____. *Mysticism in the World's Religions.* New York: Oxford University Press, 1979.

_____. *Witchcraft: European and African.* London: Faber & Faber, 1963.

Parshall, Phil. *Bridges to Islam: A Christian Perspective on Folk Islam.* Grand Rapids: Baker Book House, 1983.

Peters, George W. *A Biblical Theology of Missions.* Chicago: Moody Press, 1972.

Poland, Dorrie. "Animist Journal," Columbia Graduate School of Bible and Missions, Columbia, S. C.: unpublished manuscript, 1985.

Preston, James J., ed. *Mother Worship: Theme and Variations.* Chapel Hill: University of North Carolina Press, 1982.

Radin, Paul. *Primitive Religion, Its Nature and Origin.* New York: Oxford University Press, 1958.

Rappaport, Roy A. *Pigs for the Ancestors.* New Haven: Yale University Press, 1967.

Ray, Benjamin C. *African Religions.* Englewood Cliffs, N.J.: Prentice Hall, 1976.

Reid, Janice, ed. "Body, Land, and Spirit: Health and Healing," in *Aboriginal Society.* St. Lucia; New York: University of Queensland Press, 1982.

Richards, Audrey I. *Chisungu.* London: Faber & Faber, n.d.

Richardson, Don. *Eternity in Their Hearts.* Ventura, California: Regal Books, 1981.

Ringgren, H. *Sacrifice in the Bible.* London: Lutterworth Press, 1962.

Robert, and Hamill. *Fetishism in West Africa.* Nassau, New York: Negro Universities Press, 1904.

Robbins, Russel Hope. *The Encyclopaedia of Witchcraft and Demonology.* New York: Crown Publishers, 1959.

Roche de Coppens, Peter. *The Nature and Use of Ritual: The Great Christian Documents and Traditional Blue-prints for Human and Spiritual Growth.* Washington, D.C.: University Press of America, 1979.

Roy, Asim. *The Islamic Syncretistic Tradition in Bengal.* Princeton, N.J.: Princeton University Press, 1983.

Rushdoony, R. J. *The Institute of Biblical Law.* Nutley, New Jersey: Craig Press, 1973.

Ruud, Jorgen. *Taboo (A Study of Malagasy Customs and Beliefs).* Oslo: University Press, 1960.

Sanneh, Lamin. *"Amulets and Muslim Orthodoxy."* International Review of Missions 63 (October 1974):515-29.

Simmons, Leo W., ed. *Sun Chief. The Autobiography of a Hopi Indian.* New Haven: Yale University Press, 1942.

Siskin, Edgar E. *Washo Shamans and Peyotists: Religious Conflict in an American Indian Tribe.* Salt Lake City, Utah: University of Utah Press, 1983.

Skeat, Walter William. *Malay Magic.* New York: Dover Publishers, 1967.

Smalley, William A. ed. *Readings in Missionary Anthropology.* Tarrytown, New York: Practical Anthropology, 1967, reprinted by Wm. Carey Library, So. Pasadena, 1984.

Smart, Ninian. *The Religious Experience of Mankind.* New York: Charles Scribner's Sons, 1969.

Smith, Edwin W. *The Secret of the African.* London: United Society for Christian Literature, 1943.

Smith, Elmer L. *Pennsylvania Dutch Folklore.* Lebanon, Pa.: Applied Arts Publishers, 1960.

Smith, Jane I. "Concourse Between the Living and the Dead in Islamic Eschatological Literature." *History of Religions* 19, (February 1980): 224-36.

Sneck, William Joseph. *Charismatic Spiritual Gifts: A Phenomenological Analysis*. Washington, D.C.: University Press of America, 1981.

Song, Choan-Seng. *Tell Us Our Names: Story Theology From an Asian Perspective*. Maryknoll, NY: Orbis Books, 1984.

Spence, Lewis. *An Encyclopaedia of Occultism*. New York: University Books, 1960.

Starkloff, Carl F. *The People of the Center*. New York: The Seabury Press, 1974.

Steltenkamp, Michael F. *The Sacred Vision: Native American Religion and Its Practice Today*. New York: Paulist Press, 1982.

Stewart, Louis. *Life Forces: A Contemporary Guide to the Cult and Occult*. New York: Andrew and McMeel, Inc., 1980.

Streng, Frederick J. *Understanding Religious Life*. 2d. ed. Belmont, Calif: Wadsworth Pub. Co., 1976.

Stutley, Margaret. *Ancient Indian Magic and Folklore*. Boulder: Great Eastern, 1980.

Subhan, John A. *Sufism: Its Saints and Shrines*. Lucknow: Lucknow Publishing House, 1938.

Sundkler, B.G.M. *Bantu Prophets in South Africa*. New York: Oxford University Press, 1970.

Swidersky, Richard. "Italian-Americans from Folk to Popular: Plastaic Evil Eye Charms" in *The Evil Eye*, ed. Clarence Maloney. New York: Columbia University Press, 1976.

Talayesva, Don C. *Sun Chief: The Autobiography of a Hopi Indian*. edited by Leo W. Simmons. London: Yale University Press, 1942.

Tambiah, S. J. *Buddhism and the Spirit Cults in Northeast Thailand*. Cambridge: University Press, 1970.

Taylor, John V. *The Primal Vision*. London: SCM, 1963.

Tillich, Paul. *Christianity and the Encounter of World Religions*. New York: Columbia University Press, 1973.

Times of Zambia. Lusaka. July 27, 1981.

Toirac, Florent D. *A Pioneer Missionary in the Twentieth Century*. Winona Lake, Indiana: By the author, P.O. Box 542, Winona Lake, Ind. 46590. n.d.

Trimingham, J. Spencer. *The Christian Church and Islam in West Africa*. London: SCM Press, 1955.

Tschopik, Harry Jr. "The Aymara of Chucuito Peru." in *Anthropological Papers of the American Museum of Natural History*, 44, Pt. 2: 1, Magic. New York: The American Museum of Natural History, 1951.

Tylor, Edward B. *Primitive Culture*, 2. New York: Harper, 1958.

Tippett, Alan R. "The Evangelization of Animists," in *Let The Earth Hear His Voice*, ed. J. D. Douglas. Minneapolis: World Wide Publications, 1975.

_____. "Possessing the Philosophy of Animism for Christ," in *Crucial Issues in Missions Tomorrow*. ed. Donald A. McGavran. Chicago: Moody Press, 1972.

_____. *Verdict Theology*. So. Pasadena: William Carey Library, 1972.

Tippett, Alan R. editor. *God, Man and Church Growth*. Grand Rapids: Wm. B. Eerdmans Publishing Company, 1973.

Van Der Leeuw. *Religion in Essence and Manifestation*. New York: Harper & Row, 1963.

Van Til, Cornelius. *The Defense of the Faith*. (rev. ed.), Philadelphia: Presbyterian & Reformed, 1963.

Vos, Howard F. editor. *Religions in a Changing World*. Chicago: Moody Press, 1959.

Walker, J. R. "The Sun Dance and Other Ceremonies of the Oglala Division of the Teton Dakota," in *Anthropological Papers of the Museum of Natural History*, 16, 1917.

Walker, Sheila S. *Ceremonial Spirit Possession in Africa and in Afro-America*. Leiden, Netherlands: E. J. Brill, 1972.

Webster, Hutton. *Taboo: A Sociological Study*. Stanford: Stanford University Press, 1942.

Westermarck, E. A. *Early Beliefs and Their Social Influence*. London: McMillan, 1932.

Westermark, Edward. *Ritual and Unbelief in Morocco*. London: McMillan, 1926.

Willoughby, W. C. *The Soul of the Bantu*. New York: Harper & Row, 1928.

Wilson, Clifford and Weldon, John. *Occult Shock and Psychic Forces*. San Diego: Master Books, 1980.

Wright, G. Ernest. *God Who Acts*. London: SCM Press, 1973.

_____. *The Old Testament Against Its Environment*. London: SCM Press, 1950.

Wright, Michael A. "Some Observations on Thai Animism," in *Missionary Readings in Anthropology*, ed. W. A. Smalley. So. Pasadena: William Carey Library, 1984.

Zahan, Dominque. *The Religion, Spirituality and Thought of Traditional Africa*. Chicago: University of Chicago Press, 1979.